BUGLERS ON THE HOME FRONT

SUNY Series in Chinese Philosphy and Culture
David L. Hall and Roger T. Ames, editors

BUGLERS ON THE HOME FRONT

The Wartime Practice of the
Qiyue School

Yunzhong Shu

State University of New York Press

Published by
State University of New York Press, Albany

© 2000 State University of New York

All rights reserved

Printed in the United States of America

No part of this book may be used or reproduced in any manner whatsoever without written permission. No part of this book may be stored in a retrieval system or transmitted in an form or by any means including electronic, electrostatic, magnetic tape, mechanical photocopying, recording, or otherwise without the prior permission in writing of the publisher.

For information, address State University of New York Press
State University Plaza, Albany, New York 12246

Production by Dana Foote
Marketing by Michael Campochiaro

Library of Congress Cataloging-in-Publication Data

Shu, Yunzhong, 1955–
Buglers on the Home Front : the wartime practice of the qiyue school / Yunzhong Shu.
p. cm. — (SUNY series in Chinese philosophy and culture)
Includes bibliographical references and index.
ISBN 0-7914-4437-6 (alk. paper) — ISBN 0-7914-4438-4 (pbk. : alk. paper)
1. Chinese literature—20th century—History and criticism. 2. Sino-Japanese Conflict, 1937–1945—Literature and the war. 3. Hu, Feng, 1902–1985. 4. Ch°' yëëh (Wuhan, China) I. Title. II. Series.
PL2303.S625 2000
895.1'09358—dc21   99–053411

10 9 8 7 6 6 5 4 3 2 1

To my family and to the memory of my grandmother and father

Contents

ACKNOWLEDGMENTS/ix

INTRODUCTION
Toward an Energetics of Literary Production in Modern China/1

ONE
From a May Fourth Youth to Lun Xun's Ally:
Hu Feng's Intellectual Evolution/23

TWO
Antidote to Wartime Heroics:
Early *Qiyue* Reportage/43

THREE
From Reflection to Lyricism:
The Transition from *Qiyue* Reportage to *Qiyue* Fiction/65

FOUR
Image Making, Legacy Clarification, and Agenda Formulation:
Hu Feng's Interpretations of Lu Xun, May Fourth, and
the "Subjective Fighting Spirit"/87

FIVE
Different Modes of Intellectual Intervention:
Lu Ling's Short Stories/107

SIX
Manifestations of Self-Transcendence:
Lu Ling's *Children of Wealth*/129

Contents

SEVEN
(Re)presentation of Historical Particularities:
Ji Pang's *Night Travellers*/153

EPILOGUE/175

NOTES/183

BIBLIOGRAPHY/195

INDEX/205

Acknowledgments

The journey of this book started with a dissertation that I wrote in 1994 under the direction of Professor David Der-wei Wang, who deserves my heartfelt thanks for his unstinting professional help during and after my Ph.D. program. I am grateful for a 1995 travel grant from CUNY Research Foundation that enabled me to make a trip to China to gather some of the primary materials for this book and to interview some surviving *Qiyue* members. I appreciate the assistance from Professor Cheng Guanglin at the Chinese Academy of Social Sciences in locating and photocopying most of the materials I needed. I was fortunate to be able to interview Hu Feng's widow Mei Zhi, his daughter Zhang Xiaofeng, and *Qiyue* poets Lü Yuan and Niu Fang. Particular mention should be made of Shu Wu and Ji Pang, whom I also interviewed on my trip, for answering my specific questions afterwards through correspondence.

I owe many debts of gratitude to Jesse Dudley, Charles Laughlin, and Kris Torgeson for their thoughtful comments on either the entirety or parts of earlier versions of my manuscript; to the two anonymous readers at the State University of New York Press for their valuable comments on my manuscript; to Professor Kirk Denton for his suggestions; and to Zhang Rongxiang at the Starr East Asian Library at Columbia University for her continuing help.

I remain grateful to my colleagues at the Department of Classical, Middle Eastern and Asian Languages and Cultures at Queens College, CUNY for their professional and moral support as well as creating the congenial work environment I have enjoyed ever since I started my teaching career in 1993.

The following people at the State University of New York Press should be thanked for their support and editorial help: Nancy Ellegate, Dana Foote, and David Hopkins.

I simply cannot find adequate words to express my gratitude to my mother, who has helped me in her quiet ways; to my wife, who has

Acknowledgments

never failed to show her understanding, patience, and support at times I needed them the most; and to my son Benjamin, who has brought joy into my life.

Of course it goes without saying that the errors and weaknesses that still remain in this book are entirely my own responsibility.

Introduction

Toward an Energetics of Literary Production in Modern China

When the war against Japan broke out on a full scale after the Marco Polo Bridge Incident in 1937, Chinese literature, like Chinese society, reached a critical moment. Confronted with an altered situation in which national survival became the top concern for the whole nation, writers who had followed the May Fourth tradition of cultural criticism urgently felt the need to change their agenda. Many gave up Western-influenced vernacular fiction and began to use the formats and techniques of folk literature to arouse the broad masses for the war effort. Some even went so far as to suggest that writers throw away their pens and join the army to serve their country more directly. Among those who continued to write in the vernacular, patriotism pervaded their praises of national heroism in reportage, a genre newly prominent because of its topicality. With the war as the center of attention and national salvation as the imperative task, Chinese literature at this point displayed a general "centripetal" tendency.[1]

It would be historically inaccurate, however, to regard the literary scene as one composed of nothing but "centripetal" forces even at this early, most intense stage of the war. To begin with, writers of different political persuasions still retained their allegiances to various degrees, so the boundaries separating different camps were not completely erased. Within the leftist camp, a group of writers, headed by the critic Hu Feng and affiliated to his journal *Qiyue* (July), continued to launch vigorous challenges at prevalent patriotic beliefs. First inspired by the

Introduction

position of domestic cultural criticism that Lu Xun held in the famous debate over the "Two Slogans," the *Qiyue* group set itself determinedly against the dominance of what it perceived as "resistance formulism." As this confrontational group stood its ground against the leftist mainstream in the successive stages in its evolution, it managed to diversify and enrich wartime literature in areas such as reportage, literary criticism, poetry, fiction, and even the familiar essay. Although its life was eventually cut short by the brutal purge of the "Hu Feng anti-Party and antirevolutionary clique" after the Communist takeover and for decades its existence was not even acknowledged in official literary histories sponsored by Mao's government, its modus operandi still merits our attention because it, when taken note of, can help shatter monolithic views on the wartime literature. With that goal in mind, this study will delineate the genesis and development of the *Qiyue* school through presentations of its historical circumstances and analyses of representative theoretical and literary works by its key members.

Before I proceed with my discussions of the *Qiyue* school, I want to make it clear at the outset that I have no intention of claiming its typicality in the wartime literature. In fact, typicality is precisely the notion that I, inspired by *Qiyue* writers, come to question. The literary world in the wartime, if there was one, was highly divided along geopolitical lines. As the war went on there was an increase in literary activities not only in Guomindang areas but also in areas occupied by the Japanese, such as the northeast, north China, and Shanghai, and in Communist areas. Within each subfield there were forces working for different agendas and refusing to cohere. Since the conditions and the trajectories of literature in these areas were so diverse, any attempt to crystallize a common mode of wartime literary production is bound to fail. Of course, that does not mean we cannot find any common interests between the *Qiyue* school and writers living and working outside Guomindang areas. Indeed, to find out such parallels would certainly be a rewarding project. Unfortunately, due to the limit of space, this project lies beyond the scope of the present study.

I also want to make it clear that I do not want to claim for myself the ability to solve all the questions, and mysteries, about all *Qiyue* writers and texts, either. To make sense of a literary group that had involved, in different degrees, about a hundred men of letters writing as poets, fiction writers, critics, and essayists for more than a decade, it becomes unavoidable for me to make certain selections. Conse-

Introduction

quently, my study takes on a certain constructedness. The question we should ask, however, is not whether we should do away with construction in our research, since all literary scholarship is inevitably bound up with construction. Rather, we should ask ourselves the following questions: How successfully do our constructions bring out the crucial characteristics of the phenomena under examination? how close do they stand in relationship to what had really happened in history? and what are their relationships to other constructions of the same phenomena? Specifically, I am fully aware of the contemporary rediscovery of the *Qiyue* school in mainland China after the official rehabilitation of the Hu Feng group and to me the large amount of primary materials, such as reprints of original works, diaries, letters, and so on, and some secondary materials, such as biographies, memoirs, and the like, was indispensable in shaping my views. As for the spate of mainland critical scholarship on the *Qiyue* school, I find that, commendable as it is, it has in general regrettably, though understandably, refrained from putting in the spotlight the most sensitive political issues related to the *Qiyue* school. As someone who does not have to worry about the political consequences of his research, I feel obligated to fill this lacuna that no one, including scholars in the West, has filled. In so doing I decided to work mainly on a few genres and seven writers because I believed they best represent the thrust of the school as well as the important problems it tried to tackle. With neither inclusiveness nor conclusiveness as its aim, my study, in other words, is intended to recover a dissenting voice in modern Chinese literature and its attempts at self-transcendence that have been overlooked for too long.

THE CONSTITUTION OF THE *QIYUE* SCHOOL

To understand the *Qiyue* school as a historical phenomenon, we should begin by putting it into its historical context. As a start, we should realize the cultural world in which it existed was not hegemonic to the degree of stamping out all dissident elements. In spite of the popular impression of its high-handed governance, the Nationalist (Guomindang) regime had instituted fundamental political changes during the period of 1928–49 that led to a viable civil society allowing for voluntary associations and private publications. Government censorship was surely exercised during the wartime, but it was ineffective, often limited to the level of wording. As for the Chinese Communist Party (CCP), with its headquarters in the remote area of northern Shaanxi, the lack of political power prevented it from achieving total dominance over the leftist writers, not to mention writers of other political leanings, who lived in Guomindang (GMD) areas. As a dissident school that operated mainly in Guomindang-controlled urban areas, *Qiyue* writers could be said to have existed in the cracks created by the GMD's and the CCP's incomplete control of cultural affairs.

Compared with the GMD and GMD-leaning writers, the CCP and the mainstream leftist writers under its influence certainly had a tremendous impact on the practice of the *Qiyue* school. As the school's adversaries, they defined its agenda, which to various degrees consisted of a series of subversions of the common practices in the leftist camp at different times. Yet the Party and the leftist mainstream by no means formed a monolith with a well-planned cultural program. As a matter of fact, Hu Feng was helped several times by Zhou Enlai, the vice chairman of the CCP and its chief delegate to the Chongqing GMD government during the war, including getting a considerable sum of money from Zhou as a financial guaranty to start his journal *Xiwang* (Hope). In view of the CCP's lack of a consistent cultural policy in Guomindang areas (such a policy was not formulated even in Communist areas until Mao gave his famous "Yan'an Talks" in 1942) and the complicated makeup of the leftist camp, intertwined for much of the wartime with the united front in the cultural field, we may argue that the unity *Qiyue* writers saw in the leftist mainstream was more imagined than real, a unity largely derived from their need, as dissidents, to define and clarify their own position vis-à-vis a center.

Ensconcing itself in the space created by the incomplete control of the cultural world by the political world, the *Qiyue* school was able to respond to important issues in ways it saw fit. Although at each stage the concerns and interests of the literary world were not up to the individual members of the school to determine, they remained free to choose their own positions and strategies to secure and strengthen their positions. Belligerent in principle, they were so engrossed in their competition against the leftist cultural establishment that they had practically ignored the cultural forces outside the leftist circles; this became all the more obvious as the literary scene began to diversify later in the war. Thus shot through with oppositional zeal, their works,

Introduction

regardless of their generic categories, constituted efforts to gain legitimacy and power at the cost of contemporary leftist orthodoxy.

How did the *Qiyue* school come into possession of its oppositional propensity, which generated a consistent pattern of antagonistic interaction with the leftist mainstream? The following remarks by Pierre Bourdieu about literary or artistic production in general throws some light on this question:

> The literary or artistic field is a *field of forces*, but it is also a *field of struggles* tending to transform or conserve this field of forces. The network of objective relations between positions subtends and orients the strategies which the occupants of the different positions implement in their struggles to defend or improve their positions (i.e. their position-takings), strategies which depend for their force and form on the position each agent occupies in the power relations.[2]

Bourdieu's rather economicist conception of the literary field, however, can only help us understand the *Qiyue* school to a certain degree. According to Bourdieu, once a dominated group in the literary field achieves recognition, it tends to disintegrate as a result of its internal competition in the wake of the uneven distribution of the symbolic profit of that recognition.[3] This Francocentric observation apparently does not hold true for the *Qiyue* school, which demonstrated a unity both before and after it had won recognition. Premised on the political convictions *Qiyue* writers shared, the persistent cohesion of the school proves that power or symbolic capital was not the only thing that mattered in its existence. Bourdieu's other weakness, it seems to me, is his relative inattention to the operation of power within each position in the literary field, as he maintains that the power of each occupant in the field is directed outwardly against the competitor(s). *Qiyue* writers, particularly Lu Ling and Ji Pang, as we shall see, spent as much energy on questioning their own presumptions and conclusions as on challenging the leftist orthodoxy. Consequently, the politics of power in their works was quite different from the kind we see in Bourdieu's study of the nineteenth-century French literary field.

The most crucial difference between the *Qiyue* school's environment and the nineteenth-century French literary field was that in the former literary or artistic concerns more often than not played second fiddle to contemporary political and cultural issues. The nature of these issues was so weighty that participants in the field had to take open stands to maintain their legitimacy, measuring, in the meantime, the validity of their own views and the invalidity of their opponents' views in kind rather than in degree. The ascendancy of some positions, however, did not always result in the disappearance of their rivals. Instead, it could evoke a sense of crisis in the adherents of the programs under eclipse and make them argue all the more strongly for the necessity of their agendas, as *Qiyue* writers did in their defense of the May Fourth legacy against what they considered shortsighted patriotism and vulgarized Marxism. Consequently, long-term projects, such as cultural criticism, could persist or even expand despite the unfavorable conditions, as we witness in the continued exposure of China's domestic ills in *Qiyue* reportage. Propelled by their strategy-generating May Fourth predispositions, what Pierre Bourdieu might call *habitus*,[4] *Qiyue* writers managed to adhere to their own path as they coped with unforeseen, ever-changing situations. The persistence and consistency of their predispositions were further enhanced by the structure, or the lack thereof, of the school. Here an interesting contrast can be found between the *Qiyue* group and the Literary Association (Wenxue yanjiu hui), the generally acknowledged first society for China's "new literature." Unlike the Literary Association, which, as Michel Hockx recently shows us, had a rather democratic structure stipulated by its by-laws and depended on voting for the recruitment of its members and for the editing of its series,[5] the *Qiyue* group was influenced by one person, Hu Feng, particularly in its early stage when Hu Feng was virtually in charge of all its publication projects. From that position he could easily screen out those writers who disagreed with him on important issues. Last but not the least, the pressures from its opponents, real or imagined, also strengthened the standpoint and the internal unity of the *Qiyue* group.

The affective constitution of the *Qiyue* school contributed no less importantly to its operation. Polemic in disposition, Hu Feng largely defined his position with his hostility toward Zhou Yang, the Communist cultural doyen in Shanghai, as he became a contender for power in the leftist literary circles in the 1930s. Fired by differences in opinion as well as personal animosity, the running debates they had, which culminated in the debate over the "Two Slogans" that fundamentally

Introduction

determined the orientation of the *Qiyue* school, were as intellectual as they were emotional. The list of enemies, by no means limited to Zhou Yang and his associates, also included Mao Dun, who in 1935 tried to alienate Lu Xun from Hu Feng with rumors about Hu Feng's clandestine connection with the GMD, and Guo Moruo, one of the most ardent apologists for the "National Defense Literature," who was promoted by the CCP in 1938 as Lu Xun's successor and national leader of leftist writers. As the epitomes of "objectivism" and "subjectivism" respectively, Mao Dun and Guo Moruo subsequently served as the two main obstacles *Qiyue* writers tried to overcome under the guidance of Hu Feng's "subjective fighting spirit."[6] Thus conditioned by and expressive of the *Qiyue* writers' affective makeup, their texts could be regarded to a large degree as literary transfigurations of their resentment against their enemies.

Hu Feng undoubtedly played a pivotal role in the formation and sustenance of the *Qiyue* school, so a brief look at the constitution of his position will help us understand the school as a whole. A romantic, idealistic rebel growing up in the May Fourth era, Hu Feng in his formative years, like so many in his generation, came to adopt an iconoclastic attitude toward what was considered China's feudal tradition. Bent on rejecting the tradition *in toto*, this early intellectual entelechy became for him a natural view of Chinese society, predisposing him to a hypercritical mode of thought, feeling, and action with regard to China's traditional cultural heritage. As Karl Mannheim noted with regard to how different generations are formed and defined, all one's later experiences tend to receive their meaning from the original set of early impressions, whether they appear as the verification and fulfillment of the original set or as its negation and antithesis.[7] In Hu Feng's case, the original set of early impressions was strengthened to the point of inviolability since all his later experiences turned out to be nothing but its confirmations.

With his participation in the Japanese proletarian literature movement in the late 1920s and early 1930s, Hu Feng came under the sway of Fukumotoism, a political theory influential among Japanese Communists that emphasized the necessity of separating genuine revolutionary elements from fellow travellers and the importance of theoretical struggles. For Hu Feng the influence of Fukumotoism eventually resulted in his obsessive concern, not unmixed with sectarianism, for the purity of the revolutionary ranks, particularly his own camp, and his strong inclination to polemics launched to maintain the purity of his own theory. We should note that the appeal of Fukumotoism to Hu Feng was by no means an exception in Chinese leftist literature. Dating back to the debate over the issue of revolutionary literature between the Creation and Sun Societies and their joint attacks on Lu Xun in 1928,[8] the influence of Fukumotoism contributed to the internal rivalry that characterized Chinese revolutionary literature from its inception. In that regard Hu Feng's practice as a polemicist followed a larger pattern of competition.

Though attributable to the influences of the May Fourth *Zeitgeist* in his youth and Fukumotoism in the early phase of his career as a leftist critic, Hu Feng's insistence, after he came to the Shanghai leftist literary scene in 1933, on an almost exclusively antifeudal cultural agenda and his perseverance in debate after debate had a great deal to do with his position in the cultural field. A latecomer to the leftist literary scene, he sided with the increasingly radical Lu Xun, particularly in the debate over the "Two Slogans," to improve his status as a competitor against powerholders such as Zhou Yang and his associates. As he afterwards appointed himself to the prestigious position of Lu Xun's only bona fide successor, the stakes only increased. In order not to lose his appeal to the public and, especially, to his young followers, he had to keep alive Lu Xun's agenda of cultural criticism under all circumstances and at all costs. For him it was this ever-present need to affiliate himself closely to Lu Xun's agenda that made him launch *Qiyue* in the first place and keep it on an unchanging course thereafter. In that sense his identity and fate were defined by their adherence to Lu Xun's advocacy of cultural criticism. With his program thus determined, Hu Feng in turn tried to bring Lu Xun's complicated life experience into sharp focus by streamlining it into a legacy of tenacious fighting against feudalism. Now the image of Lu Xun radicalized in his hands served to enhance the validity of his own program. The same could be said of his crystallization of the combative spirit of May Fourth, which in his opinion was epitomized by Lu Xun. At a time when Lu Xun and May Fourth were subjected to diverse interpretations and, in the latter's case, even to criticism, Hu Feng's all-out efforts to clarify the complicated legacies of both were, once again, necessitated to a large extent by his position in the cultural field and the need to distinguish himself from advocates of other platforms. Appearing as a spokesman for an agenda currently under

Introduction

eclipse yet still retaining its legitimacy, a risky but sure way to make his presence felt, he had to tie cultural authorities such as Lu Xun and May Fourth to his own platform in unambiguous terms. In sum, the relationship between Hu Feng and the legacies of Lu Xun and May Fourth was reciprocal in that the latter inspired Hu Feng, who, out of the need to maintain his position, gave clarity to the latter.

Why should Hu Feng persistently call for the total rejection of tradition at a time when even May Fourth veterans came very close to renouncing their old antifeudalist stance? Part of the answer lay in the public image he assumed. With little political, institutional, or financial power at his disposal, Hu Feng was what Max Weber describes as a "charismatic" leader, a leader who derives his authority only from his exceptional personal qualities.[9] As such his power came almost exclusively from his image as Lu Xun's heir. To maintain this symbolic power and to improve his position, he had to remain unswervable from what the public, especially his own followers, perceived as Lu Xun's legacy, which included fortitude, a relentlessly critical view of Chinese society, and constant vigilance against the danger of betrayal in the revolutionary ranks. The net effect of the perpetual need for him to follow in Lu Xun's footsteps was at once energizing and confining. While it molded his intense personality and his career by giving him a strong sense of mission, the investiture he bestowed upon himself as heir to Lu Xun and May Fourth also created a pressure under which he had to behave like a worthy heir in order to keep his title. His was, in short, a typical example of what Pierre Bourdieu might describe as an heir being inherited by a heritage.

As for his *Qiyue* followers, we should note that when they made their entries into the literary world they were mostly unknown young writers. For them, one way to enhance their status was to assert their difference from the standard practice in the literary field. In so doing they naturally constituted a revolutionary force intent on breaking through the monopoly of the orthodoxy. Moreover, being passionate youths keenly aware of the insufficiency of the prevailing modes of thought in the face of unusual circumstances, they were in search of an authority in close touch with the vital issues of the time. They found such an authority in Hu Feng, or, to be more exact, Hu Feng and his young followers found each other as allies with a common interest in displacing the dominance of the leftist mainstream. In the end what appeared was a group of writers unified by their conviction in cultural criticism and their openly challenging attitude toward the status quo in the leftist cultural world.

THE EVOLUTION OF *QIYUE* TEXTS

While highlighting the consistency and continuity of the *Qiyue* school, we should not overlook the internal changes in its position. Extraordinary historical circumstances of the time had brought changing concerns to the cultural world and the *Qiyue* school in turn shifted the thematic foci of its literary texts as it responded to different historical situations. As producers of texts, *Qiyue* writers vented their discontent with the leftist mainstream through attempts to rectify various prevailing "formulisms" (*gongshi zhuyi*). In our examination of *Qiyue* works across the generic and chronological boundaries, we see that they were in turn mainly directed against patriotic romanticism, socialist realism, and, to a lesser degree, naturalism. On the whole *Qiyue* texts constituted a series of efforts, best summarized by Hu Feng's notion of the "subjective fighting spirit," to wrest writers' individual perceptions from the tyranny of the prevalent paradigms. While adhering to the paradigm of May Fourth critical realism for their sociohistorical vision, *Qiyue* writers, as we shall see later in this study, injected new interests, particularly the preoccupation with the role of subjectivity in the cognitive process, that significantly changed the terrain of critical realism.

To *Qiyue* writers the dominant formulaic works of their times deserved to be debunked urgently and forcefully because of their harmful influence. As they conscientiously set out to demonstrate the essential gap between the various myths in the dominant works and the complex truths of reality, *Qiyue* writers all remained bent on conveying their central message that, whereas the popular myths were partial, abstract, and inflexible, reality was nonconceptual, concrete, multifaceted, and close at hand. The strong distrust of the conceptual approach to reality, a key characteristic of the *Qiyue* school, can be traced all the way back to some of Hu Feng's early articles in which he criticized oversimplified Marxist social analysis in leftist literature. Once the war against Japan was under way and patriotic romanticism assumed sway in the form of uncritical panegyrics on the Chinese nation's heroism, *Qiyue* reportage writers quickly resorted to their personal experiences on or behind the front line to expose the collective myth of courage and bravery as reductionistic and untruthful. Thus endowed with an unmistakable argumentative edge, the "facts" they offered in a supposedly "realistic" genre were characterized, first and foremost, by their belligerence, not their neutrality.

As the wave of patriotic enthusiasm subsided later in the war and leftist writers resumed fiction writing from a Marxist scientistic approach, Hu Feng emphasized literary creativity as a dynamic, transformative process in which neither the writer nor his subject matter remains inert or impervious to the influence of the other. Under his tutelage, the *Qiyue* writers Lu Ling and Ji Pang tried hard to break out of the conceptual straitjacket of simplified Marxist doctrines. Both of them called attention to the amorphism of lived experience and questioned the revolutionary millennial dreams about the inevitable emancipation of working classes, but Lu Ling distinguished himself with his incessant and unabashed efforts to press forward the explorations of the authorial discourse while Ji Pang emphasized the impact of historical authenticity on the authorial consciousness. They complemented each other in showing that truth about reality was an expansive process that did not result in an all-inclusive proposition and that, to maintain its adequacy, consciousness needed to interact not only with its object but with itself as well. As a self-reflective act, their emphasis on mobility, both the mobility of knowing subjects and that of the world they tried to know, indicated their desire to free themselves from both a dogmatized, reified Marxism and a totalized, fully constituted Self.

The power inequality between the *Qiyue* school and its orthodox opponents notwithstanding, the competitions it launched throughout its existence bore a certain resemblance to what Karl Mannheim terms "atomistic competition," a type of thinking an isolated social group employs as it tries to take over the official interpretation of the world from other similar groups.[10] Representing a democratizing tendency, the *Qiyue* school eventually developed a mode of thinking that was not concerned with fitting new facts into a preexistent model but with an increasingly radical rejection of all externally given models. Pushed to its extreme, it even raised doubts about its own premises and conclusions, as Lu Ling's and Ji Pang's questioning of the intellectual self fully demonstrated. With an intensified awareness of the distance between multifaceted reality and all reductive thinking, especially the sinicized vulgar Marxism, it started with drawing attention to the sur-

Introduction

plus of the Real to which current modes of symbolization failed to do justice and ended with challenging all symbolizations. In the end the Real, struggling against ideological subjection, became a force of negativity that questioned every given, objectified status imposed on it from the outside.

In retrospect, we notice a gradual shift in the *Qiyue* school's modus operandi. Whereas *Qiyue* reportage started by directing its force outward against current vogues in the literary field, *Qiyue* fiction ended up aiming its energy inward at self-transcendence and self-transformation, though at no time was one tendency completely displaced by the other. The shift in orientation shows, for one thing, that the power-relations of the *Qiyue* school should not be understood too mechanistically—as mere reactions to external circumstances. Full of internal tension and instability, power was exercised by the *Qiyue* school for the transformation of both the contours of the literary field and its own conditions. It was a disposition that refused to stop at a final state and, as such, it strove for a continuous process of "becoming." Hence thinking, a symptom of power, was not in the least afraid of throwing doubts upon or even doing violence to its own products. Intent on freeing life, with all its particularity and negativity, from the prison of ideas, thinking in the case of *Qiyue* writers refrained from offering any conclusive theoretical solution to life. Instead, it kept activating and rejuvenating both life and itself simultaneously.

Viewed as an ensemble of cognitive enterprises, *Qiyue* texts display a general movement from the exposure of the noncorrespondence between beliefs and reality to the revelation of the conditions and processes of the search for truths. Whereas in the former case none of the prevalent beliefs is regarded as holding true in front of the complicated world, in the latter case attention is focused on the construction of truths and its restraints. In both cases *Qiyue* writers refute the fallacies of an independently existing "world in itself" and "truth in itself" waiting to be finalized and fully grasped once and for all. Instead, truths are shown to be relational and perspectival, conditioned by their interactions with other propositions and by the standpoints and concerns of those who assert them. In other words, *Qiyue* writers, wittingly or unwittingly, prove that the search for truths necessarily unfolds in the context of human life, and that intellectual operations inescapably reflect the features of human power involved in historical circumstances. While *Qiyue* reportage, still bound to a certain extent by its generic requirements for facts, calls attention to the pivotal importance of perspective in the interpretation of facts, *Qiyue* fiction takes a further step in stressing that truth is not something determined in itself that can simply be found or discovered. Rather, it is something that has to be created in an endless process that, while remaining creative, has its own share of restraints imposed by an intractable human society. Whether the focus falls on the creativity in truths or on their restraints, the search for truths and truths themselves are rendered dynamic with the inclusion of human agency on both ends of the interpretive tug of war.

Standing in opposition to the hardening positivist and scientistic approach in vulgar Marxism, the aesthetics of negation embraced by *Qiyue* writers entailed a significant change in the conception of literature. As a literary critic in the ideologically and aesthetically divided Marxist camp, Hu Feng had always sided with Marx, Engels, and, to no less a degree, Lukács in their preference for pictorial representation over conceptual representation. On the other hand, he had remained critical of the Leninist/Zhdanovian approach of political tendentiousness and partisanship that culminated in Stalinist socialist realism. More significantly, we should note that, with his emphasis on literary creativity as dynamic praxis, he parted company with the crucial Marxist materialist assumption about the mimetic role played by literature vis-à-vis the objective reality. As he injected activism into literary creativity and put the writer in the center stage as an agent engaged with the vital issues of contemporary times, literature became for him, and his followers, a force of history and not its epiphenomenal reflection.

At this point I would like to venture a brief comparison, at the obvious risk of oversimplification, of the *Qiyue* school with the Western Marxists, mainly the Frankfurt School. Both being dissidents within the Marxist camp, *Qiyue* members and the Critical Theorists shared certain thematic concerns, for example, the resistance to the ossification of an "official Marxism" and the emphasis on man as the subject or creator of history. There was, however, an important difference between them. The Critical Theorists, living in an age marked by the stabilization of advanced capitalism and the ebb of the European proletarian movement, not to mention the rise of fascism, adopted a basically contemplative, though critical, position toward an all too powerful society with their retreat from politics into theory, and an increasingly abstruse and hermetic theory at that. The *Qiyue* school, in contrast, boldly confronted some of the most powerful ideological forces of its time and, in so doing, directly engaged itself in practical politics.

In view of this major difference, it is more meaningful, I believe, to compare the *Qiyue* school with an earlier group of dissidents in the international Marxist movement, that is, Karl Korsch, the early Georg Lukács, and Antonio Gramsci. As political theorists and revolutionary leaders with a strong activist bent rather than philosophers, these early dissidents all combatted vigorously the degeneration of Marxism into a dogma in the hands of orthodox Marxists. To them the raison d'être of revolutionary theories was that they should become instruments of revolutionary change, rooted in and responsive to the struggles, needs, and goals of multiple revolutionary movements. Since they were motivated by a strong voluntarist urge, their critique of the crude attempts to create an objectivistic "scientific Marxism," a Marxism premised philosophically on the copy theory of knowledge and the correspondence theory of truth, bore an obvious resemblance to the "subjective fighting spirit" of the *Qiyue* school. To a certain extent a historical link can be established between this activist Marxist tendency and Hu Feng's position, as I will demonstrate in chapter 1. Historically situated before Stalinism and Maoism completely gained the upper hand in different contexts, Korsch, Lukács, and Gramsci, on the one hand, and Hu Feng and his *Qiyue* followers, on the other, could be said to have waged battles against the ossification of Marxism from similar standpoints.

Since I will discuss Hu Feng's relationship with Lukács on later occasions, I will, for now, concentrate on Hu Feng's similarities to Korsch and Gramsci. As far as Korsch is concerned, we should note that his application, in his 1923 work *Marxism and Philosophy*, of the materialist conception of history to Marxism itself and, more importantly, his criticism of the increasing divergence of Marxism from the workers' movement remind us of Hu Feng's antidogmatic stand. Both Korsch and Hu Feng were aware that Marxism, once separated from revolutionary practice, faced the danger of becoming a false consciousness that would impede revolution. Korsch's left-oppositionalist position vis-à-vis the orthodox center of the Soviet Communist Party and the Comintern, his advocacy for "party democracy" and freedom of discussion, and his criticism of Stalinist opportunist politics in forming an alliance with Nazi Germany also paralleled Hu Feng's views. As

Introduction

leaders of splinter groups confronted with the political pressure from the bureaucracy in the revolutionary ranks, Korsch and Hu Feng both determinedly and courageously tried to preserve the integrity, purity, and consistency of their own standpoints at all costs, thus enriching the revolutionary movements in which they participated.

Sharing a critical view on the schematized and vulgarized materialist Marxism with Korsch and the Lukács of *History and Class Consciousness,* Antonio Gramsci remained opposed to the deterministic conception of history and in that respect his position was very close to Hu Feng's, since both emphasized the importance of revolutionary praxis, premised on a critical subjectivity and intentionality, in bringing about historical change. Gramsci was also similar to Hu Feng in stressing the materiality and durability of ideology as an essential constituent of historical reality and in subsequently emphasizing the necessity of cultural reformation. Their comparable voluntarist stances gave rise to the most important similarity between Gramsci and Hu Feng—their "hegemonic" perception of the social function of literature and art. To Gramsci, hegemony, indisputably the central concept of his political and cultural theory, not only referred to the consensual control over society that a ruling social group could achieve by disseminating its ideology among the oppressed through its sociocultural institutions but also, no less significantly, drew attention to the opportunities for political articulations as counterhegemonic measures in the incomplete, unstable, and open social spaces in civil society. In other words, the Gramscian notion referred to a process in which counterhegemonic maneuvers could fight hegemonic attempts. While certainly engaged in counterhegemonic battles, Hu Feng and his followers went a step further by directing their struggles against a burgeoning totalitarian ideological formation sponsored by the Communist Party. As it combatted the stagnancy that arose from what Gramsci viewed as the vanguard of revolution and the political center of a new hegemony, the *Qiyue* school could be said to have removed the residual static elements from the Gramscian notion and turned it into a never-ending process, a process best illustrated by Lu Ling's and Ji Pang's contemplations on subjectivity. In the end what *Qiyue* writers wanted to achieve was a democracy in which no universal class, party, or subject would deprive other historical agents of their roles in history.

On the other hand, we should realize that the counter-hegemonic struggles of the *Qiyue* school could only be conducted in a historical environment characterized by its porosity. When it tried to wage the same struggle in Communist China, in which the cultural realm was effectively sutured by the CCP, its efforts were doomed to failure. In that sense Hu Feng's post-1949 advocacy for dispersed "cultural centers" largely independent of government control should be viewed, not as a position comparable to Gramsci's theories of "civil society" and the "public sphere," as Liu Kang has recently argued,[11] but as an anachronistic strategy that backfired because it did not realize the consequences of the fundamental structural changes the new totalitarian regime brought to the cultural field.

By way of a digression, I want to offer here another word of self-reflection, this time from a Gramscian perspective. Gramscian in the sense that it locates beneath the surface of cultural artifacts the elements of a hegemonic process, my study is aimed at giving an order to the existence of the *Qiyue* school by taking into consideration the sociohistorical, biographical, thematical, and formal factors that either gave rise to or exhibited the oppositions, conflicts, paradoxes, solidarities, continuities, and changes in the school's literary texts. As an exercise in literary sociology, my study is meant to reflect on the dynamics of human consciousnesses, consciousnesses that were engaged in active sociopolitical relationships and, at the same time, in literary production to express their needs, intentions, and powers. While selecting, evaluating, and critiquing *Qiyue* texts, I am fully aware that I myself am situated in a hegemonic process. Specifically, my goal as an agent in such a process is to challenge, with the example of the *Qiyue* school, the reductionist views on the wartime literature in China. Following in the footsteps of the writers I study, I aspire after a democratic prospect in which perceptions and ideas can be freely exchanged and questioned. In my case the first step I take toward such a prospect is to call attention to a mode of literary production significant in its own right and yet unduly overlooked by literary scholars.

While comparing Gramsci with Hu Feng, we should not overlook the significant differences between them. The most important difference, in my view, can be seen in their conceptions of popular culture. To Gramsci popular culture appeared as a site of disaggregated sentiments, ideals, myths, beliefs, norms, values, and so on in which the organic intellectuals of the subaltern classes could first search for a healthy nucleus of ideas and experiences and then turn the nucleus

Introduction

into a superior conception of the world to supersede the prevailing ideology in society. To Hu Feng, as we shall see more clearly in chapter 4, popular culture, saturated with feudal ideology, remained little more than a means for the feudal tradition to enslave the working masses spiritually and to keep their spontaneous rebellion in its most primitive state. Gramsci's and Hu Feng's contrasting views have to be understood in terms of their different historical origins. Whereas for Gramsci, who started his revolutionary career as a journalist heavily involved with labor movement, popular culture was seen as a battlefield where counterhegemonic struggles could and should be waged to educate the masses and gain their support, Hu Feng inherited the May Fourth iconoclastic view on popular culture as part and parcel of the repressive feudal tradition in China. In the final analysis Hu Feng's negative view on popular culture was tied up to his May Fourth conception of the masses. Unlike Gramsci, Hu Feng did not try to link the revolutionary intellectual worldview and the mass belief system within the same historical totality. Intellectuals and the masses, in his view, were not shaped by the same historical and ideological processes. Instead of envisioning the intellectuals and the masses being constituted by the same historical subjectivity in different degrees and waging the same historical struggle in unison, Hu Feng and his followers often followed their May Fourth predecessors in revealing the distance and the uneasy relationship between these different historical agents. In short, in any comparative study of the *Qiyue* school we should not lose sight of its historical heritage.

A significant part of the historical heritage that shaped the *Qiyue* school, and the literary production in modern China in general, was the intensely polemical atmosphere in the literary field from the May Fourth literary revolution to the Communist takeover in 1949. The major concerns and criteria in modern Chinese literature were in a large measure determined by a series of rivalries and debates. In this environment, even an indifference to an ongoing contention amounted to a competitive position aimed at overriding the parties involved in the contest. That theoretical debates often preceded rather than followed literary practice further sharpened the thematic foci of literary texts as vehicles for the urgent expression of views in contradistinction to other views. The mode of literary production thus engendered was highly political. The *Qiyue* school certainly illustrated this mode.

Introduction

A BRIEF SUMMARY OF THIS STUDY

An analytical account of the genesis and development of the *Qiyue* school is offered in the following pages. While tracing the history of the school, I bear in mind that, instead of embarking on a grand journey toward an abstractly conceived destination, *Qiyue* writers were trying to tackle historically situated issues with theoretical and narrative tools at their disposal. Hence I always keep an eye on their historical terrain, even at the time when I am offering technical analyses of their imaginative works. In order to understand the school relationally, I devote a considerable amount of space to the description of its historical background, especially in the chapters dealing with Hu Feng's growth as an unorthodox Marxist critic, early *Qiyue* reportage as a corrective reaction to wartime heroics, and Hu Feng's wartime exegeses of Lu Xun and May Fourth. Whether rendered explicit or implied, a historical narrative remains the backbone of my theoretical reflections. By inserting them into their immediate historical context, I intend to prove that, instead of concerning themselves with the large problematic of Chinese modernity, as Kirk Denton recently argues with his interpretation of Hu Feng and Lu Ling,[12] *Qiyue* writers were far more engrossed in close-range fighting in leftist cultural circles.

In view of the crucial role Hu Feng played as the founder and guiding spirit of the *Qiyue* school, chapter 1 of this book traces his growth from a rebellious May Fourth youth to an independent-minded Marxist literary critic and eventually to a disciple of Lu Xun who would not hesitate to do battle with his adversaries in the leftist camp over matters of principle. Special attention is paid to the formation of his activist orientation in the May Fourth emancipatory *Zeitgeist*, the influence of Georg Lukács's *History and Class Consciousness* in connection with Marx and Engels's aesthetic views, and the position of the Lu Xun camp in the famed debate over the "Two Slogans," all of which contributed crucially to the course of his future career as the pacesetter of the *Qiyue* school. By the time Hu Feng came out of the debate over the "Two Slogans," he had already formulated an agenda and gathered a group of core writers for the journal he was soon to launch.

In chapter 2, after a brief overview of the Chinese reportage in the 1930s that culminated in its collective heroization of the Chinese nation at the beginning of the Anti-Japanese War, an analysis of Cao Bai's personalized, de-idealized reportage is offered in connection

Introduction

with Lu Xun's and Hu Feng's influences on him. It is followed by an analysis of Qiu Dongping's deflation of combat heroics in his battlefield reportage. Chapter 3 starts with a section on A Long's deepening understanding of warfare, reflected in his war reportage, as the Anti-Japanese War dragged on. The increase in authorial intervention, already discernible in Qiu Dongping's later reportage pieces, is the focus of the next section in the chapter, an analysis on A Long's book-length reportage work *Nanjing*. By embedding a pervasive authorial presence as a moral/intellectual center in this intensely emotional work, A Long broke away from the final structural constraints of reportage and paved the way for subsequent psychology-oriented *Qiyue* fiction. In the field of fiction, we find an early example of the restitution of subjectivity in the first-person stories by Jia Zhifang, who started out his career by following Lu Xun but increasingly departed from Lu Xun's path as he came under the influence of Hu Feng's "subjective fighting spirit." The last section of chapter 3 focuses on this transformation.

On the theoretical front, Hu Feng's exegeses, defense, and development of the spirit of Lu Xun and May Fourth in the adversities of the wartime constituted an essential part of his cultural program. On account of the *Qiyue* school's crucial relation to Lu Xun and May Fourth, chapter 4 is devoted to, first, Hu Feng's two-pronged radicalization of Lu Xun and May Fourth and, then, the genesis of his important notion of the "subjective fighting spirit." While intended to continue the legacy of cultural criticism bequeathed by Lu Xun and May Fourth, a legacy imitable only through practice, the "subjective fighting spirit" also tried to stave off the despondent atmosphere in Guomindang areas in the last phase of the war and, more importantly, the ideological regimentation imposed by the Communists in the wake of Mao Zedong's "Yan'an Talks." As it called on the writer to function as a revolutionary agent, the "subjective fighting spirit" entailed a flexible approach to writing that took into consideration the interactions between self and society, an approach that soon bore fruit in the works by Hu Feng's disciples.

Chapter 5 analyzes the various approaches Hu Feng's favorite follower Lu Ling adopted to implement the "subjective fighting spirit" in his short stories and novellas. Starting with a section on the authorial intervention in his fiction as a rehabilitation of intellect and the intellectual, this chapter then moves on to his focus on the abject

Introduction

and the "primitive vitality" as the antithesis to revolutionary progressivism. Related to the paradigm contest between critical realism and socialist realism, Lu Ling's hostility toward millennialism eventually found an outlet in the satiric stories he wrote in the last years of the war. As he increased his moral and intellectual distance from his caricaturized targets, however, satire, with its implicitly static moral vision, turned out to be a medium not entirely appropriate for the "subjective fighting spirit."

To overcome the implicit stasis in satire Lu Ling had to move to a different ground, a ground where the writer could transcend the meanings he had achieved. That is what we find in his magnum opus *Children of Wealth*, the focus of chapter 6. In this most unusual work, discursive to a degree unprecedented and unsurpassed in the history of modern Chinese fiction, all of its major constituents—time, space, characters, themes and, most importantly, the narratorial perspective—are rendered fluid and expansive to convey the message that the world and its comprehension are not yet and should not be completed. A field of energy that entails endless activities rather than a finished product of artistry, this novel refuses to conform to the formal requirements of any novelistic genre, be it *roman à thèse* or *Bildungsroman*. An attempt is made, in my analysis, to relate this novel's formal anomalies to its young author's burning desire to break through the doxic mode in Chinese literary realism with the reintroduction of refractory human agency and psychology.

Chapter 7 analyzes the implementation of the "subjective fighting spirit" by Hu Feng's another disciple Ji Pang in *Night Travellers,* a novel focused on the difficulties of Chinese peasants' spiritual enlightenment. Cautiously aware of the gap between lived experience and idea, Ji Pang focused on concrete historical particularities as heterogeneous and multidirectional elements resistant to any totalizing, reductive theoretical thought. As he maintained a sensory reality characterized by contingency of individual actions and, in particular, psychological idiosyncrasies, he questioned the perceptive and predictive authority of Marxist progressivism founded on the belief in historical rationality. The low profile his self-effacing and self-doubting narrator kept vis-à-vis such an intractable reality indicated an unwillingness to offer an overall explanation for the past and the present or to delimit the rich possibilities for the future. In liberating human potentiality from the straitjacket of Marxist historical vision, Ji Pang,

Introduction

like his *Qiyue* colleague Lu Ling though from a different angle, presented the movement of history as one without a telos.

The present study ends with an epilogue that offers a brief account of the CCP's persecution of the *Qiyue* group. Once the Communist orthodoxy implemented fundamental structural changes in the cultural field and put a stranglehold on literature after 1949, the sociopolitical space for any open dissent was effectively closed. Yet the dissident stance of the *Qiyue* school has not been completely lost on later generations of intellectuals, for its echoes could be heard as soon as the Communist ideology became less coercive. By taking note of the similarity between Liu Zaifu's view on subjectivity and Hu Feng's "subjective fighting spirit" at the end of my study, I intend to point out the contemporary relevance of the *Qiyue* school as a precedent of dissent in the cultural field. After all, my study is aimed at an understanding of literary production in modern China, including the present.

One

From a May Fourth Youth to Lu Xun's Ally: Hu Feng's Intellectual Evolution

As the founder and pacesetter of the *Qiyue* school, Hu Feng provided his followers with general guidelines as well as practical advice in his capacity as a critic and an editor. To understand his consistent standpoint it is necessary for us, as a start, to trace his intellectual growth from a rebellious May Fourth youth to a critic who finally found a direction and the right company for himself after wading through the troubled waters of the Communist movement at home and abroad. Without such a first step, we would not only miss some of the most crucial influences on his eventual position but lose sight of its historical bearing. Hence in what follows I will proceed to outline the development of some of Hu Feng's most important ideas and positions. As we near the end of this chapter, we will see that the fundamental orientation of his future journal *Qiyue,* and by extension the school he was about to lead, was already determined by his alliance with Lu Xun in the well-known debate over the "Two Slogans."

In tracing Hu Feng's intellectual growth, I will focus on the formation of a coherent network of interrelated views that he achieved through his creative assimilation of different schools of thought. In contrast to the position adopted by the leftist orthodoxy of the time, which shifted significantly under the sway of changing political priorities, this ideational network on Hu Feng's part was enduring and capable of withstanding political and ideological pressures. Its paradigmatic importance, as the works discussed in the later chapters of this study will fully bear out, lay in that it provided Hu Feng and his followers with a critical perceptual scheme, a combative understanding of the function of literature and a nonconformist ethic. It, in other words, was what distinguished the *Qiyue* school from the majority of contemporary leftist writers.

A REBELLIOUS ACTIVIST IN A REVOLUTIONARY ERA

Born in 1902 when Chinese society was undergoing dramatic upheavals, Hu Feng spent his formative years restlessly. Like many young men of his time, he was unhappy with traditional Confucian education, so after he started school at eleven he went through six different tutors in six years before finally enrolling in a modern-style elementary school. Thereafter the restlessness led him to Wuchang in 1921 and then to Nanjing in 1923 in search of a better high school education, a significant part of which consisted of reading May Fourth vernacular literature. The following is his own account of his voracious reading experience at the time:

> I read *Experiments* (*Changshiji*, by Hu Shi) as well as *Resurrection of the Goddess* (*Nushen zhi zaisheng*, by Guo Moruo). I read *Guide* (*Xiangdao*) as well as *Effort Weekly* (*Nuli zhoubao*). . . . But what made me really come close to literature as well as human life was two little-known booklets: *Lake Side Poems* (*Hupan shiji*) and Wang Tongzhao's *A Leaf* (*Yiye*). The former gave me the feelings of a young man awakened by the May Fourth movement to his "self" and saved me from being frustrated by my surroundings; the latter, in spite of its sighs after disillusionment, called forth in me a desire for pursuit and made me indescribably sad for a long time.[1]

Typifying the romantic ethos of the time, *Lake Side Poems*—a collection of poems by the so-called "Lake Poets" Pan Mohua, Feng Xuefeng, Ying Xiuren, and Wang Jingzhi—consciously followed the lead of the British romantic Lake Poets Wordsworth, Coleridge, Southey, and Leigh Hunt in singing praises of nature and love and *A Leaf*—a novella by a founding member of the Literary Association—

lamented over the endless human suffering and the irreconcilable conflicts between ideals and reality in a tone no less sentimental. Two minor yet representative works of the early 1920s, both displayed a yearning for an idealized, beautified life while implicitly or explicitly criticizing the flaws of the mundane world, echoing the wishes and the discontent of a whole generation of educated youths. In Hu Feng's case, the discontent with society would soon go beyond the interest in the vernacular literature and materialize in his active participation in student movements.[2]

Growing up amidst tremendous changes in society, the young Hu Feng belonged to a generation that, under the impact of historical circumstances, came to adopt a radically new approach to the cultural heritage of China. As Karl Mannheim points out:

> When as a result of an acceleration in the tempo of social and cultural transformation basic attitudes must change so quickly that the latent, continuous adaptation and modification of traditional patterns of experience, thought, and expression is no longer possible, then the various new phases of experience are consolidated somewhere, forming a clearly distinguishable new impulse, and a new centre of configuration. We speak in such cases of the formation of a new generation style, or of a new *generation entelechy*.[3]

For May Fourth youths like Hu Feng, their generation entelechy was saliently characterized by an iconoclastic attitude toward what they considered China's feudal tradition. Unlike those older May Fourth participants reared on Confucian doctrines, they only had a tenuous relationship with the traditional culture. As a result of their intellectual and emotional distance from the feudal past, they tended to judge it monolithically without bothering themselves too much about sorting out its pros and cons. Theirs was a generation that could carry out the attack on tradition without being haunted by a guilty conscience or a feeling of complicity. In view of this wholly negative conception of tradition, for which more evidence will be adduced later in this study, particularly in chapter 4, we have reason to question Kirk Denton's recent attempt to trace Hu Feng's lineage back to Neo-Confucianism, an attempt not directly supported by Hu Feng's own writings.[4] We should realize that Hu Feng's generation gave their

Chapter One

allegiance to the New Culture, venerating May Fourth in absolute terms as the nemesis of China's feudal tradition as they rejected the latter in toto. We should further note that the institutionalizations of May Fourth were under way right after it took place,[5] and the passionate young iconoclasts like Hu Feng, in turn, put a radical spin to its legacy.

That was precisely how Hu Feng regarded Lu Xun, the epitome of May Fourth in his eyes and the most crucial influence on him in his youth. Here is his recollection of his first encounter with Lu Xun's preface to *Call to Arms* (*Nahan*) in his high school days:

> Of course, I did not understand it, but I intuitively felt that he [Lu Xun] was writing, with a heavy heart, about the soul of our ancient country. Later *Call to Arms*, in its red cover, was published and I immediately bought a copy. Of course I did not understand the book either, but, once again, I intuitively felt that what he described was the darkness and pain that had surrounded me. Thereafter Lu Xun became the dearest name to me. Like today's young people, I dreamed about light and friendship in my youth. I always wanted to give something to those friends I held respectable and the best gift was of course books, most valuable because I thought they could bring light. I remember I bought four or five copies of *Call to Arms* in its red cover and gave them, with my passion, to friends about to leave or living elsewhere.[6]

Associating Lu Xun with light, the future, and the young generation, Hu Feng's intuitive understanding projected Lu Xun as a dauntless fighter against China's feudal tradition while glossing over his admitted involvement with the past and his self-doubts as its critic. In Hu Feng's youthful view, the image of Lu Xun was already radicalized.

Both Hu Feng's hostility towards tradition and his admiration for Lu Xun had stemmed from a humanist standpoint shared by many May Fourth youths. As an "idealist" pining for love and social justice, to borrow an epithet from the title of one of his autobiographical sketches,[7] he in turn fell under the spell of Leo Tolstoy's *Resurrection*, Hermann Sudermann's *Frau Sorge* (*Dame Care*), a novel taking as its subject matter the maturation of a sensitive youth, V. Ropshin's *Pale Horse*, a novel about a Russian terrorist that was received by Chinese intellectuals in the 1920s as an insightful delineation of the development of a revolutionary soul, and the works of Arishima Takeo, a Japanese novelist known as "the man of love" in his country. The attraction of these works and authors, as Hu Feng tells us, came from what he perceived as their passion for life. Being a young man with the same passion, he also discovered the unembellished truth of human life and life struggle in China's New Literature.[8] In that regard he was close in spirit to the members of both the Literary Association (Wenxue yanjiu hui) and the Creation Society (Chuangzao she), who had focused either on the revelation of human and social realities in a "literature for humanity's sake" or on unrestricted personal expression and individual protest. Given his valuational agreement with these two groups of writers responsible for the literary revolution in the early 1920s, his subsequent endorsement of the New Literature, as we shall see in the following chapters, tended to be sweeping, unproblematic, and unconditional.

With regard to the prevailing mimetic view that had worked hand in glove with the humanitarian concerns in the New Literature, Hu Feng brought along the important addition of voluntarism in his understanding of the function of literature, thanks mainly to the influence of *Symbols of Agony* (*Kumen de xiangzheng*), a book written by the Japanese critic Kuriyagawa Hakuson (1880–1923) in 1921 and translated by Lu Xun in 1924.[9] Largely a synthesis of Henri Bergson and Sigmund Freud, *Symbols of Agony* interpreted human life as a struggle of human vitality—or Bergsonian "*élan vital*"—against social restraints, with art and literature as pure expressions of life, freedom, independence, and individuality.[10] As an acolyte of psychoanalysis, Hakuson highly valued the cathartic function of literature, therefore to him there was little functional difference between tragedy, presumably the highest literary genre, and the conversation therapy used by psychoanalysts in the treatment of hysteria, since both could locate hidden mental damage in the unconscious and, through unobstructed expression, relieve the damage by transferring it to the conscious level. Art that did not symbolize the agonies or mental injuries hidden in the depths of the subconscious, in his view, simply was not great art.[11] This view, as our subsequent discussions will bear out, would contribute crucially to Hu Feng's choice of the "spiritual scars" left by the protracted feudal tradition on the Chinese nation as the most important subject matter for literature.

Hakuson's most important message for the young Hu Feng lay in his interpretation of literary creativity as a dynamic process in which human subjectivity unabashedly took the initiative. He made the truthful reflection of the external world play second fiddle to the writer's search into the depths of his own mind and prioritized the expressive, affective functions of literature over its cognitive, intellectual functions. In contrast to the mimetic view prevalent at the time, Hakuson's was an alternative approach that emphasized the writer's crucial involvement in the creative process as a conscious agent, a psychological therapeutist, and a liberator of pent-up psychic energy. On a broader scale, the importance Hakuson placed on human subjectivity reinforced a conception of life as a process of individual experiences rather than a given scheme revealing itself objectively in a rational order, a view held by Chinese romanticists such as Yu Dafu, Xu Zhimo, Guo Moruo, and Jiang Guangci in the 1920s, as Leo Ou-fan Lee notes.[12] Being a radical activist committed to the lofty cause of changing the society, Hu Feng was naturally susceptible to Hakuson's performative emphasis. To him literature was no longer a mere mirror held up to reflect a social reality outside itself. Instead, imbued with willpower and strength of purpose, it became, first and foremost, an important tool for social revolution.

It was this strong will to change society by means of literature that produced the content and the organizing principles of Hu Feng's social knowledge. For the young radical, social knowledge did not arise out of disinterested theoretical cogitation. Rather, it was centrally derived from a volitional and emotional act motivated to transform or destroy a given social condition to such an extent that it only saw the negative attributes of the society in question. In other words, Hu Feng's approach to social knowledge aspired after action, not contemplation, on social issues. Thus from the start of his intellectual journey Hu Feng had adopted an activist view on literature and approached May Fourth literature accordingly. Under the influence of activism, literature became for him a force immanent in history and the writer a conscious agent of change in an incessantly dynamic world. While putting a high premium on being with one's time, the activist view refused to impose a transcendental, predetermined pattern on history. The future, in short, was yet to be created necessarily through human interventions and interactions. Generally irresponsive to Marxism, an increasingly popular belief system among Chinese leftist intellectuals after the mid-1920s, Hu Feng the activist would eventually take issue on its major pitfall—economic determinism.

COMING TO GRIPS WITH MECHANISTIC MARXISM

After participating in radical peasant movements in his hometown Qichun, Hu Feng had to flee to different cities to escape the white terror in the wake of the traumatic split between the GMD and the CCP in 1927. In September 1929 he went to Tokyo and enrolled in a language school to learn Japanese. Soon he became engrossed in Japanese proletarian literature, which was then in vogue. Especially attractive to him were the short dispatches from workers and peasants carried in the journals associated with Japanese proletarian literature. Standing in contrast to what he considered the programmatic works by members of the Creation Society and the apathetic works by Mao Dun, these dispatches impressed him as sincere, passionate, and down-to-earth.[13] As he began to cultivate friendship with important Japanese proletarian writers such as Eguchi Kiyoshi (1887–1975) and Kobayashi Takiji (1903–33), he joined their discussion groups, wrote articles on Chinese left-wing literature for their magazines, translated their works and acted as a liaison between them and their Chinese peers.

During Hu Feng's stay there the Communist movement in Japan was still under the sway of Fukumoto Kazuo, a theoretician–turned–Communist Party leader who was the first systematic introducer of Marxist dialectics in Japan in the 1920s. Critical of the parliamentarianist and gradualist position embraced by Yamakawa Hitoshi, a Communist leader influenced by the Second International, Fukumoto emphasized, among other things, the necessity of separating genuine Marxists from fellow travellers before crystallizing the former group into a well-organized party, the self-determining, active role of revolutionary intellectuals in adopting Marxist principles and the importance of theoretical debates in promoting proletarian class consciousness. The impact of Fukumotoism on Chinese leftist writers in the 1920s was significant, especially in the quarrel between the Creation and Sun Societies and their later joint attack on Lu Xun in 1928.[14] As far as Hu Feng was concerned, we can certainly detect the influence of

Fukumotoism in his preoccupation with the purity of the revolutionary ranks, his strong polemic proclivity, and his emphasis on the role of the revolutionary intellectual as a progressive historical agent. Reinforcing the May Fourth cultural-intellectual approach to social issues and Hakuson's voluntarism that Hu Feng came to adopt in his youth, Fukumotoism further strengthened the activist orientation of Hu Feng's thinking while leading it in a Marxist direction.

While talking about Fukumotoism, we should bear in mind that in an important way it was derived from Karl Korsch's *Marxism and Philosophy* (1923) and Georg Lukács's *History and Class Consciousness* (1923), the twin fountainheads of Western Marxism that Fukumoto came to know when he studied Marxism in Europe. Lukács's book was especially significant in that, when published in Japanese translation in 1927, it introduced important notions such as alienation, reification, dialectics, and totality into Japanese Marxists' social understanding. Li Huoren has rightly pointed out that Hu Feng's application of the concepts of totality and dialectics in his articles against the "third-category" writers, written between 1932 and 1933 in Japan, were heavily indebted to Lukács's book, especially its first chapter "What Is Orthodox Marxism?"[15] Later dismissed by Hu Feng himself for their rigid subscription to the Marxist social analysis vulgarized by the RAPP (Russian Association of Proletarian Writers) and eventually excluded from his collected works compiled in the mid-1980s, these articles, however, only partially bore out Lukács's influence. Compared with the notions of totality and dialectics, a more latent and more lasting influence lay in other views in Lukács's complicated book.

Consisting of essays written between 1919 and 1922 in the light of the success and survival of the Russian Revolution and the gradual dissolution of revolutionary working-class movements in Europe, two historical developments Marx himself had not expected, *History and Class Consciousness* made important revisions of classical Marxism. It represented, in Gareth Stedman Jones's words, "the first major irruption of the romantic anti-scientific tradition of bourgeois thought into Marxist theory."[16] As such, it was strongly opposed to the application of the ideal of natural science to society, for "it turns out to be an ideological weapon of the bourgeoisie. For the latter it is a matter of life and death to understand its own system of production in terms of eternally valid categories: it must think of capitalism as being predestined to eternal survival by the eternal laws of nature and reason."[17]

With its implicit emphasis on the importance of human agency, Lukács's book came very close to the voluntarist stance Hu Feng had adopted. Hence it is small wonder that Hu Feng was attracted to some of its crucial ideas.

One of the most crucial theories developed in *History and Class Consciousness* is about "reification," or generalized fetishism that conceals, in all areas, the actual human "content" of social life in capitalism. To Lukács the proletariat is not immune to the harm of reification and, as a result, its actual thoughts, feelings, and desires can be nothing more than a "class-conditioned *unconsciousness*."[18] Political consciousness, in other words, is not a matter of course for the proletariat as Marx had assumed. To a certain extent, the influence of Lukács's line of thought can be detected in Hu Feng's later insistence on the revelation of the spiritual deformities of the working classes. While calling for the disruption of the reified phenomena and categories in capitalist existence by means of mediation or practice, Lukács maintained that "the nature of history is precisely that every definition degenerates into an illusion: *history is the history of unceasing overthrow of the objective forms that shape the life of man.*"[19] In the final analysis, the danger of reification can only be offset with an anthropocentric approach to history, an approach that Hu Feng the young voluntarist could readily accept.

In retrospect, Lukács's concept of "reification" served for Hu Feng as something more than a critique of formalistic rationality that pervaded capitalism and obscured its living human substrata. Itself being a theoretical mediation, the Lukácsian concept set out to overcome, among other things, the reification of consciousness from a historicist perspective. We should note that to Lukács reified consciousness included the Marxism dogmatized in the hands of theorists like Bukharin. In order to avoid the trap of dogmatism, Lukács specifically warned that, with capitalist society as the classical terrain for its analysis, Marxist historical materialism should not be applied indiscriminately and mechanically to the analysis of precapitalist societies.[20] Lukács's application of the method of ideology critique to orthodox historical materialism, as can be seen in his acknowledgment of Marxism's interpretative limitations, was to be pushed to an extreme by Hu Feng in his tirades against Marxist "formulism."

Interestingly, as it shifted the focus of its discussions by drawing on the early Marx's interest in consciousness, culture, and subjectivity, aspects underplayed by the Marxist orthodoxy of the time, *History and Class Consciousness* started a trend that would be reinforced by Western Marxism. In that respect Hu Feng's preoccupation with issues of culture, intellectuals, and subjectivity in his career bore a certain resemblance to some of the theoretical concerns of Lukács's heirs in the West, especially the Frankfurt School. Yet we do see a difference between Hu Feng and the Frankfurt School in their common resistance to economic determinism. Whereas the members of the Frankfurt School in their academic analyses of advanced capitalism often exhibited a political powerlessness, which eventually resulted in the shifting of their attention away from class struggle to the conflict between man and nature, Hu Feng opted for active intervention in dealing with the spiritual maladies of Chinese society. Sharing to a large degree Western Marxists' central concern over the perpetuation of oppression by the oppressed themselves, Hu Feng, with his adoption of the "cultural-intellectualistic" approach of May Fourth, was nonetheless able to locate revolutionary agents in critical intellectuals as independent individuals. On this point he parted company with the Lukács of *History and Class Consciousness,* who regarded the Communist Party as a concrete embodiment of true proletarian class consciousness that would make revolution possible. As he departed from Lukács on the issue of revolutionary agent, Hu Feng offered, probably unwittingly, a solution to the problem of bureaucratization, a nascent tendency Lukács himself had noticed in the Communist movement but had no remedy.

We should reiterate here that the influence of the Lukácsian concept of "reification" did not come to full fruition in Hu Feng's thinking until years later. A more direct inspiration for his final farewell to the schematic approach in leftist literature came from a more authoritative source: the aesthetic views of Marx and Engels. In an autobiographical sketch written in 1979 Hu Feng mentioned that in the early 1930s the newly found letters by Marx and Engels on literature, accompanied by the struggle against the dogmatism of the RAPP in the Soviet Union, deepened his understanding of China's New Literature and its problems. He began to realize, he went on to say, that the path of realism could only be blazed with the actual conditions of the working people and the middle classes in view and that realism had to include the whole society in its political content and be predicated on sensual particularity in its aesthetics. Thereafter he launched his theoretical inquiries to break through the dominance of doctrinairism.[21]

For a proper understanding of Hu Feng's assimilation of the aesthetic views of Marx and Engel, a brief look at his environment is in order at this point. First of all, we should bear in mind that the leftist literary scene worldwide was swayed at the time by the literary activities and official literary policies in the Soviet Union. As far as the Soviet literary scene was concerned, the early 1930s was marked by two important milestones: the formulation of "socialist realism" and the systemization of Marxist aesthetics. In November 1932 the Soviet Communist Party dissolved the clannish RAPP and replaced its "method of dialectic materialism" with "socialist realism" as the guideline for literary production. Soon afterwards the new concept was introduced into Japan and China. In November 1933, in an article titled "On Socialist Realism and Revolutionary Romanticism" (Guanyu shehui zhuyi de xianshi zhuyi yu geming de langman zhuyi), Zhou Yang interpreted "socialist realism" as a "dynamic" realism aimed at capturing the progress of socialism and imbuing its readers, by means of a simple language, with the spirit that they should fight for the better future of mankind.[22] Though conceived as a corrective measure against the RAPP's doctrinaire "method of dialectic materialism," "socialist realism," in Zhou Yang's view, called for the strengthening, not the dismissal, of dialectic materialism on the writer's part.[23] In a nutshell, "socialist realism" still entailed ideological regimentation in the name of Marxist world outlook.

As "socialist realism" was formulated and transmitted, the systemization of Marxist aesthetics got under way in the Soviet Union after the surviving texts of Marx and Engels were collected in the early 1930s, with none other than Lukács as a key player in the project. Like the concept of "socialist realism," Marx and Engels's opinions on literature were soon introduced into China. In 1932 Qu Qiubai, the leading Chinese Marxist literary theoretician, translated Engels's letters on realism. Later, in an article titled "Marx, Engels, and Realism in Literature" (Makesi, Engesi he wenxue shang de xianshi zhuyi) that came out in the journal *Xiandai* (*Les contemporaines*) in April 1933, Qu expounded, among other things, Marx and Engels's preference for Shakespeare and Balzac, and their reproach of Schiller. In Qu's opinion, Marx and Engels's recommendation for "Shakespearization" and their disapproval of "Schillerization" indicated their fundamental endorsement of realism and their opposition to romantic idealization.[24]

While busy with their elaborations of "socialist realism" and exegeses of Marxist aesthetics, Marxist literary critics, in my opinion, had overlooked an inner incompatibility between the former's tendentious approach and the latter's stress on fullness and particularity. Whereas "socialist realism" aimed at a revelation of revolutionary development in reality for the purpose of ideological transformation and education of workers in the spirit of socialism, Marx and Engels, both influenced by Hegel's preference for pictorial representation over conceptual representation, emphasized the importance of immediacy and sensuality in artistic expression and remained highly critical of the overt articulation of political attitude in the work of art. Put it in a different way, the incompatibility could be seen in that, while "socialist realism" was preoccupied with the advocacy of the yet-to-be-realized postulates of a socialist future, Marx and Engels were interested in realism as an accurate portrait of a historically shaped reality.

Hu Feng was one of the few critics, if not the only critic in the world at the time, who recognized the incompatibility and had the courage to take sides. In the mid-1930s, while other leftist critics were busy discussing "socialist realism," he never used the term in his writings. Instead, he resorted to Marx and Engels's criticism of tendentiousness and abstraction as a weapon against the schematic approach to reality he detected in the works of Chinese leftist writers. Eventually he dismissed the guidance of literary production by the correct worldview of Marxism—the quintessence of "socialist realism"—as lifeless "formulism." In so doing he tried to stake out a space for the writer's individual creativity.

In May 1935 Hu Feng started his tireless diatribes against "formulism" with "A Critique of Zhang Tianyi" (Zhang Tianyi lun), one of the first articles he wrote after coming to the Shanghai leftist literary scene. Calling Zhang a "plain materialist" most interested in the social colors of his characters and anxious to delineate their inevitable fates according to foregone conclusions, often simplistically and with exaggeration, Hu Feng faulted Zhang for failing to reach what he considered to be the highest goal of art—to capture the complicated truth of life—a goal reachable only when the writer delved into the depths of life with his mind and heart.[25] Hu Feng's emphasis on the writer's active engagement with reality meant that theoretical propositions should not be applied without regard for actual historical circumstances. More importantly, his prioritization of the writer's personal experience with life over abstract theory ultimately placed the initiative and power of interpretation in the writer's hands. In the face of the constraints of Marxist scientism he apparently adopted a voluntarist stand.

Hu Feng's voluntarist views were soon expanded in his explications of the "typical characters," a key term in the discussions of Marxist aesthetics. In a May 1935 article "What Are 'Typical Characters' and 'Stereotypes'" (Shenme shi 'dianxing' he 'leixing'), he argued that "typical characters," nonexistent in real life, were products of artistic synthesis and generalization. In the process of creating "typical characters," writers needed the recourse to their imagination and intuition to amalgamate their impressions of life as well as the ability to understand and analyze life so that they could extract its essence.[26] Significantly, while focusing on writers' interpretive initiative, he did not mention the role of Marxist worldview in the understanding of society. It was precisely on this point that Zhou Yang differed from him in an ensuing debate that would strain their relationship. Half a year later, in an article titled "A Preliminary Discussion on Realism" (Xianshi zhuyi shilun), Zhou Yang, after pointing out the limitations in the worldviews of nineteenth-century European realists, vigorously called on Chinese writers to take the correct worldview, namely, Marxism, as the compass in their observation and analysis of reality.[27] Although the debate between Hu Feng and Zhou Yang over "typical characters" was later sidetracked to the issue of universality versus singularity, ideological schematization in the name of Marxist worldview remained the real bone of contention.

Hu Feng's explications of "typical characters" were based on a central idea that, he complained, was ignored by Zhou Yang: literature, as a cognitive enterprise, differs from science in that, whereas science illustrates sensual particularity from a theoretical perspective, literature represents universality through particularity.[28] Underlying this central idea is the relationship between theory and practice. It follows from Hu Feng's position that literature is a search for the truths of life rather than a mere reduplication of social reality according to preexisting theoretical postulates. As a result, the social reality reflected (or, more exactly, refracted) in literature is concretized and inextricably mingled with writers' imagination, feelings, and personal views. No longer a set of self-enclosed phenomena reproducible in a scientific manner, it becomes expandable with the introduction of human agency.

Discussing Hu Feng's opinions on literature as a praxis, and his views on praxis in general, we should not overlook the importance he placed on will. Under the influence of romanticism, conveyed by Hakuson and Lukács in different ways, will in his view becomes an all-powerful force that refuses to be restrained by reason in its striving for existence. Hence its development does not follow any rational purpose or pattern. As far as literary production is concerned, Hu Feng's emphasis on will, most typically seen in his constant promotion of "hand-to-hand combat with reality," set him apart from orthodox Marxist critics, including Marx, Engels, and Lenin, who considered the philosophical category of reflection the essential function of literature and took for granted the correspondence between literature and society. In contrast, literature became for Hu Feng a willed praxis, a kind of life struggle that contends against, among other things, various coercive interpretive schemata, including vulgarized Marxism. In the following section on his alliance with Lu Xun in the debate over the "Two Slogans," we shall see that, as the national situation changed, the question of will would turn into a political issue.

KEEPING STEP WITH LU XUN

Of all the May Fourth writers, Lu Xun made the deepest impression on Hu Feng during his formative years. I mentioned previously that in his high school days Hu Feng was shocked by Lu Xun into an intuitive grasp of the darkness of Chinese society. Once he entered Beijing University in the fall of 1925, out of admiration he audited a course Lu Xun offered in the history of Chinese fiction. In his youth, however, Lu Xun remained by and large a revered yet distant teacher in spite of his intellectual impact.

Things started to change in 1933 after Hu Feng assumed the offices of the head of the propaganda department and then the secretary of the League of Left-Wing Writers and became the liaison between Lu Xun and the League. According to Lu Xun's diary, he wrote fifty-one letters and paid thirty-nine visits to Lu Xun between January

1934 and Lu Xun's death in October 1936. After he gained Lu Xun's trust, they began to edit journals and other publications in collaboration. Meanwhile, his friendship with Lu Xun further aggravated his troubled relationship with Zhou Yang, his opponent in the debate over "typical characters," of whom Lu Xun had always been suspicious.

At this point a brief analysis of the respective positions occupied by Lu Xun, Zhou Yang, and Hu Feng in the League will help us understand their interactions with each other. First of all we should bear in mind that the organization of the League, a radical assemblage constantly in danger of persecution by the Guomindang police, was loose at best. With a changing membership and a porous control over its members' viewpoints, skirmishes, including the debate between Hu Feng and Zhou Yang over the "typical characters," repeatedly broke out in the ranks of the League. Living in semi-seclusion, Lu Xun only served as its titular leader and had little sway over its day-to-day operations. In his place, Zhou Yang and his cohorts, standing for the CCP and its orthodoxy, gathered a large amount of power in their hands, but not to the degree of excluding their adversaries from the power competition. To regain his leadership in the ideological realm, Lu Xun resorted to the strategy of radicalizing himself more than the radicals and, in that vein, he wrote his most caustic essays in the last years of his life. As for Hu Feng, a newcomer to the Shanghai scene of leftist literature with little to his credit and no backing from the CCP, it was understandable for him to side with Lu Xun in order to gain a foothold in the leftist camp. Intertwined with political convictions, factionalism, and personal animus, this three-way relationship eventually gave rise to the heated debate over the "Two Slogans."

First formulated in the Soviet Union in 1930, the slogan "National Defense Literature" (Guofang wenxue) was introduced by Zhou Yang into China in January 1934, but afterwards it received virtually no attention from other writers for more than a year. As the Chinese national crisis intensified and the CCP, prompted by the Comintern, began to focus more on its cooperation with the Guomindang through a new united front, a group of leftist writers, led by Zhou Yang, started a campaign to promote "National Defense Literature" at the end of 1935. With the change in historical circumstances and the tireless propagation of the Zhou Yang group, the slogan soon gained an increasing number of supporters in literary circles.

Meanwhile, Lu Xun took "National Defense Literature" as a betrayal to the tradition of revolutionary literature as well as an abdication of the leftist camp's leadership in the literary world. In a letter dated May 4, 1936, Lu Xun told his correspondent that he had decided not to join the Writers' Association, an organization Zhou Yang had set up to implement "National Defense Literature" after he dissolved the League. Lu Xun's move marked his open rift with Zhou Yang. When Feng Xuefeng came from Yan'an, Lu Xun consulted a few associates, including Mao Dun, Hu Feng, and Feng Xuefeng, in the formulation of an alternative slogan that would extend, rather than terminate, as they believed "National Defense Literature" would, the tradition of revolutionary literature. The slogan Lu Xun finally decided upon was "Mass Literature of the National Revolutionary War" (Minzu geming zhanzheng de dazhong wenxue).

Upon Lu Xun's request, Hu Feng wrote an article "What Do the Masses Demand of Literature?" (Renmin dazhong xiang wenxue yaoqiu shenme?) on May 9, 1936, in which the Lu Xun camp's alternative slogan was publicized for the first time. "Mass Literature of the National Revolutionary War," Hu Feng argued in his article, solidified the themes of all social conflicts instead of liquidating them. In this seminal article Hu Feng advocated the following themes for current literature:

> The "Asian numbness" kept or even promoted among the masses by feudal ideology and traditionalism.
> The obstacles to and the suppression of the working people's desire for life that decrease or even destroy their enthusiasm and power.
> The extravagant lifestyle of the privileged and the abuse of power that harm the mobilization and unification of the people.[29]

These themes, focused on the domestic agenda of antifeudalism, apparently attempted to continue the May Fourth project of cultural criticism and enlightenment at a time when the domestic agenda was increasingly dominated by the agenda of anti-imperialism and national salvation, an agenda that could also find its predecessor in the May Fourth movement, although the link was certainly less direct and more mediated by contemporary factors.

In the ensuing debate over the "Two Slogans," an issue far more palpable than the tension between cultural criticism and national salvation was the concern over political compromise. We should remember that, after his clashes with the Beijing warlord regime in 1926 and his disillusionment with the Guangzhou Guomindang government in 1927, Lu Xun became increasingly radical in his political viewpoint in the last years of his life. As a staunch supporter of the League of Left-Wing Writers (the term "left-wing" was inserted into the name at his insistence), the militant Lu Xun openly associated himself with the left and with revolutionary literature in the 1930s, despite his reservations about the causes he sponsored and his leftist allies. While calling on his fellow leftists to wage a tenacious war against conservative social forces and setting himself up as their example by copiously writing essays in the manner of "dagger and javelin," he repeatedly warned them against the danger of becoming "salon revolutionaries" and backsliding into rightism. Any united front with nonradical social elements, in his view, had to be built with social revolution as its goal and with its leadership firmly in the hands of leftists. By changing the agenda of revolutionary literature from antifeudalism to antiimperialism and by adulterating the ranks of leftist writers and relinquishing their leadership, "National Defense Literature" proved to him that his apprehension was not unfounded.

Contrary to the capitulatory "National Defense Literature," "Mass Literature of the National Revolutionary War" was conceived as an attempt to continue the proletarian revolutionary literature promoted thus far by the League, as Lu Xun declared in an article he dictated on his sickbed on June 10, 1936.[30] As such, Lu Xun went on to say, its subject matter should break through the confinement of "National Defense Literature" and should include, instead, everything that happened in the contemporary life in China.[31] Lu Xun's emphasis on a panoramic view of contemporary social reality indicated that to a certain degree the debate over the "Two Slogans" was also a debate between the paradigms of critical realism and socialist realism. Five days before Lu Xun dictated his article, Zhou Yang published an article entitled "On National Defense Literature" (Guanyu guofang wenxue) in which he argued that national defense literature must adopt the method of "progressive realism." He defined "progressive realism" as "to portray reality truthfully, concretely and historically in the actual development of revolution for the sake of educating the working masses with the spirit of socialism,"[32] an unmistakable echo of the official definition of socialist realism. Keeping in view the postulate of revolutionary tendentiousness in "National Defense Literature" and the emphasis on fullness and particularity in "Mass Literature of the National Revolutionary War," we may argue that in a sense the debate over the "Two Slogans" picked up where Hu Feng left off in his earlier veiled criticism of socialist realism as "formulism."

Pregnant with political and paradigmatical significance, the debate over the "Two Slogans" was not a "silly quarrel in itself" as C. T. Hsia once called it.[33] As far as Hu Feng was concerned, in spite of the fact that he, on Lu Xun's and Feng Xuefeng's advice, refrained from embroiling himself any further after writing his only article for the debate, the Lu Xun camp's firm resolution to keep alive the tradition of revolutionary literature and critical realism fundamentally determined the orientation of his future career as a critic and the editor of *Qiyue*. Like his mentor Lu Xun, he would remain focused on the domestic agenda of cultural criticism under all circumstances and devote his attention to the danger of betrayal within the leftist ranks to such an extent that, as a very vocal critic, he would, during the wartime, keep himself away from several major debates concerning writers outside the leftist circles: the debate over Zhang Tianyi's short story "Mr. Huawei;" the debate over Liang Shiqiu's call for a literature including, but not limited to, the theme of resistance; and the debate with the so-called *Zhanguo* (*Warring state*) writers. Necessitated by the mantle of Lu Xun's only genuine successor that he increasingly came to assume after the debate over the "Two Slogans," his unswerving focus demonstrated a typical case of an heir being inherited by a heritage. Ultimately, what Theodore Huters describes as the claustrophobia in Hu Feng's wartime writings was determined by Hu Feng's position.[34]

The debate over the two slogans ended with Lu Xun's death in October 1936, but the full ramifications of "Mass Literature of the National Revolutionary War" did not play out until the inception of *Qiyue* in October 1937. From its beginning the journal unabashedly displayed its inheritance of the position held by the Lu Xun camp in the debate. In its inaugural statement "Willing to Grow with Our Readers" (Yuan he duzhe yitong chengzhang), Hu Feng defined the cultural tasks of the war against Japan with propositions that harked back to those he made in "What Do the Masses Demand of Literature?" more than a year ago. Instead of uncritically eulogizing the war as an endeavor of national salvation, as the majority of Chinese writers were doing at the time, he regarded the war as a catharsis that would expose the weaknesses of the Chinese caused by prolonged feudal oppression. The war, in his vision, was not only a military war but also a cultural war that would finally purify and strengthen the Chinese nation.[35] His advocacy of unremitting social criticism and social reform obviously followed the direction pointed out by Lu Xun during the debate over the "Two Slogans."

The genealogical relation between the Lu Xun camp and *Qiyue* can also be seen in the makeup of the journal's early contributors and, later, the way Hu Feng supported his young disciples. Major contributors to *Qiyue*, at its early stage, included Lu Xun's protégés Xiao Hong, Xiao Jun, and Duanmu Hongliang. These young but more or less established writers published in *Qiyue* personal, sometimes nostalgic, essays imitative of Lu Xun's prose. In the subsequent stages of *Qiyue*, when most of Lu Xun's associates no longer played important roles in the journal, Hu Feng's promotion of new writers bore a strong resemblance to Lu Xun's sponsorship of his followers.[36] From his personal correspondence we can see that, like Lu Xun, Hu Feng devoted much of his energy to training a younger generation of writers who would not hesitate to do battle with their enemies on matters of principle. With himself at the center of *Qiyue*, Hu Feng tried to organize his protégés into a closely knit group, demanding, again in Lu Xun's manner, ideological and political allegiance as well as personal loyalty.

All things considered, *Qiyue* should be viewed as an outgrowth of the Lu Xun camp's uncompromising stand in the debate over the "Two Slogans." Throughout its evolution Hu Feng faithfully kept step with what he understood as the spirit of Lu Xun, a highly critical perception of Chinese society that Lu Xun had achieved after decades of struggles and disappointments. The spirit of Lu Xun, in Hu Feng's interpretation, was characterized by its keen awareness of the tenacity of tradition in all walks of life, including the revolutionary ranks. While insisting on the importance and urgency of cultural criticism, it gave little room for facile optimism and constantly stayed on guard against any compromise on its agenda. Fully displayed in the debate over the "Two Slogans," it was repeatedly evoked afterwards by Hu Feng and his *Qiyue* followers to clarify their program and to castigate their opponents. In that sense it remained the guiding principle throughout the existence of the journal.

Two

Antidote to Wartime Heroics: Early *Qiyue* Reportage

On July 7, 1937, Japanese troops crossed the Marco Polo Bridge near Beijing and raided the town of Wanping. Their aggression was met with resistance from the local Chinese garrison, which quickly led to a full-scale war between China and Japan. Soon war spread to the Shanghai region. On August 13, the Japanese Marine Corps launched an attack on Shanghai and the Chinese defending army in the city immediately struck back. The war against Japan instantly inflamed the patriotic mood of the Chinese nation that had been brewing for years. As a result, the majority of Chinese writers, regardless of their political leanings, put out an all-out effort to boost the morale of their compatriots at this critical juncture in Chinese history.

Hu Feng reacted to the rapidly escalating national crisis in his own ways. Within days of seeing the Japanese bombing of the Nanshi District of Shanghai on August 24, 1937, he wrote a group of emotion-filled poems exalting the resistance against Japan. The emotional spell, however, was followed by determined work in the vein of what he had hitherto championed. On September 11 he founded a weekly *Qiyue* (July) in Shanghai as his response to the war; the journal was named after the month of the Marco Polo Bridge Incident. Predating *Literary Battlefield* (*Wenyi zhendi*, founded in Guangzhou in April 1938) and *Resistance Literature* (*Kangzhan wenyi*, founded in May 1938 in Wuhan), two leading literary journals during the war, *Qiyue* became the first major wartime literary magazine.

Chapter Two

Hu Feng financed his journal by collecting donations from his friends. The limited financial resources, compounded by other wartime material exigencies, resulted in its small circulation. However, the limited circulation also reflected Hu Feng's ideal for literary production in China—the proliferation of small, independent journals—an ideal that was to persist even in the petition he sent to Mao Zedong and the CCP Central Committee in 1954 shortly before his downfall. Thus motivated by a strong desire for independence throughout its existence, *Qiyue* differed significantly from what Hu Feng dubbed "official journals," an unflattering reference to *Literary Battlefield* and *Resistance Literature*, in subject matter and perspective. Whereas the "official journals," associated in spirit with the government propaganda apparatus, remained intent on promoting the war effort by singing praises of the Chinese nation for its heroism, *Qiyue* continued to call attention to the longstanding cultural problems China had yet to overcome during the war. Since the strategic difference first displayed itself in reportage, the genre that predominated the literary scene at the beginning of the war, the present chapter will discuss early *Qiyue* reportage in connection with its historical context.

THE BACKGROUND OF EARLY *QIYUE* REPORTAGE

In the mid-1930s reportage had already become a more or less established literary genre in China.[1] Starting out with works such as Liang Qichao's *Travels on the New Continent* (*Xindalu youji*, 1903) and Qu Qiubai's *Journeys in the Land of Hunger* (*Exiang jicheng*, 1923) and *Spiritual History of the Red Capital* (*Chidu xinshi*, 1924), Chinese reportage changed its form from travelogues to personal memoirs, such as the journal of military life by Xie Bingying, in the late 1920s. After its founding in 1930, the League of Left-Wing Writers conscientiously promoted it as a genre that could directly bring contemporary social issues to the attention of a broad audience. The strong interest can be seen, for instance, in a discussion on the theory and practice of reportage that Mao Dun set off in January 1932 when he published his translation of the Japanese writer Kawaguchi Hiroshi's article "On Reportage" in *Beidou* (Big Dipper), an official organ of the League. The discussion was carried on in many left-wing literary journals, with different degrees of intensity at different times, until 1938. In the meantime, more and more writers tried their hand at the genre.

Generically related to the news report and thematically focused on topical events, reportage enjoyed two surges of productivity and popularity in the early 1930s, the first sparked off by the Mukden Incident of September 18, 1931, and the second by the Shanghai Campaign of January 28, 1932, with the Chinese nation's immense concern over the imminent threat of Japanese invasion underlying the sudden prominence of the genre at both times. Partly inspired by the analytical approach of Marxism that emphasized social totality and partly in response to the top concern of the nation, reportage in the early 1930s began to shift its attention from the personal to the collective experience and the shift soon gave rise to a subgenre—"collective reportage." In April 1932, in the wake of the Shanghai Campaign, Nanqiang Book Company in Shanghai published the first sample of "collective reportage"—*The Shanghai Incident and Reportage* (*Shanghai shibian yu baogao wenxue*) compiled by the renowned writer and critic A Ying. In 1936, the collectivization of reportage finally culminated in *One Day in China: May 21, 1936*, a selection of 469 pieces from more than three thousand entries submitted by people from all walks of life to an ambitious project intended to reveal the entire face of China during one day.[2]

Bound up with the influence of the holistic discourse of Marxism on the one hand and, on the other, with the writers', and the reading public's, awareness of the Chinese nation as a unity under Japanese threat, the collectivization of Chinese reportage in the 1930s was deeply rooted in specific historical circumstances. The formal development of reportage from the travelogue to personal memoirs and then to "collective reportage" reflected historical demands as well as the writers' endeavors to meet the demands. The direct bearing of historical dynamics on reportage was noted by Mao Dun, an important editor and critic of reportage, as early as in February 1937:

> Every age produces its own characteristic literature. "Reportage" is the characteristic literary genre produced by our hurried and changeful age. The masses of readers cannot wait to know the changes in life that took place yesterday and writers urgently want to dissect for the masses of readers the most recent social phenomena (which take place almost every day) and journals want to display their keen sense of the times—all these are the causes for the origination and popularity of "reportage."[3]

Chapter Two

As an epitome of historical dynamics, the outbreak of the full-scale war against Japan catapulted reportage into an unprecedented position of prominence and prestige. According to an overview offered by the critic Yi Qun during the war, the erstwhile secondary genre almost filled the literary supplements of newspapers and magazines while all literary journals devoted 70 to 80 percent of their total space to reportage. With readers waiting anxiously for the publication of each new reportage piece, 80 to 90 percent of established authors, including fiction writers, poets, essayists, and literary critics, wrote at least a few reportage pieces each. Under such circumstances, reportage had reached its heyday.[4] Of course, the wartime wave of reportage could be ascribed to many causes, such as the reading public's thirst for topical truth, the lack of time for frequently dislocated writers to search for in-depth reflections on the welter of wartime happenings and the material difficulties in publishing lengthy works during the war, reportage writers' strong agitational desire, however, played a most crucial role in turning this time-bound, history-specific genre into the literary mainstream of a critical moment in Chinese history.

Reportage writers' agitational desire determined both the content and the techniques of much of the reportage written at the early stage of the war. It gave rise to an optimistic view that China, in spite of the military setbacks it had suffered so far in the war, would win the ultimate victory. This optimistic view was, for example, typically demonstrated by a large number of reportage works about the Tai'erzhuang Campaign of March–April 1938, a campaign in which the Chinese army scored one of the first major victories in the war. Treating Tai'erzhuang as a stand-in for China, writers of various political leanings, including the Communist critic Yi Qun, the Guomindang writer Sun Ling and the nonpartisan writer Xie Bingying, turned a small town in Shandong Province into a monumental symbol of China's strength and hope.

In contrast to most of the early wartime reportage characterized by its focus on the strength of the Chinese, real or imaginary, and its upbeat tone, *Qiyue* reportage started out with its attention directed to quotidian occurrences *behind* the front line and, more significantly, with an approach to Chinese society that remained determinedly in keeping with critical realism. Much of early *Qiyue* reportage consisted of eye-witness accounts of happenings in the society with the authors' highly personal and unequivocally disapproving standpoint fully foregrounded. Topical truth, the center of attention for *Qiyue* reportage as for the rest of the contemporary reportage, was divested of the narrowly defined patriotic teleology and facile optimism. Instead, it exemplified a perception of the still existing necessity of the Chinese nation's spiritual reform in the changed circumstances and the protracted nature of such an undertaking. In short, as we shall see below, a critical paradigm distinguished early *Qiyue* reportage from the contemporary agitational reportage in both subject matter and intention.

A first glimpse of the critical paradigm in *Qiyue* reportage can be obtained from "On the Sketch" (Lun suxie), an article Hu Feng wrote on January 2, 1935, in response to the growing popularity of the sketch, a shortened form of reportage. In this article, apparently intended for would-be sketch writers, Hu Feng considered the sketch a sister genre of the argumentative essay (*zawen*) that responded, in a descriptive manner, directly and critically to the daily events in a fast-changing society. With the same social purpose as the *zawen* but a different approach, the sketch, in his opinion, should adhere strictly to social reality and should, instead of describing irrelevant details, capture the essence of social phenomena. To realize such an ideal, a sketch writer would have to immerse himself in real life and equip himself with a firm viewpoint and the capability of astute observation.[5]

A more immediate source of inspiration for early *Qiyue* reportage, however, was Lu Xun's opinions in the debate over the "Two Slogans." Dissatisfied with the narrow scope of "National Defense Literature," Lu Xun argued, in an article he dictated to Feng Xuefeng on June 10, 1936, that "Mass Literature of the National Revolutionary War" should by no means be limited to the battles fought by patriotic volunteers or to the anti-Japanese rallies staged by students. Instead, its subject matters should cover everything in contemporary China.[6] Lu Xun himself practiced what he preached. For example, on August 23, 1936, Lu Xun wrote a *zawen* piece "This Too Is Life . . . " (Zhe ye shi shenghuo . . .) in which, while ridiculing the "most central theme" of National Defense Literature, Lu Xun talked in a confessional tone about his physical as well as mental exhaustion as a patient nearing death and his appreciation of the quotidian details of his life. "But people consider these ordinary things to be dregs of life without taking a look at them," he continued metaphorically, "those who strip the branches and leaves will never get the flower and fruit."[7]

Famous as a fearless fighter, Lu Xun nonetheless used a personal

Chapter Two

example to prove that not everything a fighter does in his daily life is majestic. As we shall see shortly, Lu Xun's refutation of the grandiose yet confining paradigm of National Defense Literature and his attention to the seemingly pointless details of mundane life provided a model for the *Qiyue* reportage writer Cao Bai. Faithfully keeping his eyes on the "branches and leaves" of the life he witnessed in Shanghai refugee shelters, Cao Bai would deflate the eulogy of patriotic heroism at both the collective and personal levels.

As reportage grew dramatically in volume and in importance during the war, Hu Feng provided further advice on the practice of the genre with a December 1937 article "On a Combative Literary Genre in Wartime" (Lun zhandouqi de yige zhandou de wenyi xingshi). After a brief account of the history and features of reportage, Hu Feng pointed out two weaknesses in wartime reportage—flat description and excessive sentimentalism. To remedy these shortcomings, he argued that writers should focus on the essential aspects of life and convey their emotions through concrete details selected from real life. Moreover, apparently following Lu Xun, he insisted that writers should depict patriotic heroes as complicated human beings with both strengths and weaknesses.[8] Hu Feng's advice played an important role in the maturation of *Qiyue* reportage from a more or less *journalistic* genre into a *literary* genre. If early *Qiyue* reportage contributors like Cao Bai, trying perhaps too hard to fault the pretentious paradigm of National Defense Literature, still could not help falling into the traps of flat description and unassimilated commentary from time to time, later contributors such as Qiu Dongping and A Long, heeding Hu Feng's advice, became able to turn their reportage works into organic equilibriums in which the subject matters and the authors' personal views and feelings are integrated.

Besides theoretical discussions on reportage, Hu Feng also instructed *Qiyue* reportage contributors with his editor's notes and evaluations of individual reportage works. For instance, a specified guideline for potential reportage contributors was given in November 1937 in the following editor's announcement in *Qiyue:*

> We particularly hope those who work on the front lines and in the battle zones, those who take care of wounded soldiers in hospitals, and those who work among the masses such as peasants, workers and shop clerks in the interior, will write about their personal

experience and send their works to us. However, when doing so, they should pay special attention to the following points: (1) they should seize the essential elements and avoid wordy, flat description; (2) the authors' reactions should be truthful. Neither indifference nor exaggeration is good; (3) the authors should possess a critical spirit and should expose any dark or dirty phenomenon courageously; (4) they should get rid of conceptual, abstract discourse in their use of language.[9]

Directives like the above laid the groundwork for the most important characteristics of *Qiyue* reportage—"personal" and "critical." Based invariably on firsthand experience, *Qiyue* reportage strove to show life as it appeared to the writer, apparently taking issue with trimming life for propagandist purposes. In narrating his personal experience, however, the writer would adopt a critical approach to what happened around him and convey his personal opinions either explicitly through authorial comments or implicitly through the selection of details. Since these features were first embodied in the reportage by Cao Bai, in the following pages I will proceed with an analysis of Cao Bai's works as typical examples of early *Qiyue* reportage before I move on to the battlefield reportage by another *Qiyue* reportage writer Qiu Dongping. In so doing I hope to delineate both the similarities and differences between different phases of *Qiyue* reportage.

CAO BAI: AN EXEMPLUM OF EARLY *QIYUE* REPORTAGE

One of the first writers who sought to implement Hu Feng's propositions about reportage and received, in return, Hu Feng's commendation was Cao Bai (real name Liu Pingruo). Born in Changzhou, Jiangsu Province, in 1907, Cao Bai went to the National Art School in Hangzhou, Zhejiang Province, to study wood-engraving. In 1933 he was arrested and put in jail by the Guomindang government for organizing a radical student club in school. Released in 1935, he went to Shanghai and began working as a school teacher. That summer he submitted two entries to a national wood engraving exhibition held in Shanghai and one of them, a portrait of Lu Xun, was rejected by the government censors. Angered by the rejection, he sent the portrait to Lu Xun with a letter in March 1936 and received a quick response, in which Lu Xun expressed support for Cao Bai and asked him to write a report on his experience in jail. With this encouragement Cao Bai wrote his first reportage "A Brief Account of Being in Jail" and, thereafter, became one of the old mentor's most frequent correspondents. According to the *Collected Works of Lu Xun*, from March 21 to October 15, 1936, Lu Xun wrote fifteen letters to Cao Bai, offering him personal as well as professional advice. As Cao Bai entered Lu Xun's inner circle, he befriended Hu Feng. When Hu Feng proposed to start his own journal *Qiyue* in 1937, Cao Bai immediately endorsed the idea and regarded Hu Feng's move as a correction of what he also saw as the rampant resistance formulism of the time.[10] Granting Hu Feng's request for short, prompt, and unformulaic reportage about refugees in Shanghai, for whom Cao Bai was working then as a refugee shelter administrator, he began to make submissions to Hu Feng and thus became one of the first contributors to *Qiyue*.

Belligerent to resistance formulism, Cao Bai's reportage should be understood in the context of the debate over the "Two Slogans." As Lu Xun's adherent, Cao Bai tries to carry out his mentor's call for the expansion of subject matter by premising his reportage strictly on his own personal experience so that he could offer a true reflection of a slice of life as a counterforce to the formulaic works of National Defense Literature. Hence his reportage adopts a fundamentally polemic stance and inherits many features of Lu Xun's satiric *zawen*. Comments, often unassimilated, abound in his otherwise descriptive pieces. In terms of format, his reportage mostly consists of short sketches that, as a rule, do not have a plot with a beginning, a crisis and a dénouement, a further indication of his avoidance of formulism. The "factual" authority is maintained with consistent first-person narration, yet this very device foregrounds the author's conspicuous presence. In the end what we see in his reportage is not a value-free reduplication but a refraction of a certain segment of life.

"Here, Life Is Also Breathing" (Zheli, shengming yezai huxi) is Cao Bai's first reportage work published in *Qiyue*. Immediately following Hu Feng's inaugural statement, it occupies a prominent position in the first issue of *Qiyue*. Its theme, just like its title, is obviously derived from "This Too Is Life . . . ," the essay by Lu Xun that I mentioned above. In order to keep the "branches and leaves of life," as Lu Xun recommended, Cao Bai incorporates details of his life as a refugee shelter administrator into this piece to the point of diffusion.

The first part of "Here, Life Is Also Breathing" is almost entirely taken up by an untrimmed conversation Cao Bai conducts with a refugee, in which the refugee mentions, among other things, his wife's death in a Japanese bombing in a matter-of-fact tone. Cao Bai further reveals the refugee's apathy by telling us his unwillingness to let his son go to the front line. Instead of portraying eager avengers against Japanese atrocities, Cao Bai presents insensitive and indifferent characters that remind us of the lower-class characters in Lu Xun's stories.

While tacitly criticizing the refugees, Cao Bai reserves his fiercest lashes for the Chinese bureaucrats and merchants, picking up trenchant details to show the unnecessary aggravations they have caused the refugees. The bureaucrats assign and switch refugee shelters by favoritism and their appointees, in turn, embezzle the rice allocated for the refugees in their charge. As a result, the daily ration of cooked rice for the refugees becomes lower than that for prisoners. To make things worse, the stingy owners of the movie theater where more than four hundred refugees are crammed with little fresh air only allow two fifty-watt light bulbs to be lit, adding to the general confusion in the dim theater. In comparison to the problems created by Chinese bureaucrats and merchants, the Japanese invasion becomes a far less imminent menace to the refugees. In fact, only near the end of "Here, Life Is Also Breathing" does Cao Bai mention that Japanese shelling can be vaguely heard in the distance from the shelter.

A mixture of graphic description and sarcastic commentary, "Here, Life Is Also Breathing" fires its criticism at two targets: the Chinese bureaucrats and merchants within its textual world and, the sanguine patriotic formulism outside. Untrimmed immediacy, presented in the form of details in daily life, is sought from a personal perspective to expose the fallacy of the latter. Yet as Cao Bai tries to combat patriotic formulism with the "branches and leaves of life," he cannot help being caught up between polemic intention and particularity, or, in other words, between refraction and reflection. To put it another way, his polemic intention engenders a core conception of the flawed character of Chinese society that ends up undermining his effort to preserve unadorned particularity. Thus torn between cross-purposes and pulled in different directions, Cao Bai's reportage often results in a generic hodgepodge even by his own admission.[11]

Cao Bai's next two reportage works with *Qiyue,* "In the Shadow of Death" (Zai sishen de heiying xiamian) and "Seizing the 'Living

Soul'" (Huo linghun de duoqu), are sequels to "Here, Life Is Also Breathing" both temporally and thematically. As such, they continue offering similar details and comments about his work in Shanghai refugee shelters. As he narrates his experience from a first-person viewpoint and makes intrusive comments in the "dagger and javelin" style of Lu Xun's *zawen*, the author certainly makes himself not only the vantage point for observation but also the intellectual and moral center of his work. In view of the trend of collectivization in wartime reportage, we may argue that in turning to personal life Cao Bai tries to offer an alternative approach to the emplotment of wartime experience, an approach marked, first and foremost, by its deliberate disagreement with the prevailing communal patriotic norms. We should further note that aesthetically the literary trend of patriotic collectivism works by means of sublimation, which, as Ban Wang points out in a recent book, elevates and purifies the image of the individual with the removal of what is personal, human, and idiosyncratic.[12] In contrast, by focusing his attention on what is excluded from the collectivized and sublimated image of the individual, Cao Bai expresses a strong desire for individuality and independence, a desire borne out at the formal level by the first-person singular point of view and the intimate forms of diary entry or personal letter his reportage often adopts. His effort to relativize the prevailing collective perspective of the time, however, is constantly undercut by his polemic zeal, which often blocks up interpretations different from its own.

As a consequence of his preoccupation with the mundane particularities in daily life, Cao Bai's reportage often appears to be intentionally uneventful and, sometimes, disorganized. It seems that when Hu Feng, in his December 1937 article "On a Combative Literary Genre in Wartime" that I discussed above, criticized wartime reportage for its flat description he might have Cao Bai's reportage in his mind as well. To rectify this erroneous tendency, Hu Feng asked writers to pay more attention to characterization, and his advice was promptly heeded by Cao Bai. Within a month Cao Bai submitted a reportage work "Yang Kezhong" to *Qiyue*, which came out on February 1, 1938, in the eighth issue of the journal.

One of the first wartime reportage works to focus on characterization, "Yang Kezhong" depicts the title character as Cao Bai knew him in real life. The recourse to a real-life model, with all his personal peculiarities, turns "Yang Kezhong" into a contrast to wartime heroics that draws on patriotic imagination. To begin with, Cao Bai tells us that Yang violates the regulation against smoking as soon as he comes to the refugee shelter with his friends. A taciturn artist, Yang appears haughty and untrustworthy to Cao Bai at first. Hard pressed by the shortage of personnel, he reluctantly puts Yang in charge of the educational work. Only after he is impressed by Yang's hard work does he start to get close to Yang and learn that Yang was almost used as cannon fodder by the Guomindang army because of his involvement in leftist activities. What is more, the injustices against Yang do not come to an end, for his hard work in the refugee shelter only draws jealousy and gossip. With his poor health aggravated by slanders, he eventually dies in an army hospital after several surgical operations. Enumerated one after another, the repeated injuries and hardships Yang Kezhong has to endure in his young life become the highlight of this gloomy story.

The portrayal of Yang Kezhong as an unheroic hero is, once again, largely derived from Lu Xun's perception of the fighter as a flesh-and-blood human being in a mundane world. Therefore in this unpretentious portrayal as much, if not more, attention is paid to Yang's careless appearance and manners, his reserved personality, and his sickness as to his diligent work. In the end, he impresses the reader as nothing more than an ordinary human being who has performed a particular job at full capacity for the cause of resistance. The de-idealization of the hero, however, does not stop with Yang Kezhong. It further extends to Cao Bai's self-image in the piece. Just as Yang is depicted as an unheroic hero, Cao Bai characterizes himself as a fallible man who, for one thing, frequently admits to his misunderstanding of Yang. This problematization of self-image can be viewed, beyond issues of Lu Xun's influence, as another step Cao Bai takes in deflating wartime heroism, since the exaltation of the nation during the war also engenders the aggrandizement of the self as part and parcel of the nation.

As Shanghai increasingly became a so-called "isolated island" and as the protracted nature of the war began to dawn on more and more people, Cao Bai's deflation of his own image went further and further. In the last reportage pieces he wrote before leaving Shanghai in July 1938 for the guerrilla areas in Jiangsu Province, he began to borrow Lu Xun's descriptions of Ah Q to characterize himself. The following is a wrap-up of his work in the Shanghai refugee shelters, given purposefully in the manner of a devil's advocate against the beautification of the patriotic fighter:

> Upon the heels of the "August Thirteenth Incident," I began to work for the refugee shelters on August 17 until now. What have I accomplished in work? Nothing at all as far as I myself am concerned, except that I cried five times under the pain of fighting. I admit that crying is so laughable and so petty bourgeois, . . . but for me there was no other way to ease the pain other than crying. Secondly, I have defecated in my pants under the pressure of work. That has happened three times all together. . . .
> To the fighters these are all extreme trivialities. However, I want to mention them here because I have indeed been engaged in fighting and in work. If someone forces me to tell him what my accomplishments have been in Shanghai, I will first of all mention those things and say: they are the things I listed above.[13]

Given Cao Bai's polemic intention in highlighting trivialities as a corrective to high-sounding heroics, his generous admissions of his own weaknesses, like his acknowledgments of Yang Kezhong's peculiarities, constitute an effort to bring the image of the patriotic fighter back down to human size. At once a down-to-earth worker for the cause of national survival and a distinctive, imperfect human being, the patriotic fighter in his description is characterized by a multidimensionality that the hyperbolic wartime heroics has overlooked. In the meantime, as he unfailingly follows Lu Xun's advice on the presentation of the fighter's full picture, Cao Bai seems to be unaware (or intentionally forgets?) that the same Lu Xun, in his important essay "On the Power of *Mara* Poetry" (Moluo shi li shuo) written in 1907, once constructed and extolled an idealized, gigantic body of power in aesthetic terms.[14] What emerges in his reportage, as a result, is an image of a patriot with all his physical, biological attributes, needs, functions, and infirmities.

Finally, I should point out that Cao Bai's reportage is a typical example of early *Qiyue* reportage as a whole. Like him, most early *Qiyue* reportage contributors approach their subject matter, including the most sensitive subjects of traitors and patriotic heroes, from their personal perspectives. For instance, in a sketch of the traitor You Nu Jufen, the author Gannu (Nie Gannu) presents anecdotes of hypocrisy and superstition about the wife of his former teacher of Japanese, who later worked and died for the Japanese invaders, in a sarcastic tone imitative of Lu Xun's style. In a sketch of a resistance hero, the author Duanmu Hongliang sympathetically describes the dilemma his old general Sun Dianying faced when trying to appeal to his plunderous soldiers and to the suffering civilians at the same time. Instead of glossing over the moral dubiousness of Sun, a former warlord and a resistance hero now, Duanmu describes Sun's manipulation of people's superstitious beliefs and the crude disciplinary measures he applied to his troops.

On the whole *Qiyue* reportage, like that by Cao Bai, avoided subjects most prone to stirring up patriotic zeal. The journal carried very little reportage about Japanese atrocities, a rare exception among wartime literary journals. Another difference can be seen in its reportage about hospital visits, a popular category in which many reportage writers of the time expressed their hatred of the Japanese enemy with their emotional/psychological reactions to the sights of wounds. In the fourth issue of *Qiyue,* for the first and only time, six sketches about treatments of wounded Chinese soldiers, covering diverse areas such as Kaifeng, Anqing, and Wuhan, were published under the collective title "After They Have Fought" (Tamen zhandou le yihou). These sketches invariably accentuated the maltreatments of the wounded in the hands of their compatriots and the dispiriting emotional/psychological effect on the authors. The kindred perspectives, similar details and comparable reactions in these pieces, all of them by unknown authors, displayed communal norms peculiar to *Qiyue*.

When Hu Feng first started *Qiyue,* he insisted that it should be run as a "journal for the like-minded" (tongren zazhi), a position in sharp contrast to the self-effacing efforts made by editors of other wartime journals for the sake of embracing writers of all inclinations. In early *Qiyue* reportage we see the first yield of an emerging school in the wartime literary scene. Contrary to some critics' assumption, the *Qiyue* school was not a creation of the 1950s by Communist foes like Zhou Yang and Mao Zedong for the sake of political suppression. Instead, it existed as a commonly acknowledged literary group that adhered to *Qiyue*'s position as a "journal for the like-minded," a position Hu Feng never gave up as the editor of the journal. On April 29, 1938, at a meeting attended by both *Qiyue* and non-*Qiyue* writers, Hu Feng reiterated that *Qiyue* was a journal with a certain editorial orien-

Chapter Two

tation and a tendency shared by its contributors. The non-*Qiyue* participants Feng Naichao and Lou Shiyi agreed with him on this point.[15] Due to its writers' frequent dislocations during the turbulent wartime, the membership of the *Qiyue* group underwent changes, but the existence of the school, premised on a critical agenda, was undeniable even at this early stage. As the two most frequently mentioned representatives of the *Qiyue* group at the meeting, Cao Bai and Qiu Dongping, the writer we are going to discuss next, exemplified the critical viewpoint of the *Qiyue* group most intensely at this stage, albeit in different areas.

QIU DONGPING'S SUBVERSION OF BATTLEFIELD HEROICS

Wartime heroics, the formulaic tendency Cao Bai and other writers of early *Qiyue* reportage set out to rectify, was undoubtedly displayed most directly and most ardently in the war reportage of the time. In the face of such a powerful trend, *Qiyue* writers adopted two strategies: whereas writers like Cao Bai avoided the front line altogether by focusing solely on the civilian life in the rear, writers like Qiu Dongping and A Long confronted wartime heroics head-on with their relentless exposure of the incompetence and combat trauma of the Chinese army in their battlefield reportage. Since I have already discussed Cao Bai, in what follows I will switch my attention to Qiu Dongping's correction, from a realist standpoint, of the prevailing bloated panegyrics on heroism before I move on, in the next chapter, to an analysis of A Long's combat reportage and its relation to *Qiyue* fiction.

Qiu Dongping (1910–41) was already a more or less established writer before Hu Feng started *Qiyue*. Independent-minded and ambitious from the beginning of his literary career, he once expressed his aspirations in a letter to Guo Moruo he wrote during his stay in Japan in the early 1930s:

> My works should encompass Nietzschean superman, Marxist dialectics, the religion of Tolstoy and the Bible, Gorky's correct, solemn description, Baudelaire's ambiguity, but most importantly Barbusse's correct and courageous style.[16]

With the personal experience he gained from serving in the army, he was entrusted with the writing of "Giver" (Geiyuzhe), a war novella conceived by a group of writers right after the Shanghai Incident of August 13, 1937. In November 1937 he published two sketches in *Qiyue:* "An Impression of Ye Ting" (Ye Ting yingxiangji) and "Wu Luxun and His Wife Kiko" (Wu Luxun he jizi furen). While both were written in the personal, anecdotal mode typical of early *Qiyue* reportage, the second piece, a story about a Chinese army officer's forced divorce from his Japanese wife who had gone through thick and thin with him and shown support for the Chinese during the war against Japan, obviously conveyed criticism of the excess of nationalist sentiments at the time.

Qiu Dongping's first major contribution to *Qiyue* reportage was "The Seventh Company" (Diqilian), published in January 1938 in the sixth issue of the journal. Written in the form of a monologue by a cadet-turned-company commander Qiu Jun, "The Seventh Company" delineates Qiu's initiation into the world of modern warfare from his own perspective and in his own words. Given Qiu's status as an inexperienced cadet, it starts with a description of his fear, self-doubt, and total incomprehension of the battlefield under heavy barrages. The enemy fire, on the other hand, is depicted as accurate, brutal, and overwhelming:

> The enemy artillery fire was amazingly accurate and their cannon shots followed and chased our routed soldiers closely and relentlessly like a group of spirited, running ghosts. Having thrown away their weapons, the [Chinese] soldiers, covered with blood and mud, fled in the dense black smoke like mad wolves. The enemy gunfire was fierce and it appeared all the more fierce when it created fear on the battlefield and forced our soldiers on the front line to retreat helter-skelter and pitifully, creating a frightening picture we had never seen. It not only confused our morale, it almost completely snatched away our morale. I realized that this frightening scene alone could dissipate our fighting spirit before the enemy gunfire destroyed us.[17]

Here and at other places Qiu Dongping gives a vivid description of modern warfare in which the participant's sense-perceptions precede his understanding and, consequently, battle scenes become a fragmented series of terrifying impressions on a disoriented mind.

Written as a corrective to nationalistic propaganda and civilian ignorance, Qiu Dongping's battlefield reportage makes a point of bringing soldiers' traumatic experience in combat to the reader's attention. Instead of sacralizing the War of Resistance by whitewashing the violence on the battleground, it completely strips war of its last romantic aura. An important issue in this regard is the issue of bravery. Under the circumstances of modern warfare, personal bravery carries little weight and, if misapplied, it can cause more losses than gains to the combatants. Qiu Jun illustrates this for his readers with several examples of casualties resulted from Chinese soldiers' unnecessary exposure to enemy fire in the wake of their hasty attacks by order of their thoughtless officers. As he narrates his fellow combatants' incompetence and the resultant fiascos on the battlefield, Qiu Jun's perspective gradually shifts to that of a professional army officer who has grown out of his heroic dreams and come to realize, among other things, his own faintheartedness. When he, after failing the heroic ideal of committing suicide in the event of a total defeat on the battleground, gives an anticlimactic ending to his story by telling the reader that he has not fulfilled his promise to put a piece of an enemy soldier's skull, an enemy army flag, and parts of an enemy machine gun into a leather satchel as his nephew asked him to do, the antiheroic message is made all the more poignant.

The story in "The Seventh Company" presents a process in which Qiu Jun's heroic dreams are shattered in combat as he is gradually initiated into a world of frustration, exhaustion, horror, and even absurdity. When he comes out of the battlefield with nothing but failed promises, he gains little other than the realization of his own frailty as a fallible and fallen antihero. By registering its all too human main character's painful yet sobering induction into the highly mechanized world of modern warfare, "The Seventh Company" parodies the military *Bildungsroman* from the hard-nosed perspective of a professional army officer. In tandem with this perspective is a realistic mode the author employs in his portrayal of the battle scenes. In a lapidary style, Qiu Dongping clearly and forcefully describes battlefield actions with simple sentences, giving a blow-by-blow account of successive events with neither understatement nor exaggeration. While making an effort to convince the reader that he is telling nothing but the sober truth, he includes obscenities of speech, brutalities in action, and horrific details of squalor, suffering, and death. Consequently, the reader is shocked into new imaginative comprehension of not only the reality of combat but also the vitality and virtuosity of Qiu Dongping's remarkable style.

With regard to Qiu Dongping's realistic portrayal of the battlefield, I agree with Andrew Rutherford that realism necessarily undercuts the heroic by showing war and battle as nightmare amalgams of confusion, pain, exhaustion, fear, brutality, wounds, suffering, and death rather than fields of glory and by showing soldiers as commonplace ordinary men rather than heroes.[18] Influenced by the French writer Henri Barbusse's view on the stark reality in modern warfare, Qiu Dongping refuses to make a moral allegory out of the war against Japan. In his reportage battles are largely stripped of their moral connotations and they often amount to little more than *amoral* competitions of military strength. This view, already discernible in "The Seventh Company," is more trenchantly substantiated in "We Were Defeated There" (Women zai nali dale baizhang), a reportage piece published right after "The Seventh Company." Once again a first-person viewpoint is adopted, this time that of a Chinese army commander formerly in charge of the Jiangyin Battery, and the narrator Fang Shuhong starts his account with an acknowledgment of defeat before he goes on with a series of professional questions about his army's performance after the fact of defeat. Knowing the negative answers only too well, he concludes that:

> Both victory and defeat are entirely determined by the difference in strength—Let everything be judgd by history! . . . If we, the Chinese nation, completely lose the war to Japanese imperialism, the judgment of history is fair and I can only bow to the judgement and remain silent.[19]

The story of "We Were Defeated There" is about the Chinese army's defense of the Jiangyin Battery, in which a night attack, launched by Fang's regiment to take back a town lost to the Japanese, functions as the climax of the narrative. As a gambit, Fang's soldiers successfully wipe out a small group of Japanese sentries with a surprise attack. However, the Chinese side collapses when the Japanese start to use machine guns and tanks. With graphic details Fang Shuhong recounts how his officers and soldiers fight and die bravely in the battle. Yet the acts of these heroic individuals turn out to be no contest for the powerful Japanese weaponry. Having suffered from heavy casualties, Fang's regiment has to retreat after six hours of tenacious fighting. The rest of the story mainly consists of a brief enumeration of defeats suffered by the Chinese troops, ending with a poignant statement of a fact: "By the time we reached Nanjing there were only forty-six of us left altogether."

The unembellished factual account in "We Were Defeated There," offered by a military tactician who could evaluate professionally the defeats suffered by his troops, stands out in wartime reportage for its striking lack of sentimentality. While refuting any romantic notion of war, it raises a biting question about the patriotic propaganda for the sacred War of Resistance. The view on the war against Japan, as mediated through Fang Shuhong's account, is almost naturalistic in that it largely subjects the war to the jungle law of military strength and, as a result, soldiers, in spite of their bravery, appear helpless in front of the power of weaponry. As in "The Seventh Company," wartime heroics is deflated from the perspective of a participant, this time a more seasoned military expert.

As the war against Japan dragged on and the prospect of a speedy end to the war receded in 1938, Qiu Dongping's de-idealization of combat experience took a direction that clearly pointed to the influence of critical realist fiction. The change in direction is displayed in "A Company Commander's War Experience" (Yige lianzhang de zhandou zaoyu), a relatively long piece serialized in the thirteenth and fourteenth issues of *Qiyue* in May 1938. Unlike the first-person memoirs, the form Qiu Dongping had thus far adopted for his reportage, "A Company Commander's War Experience" is recounted by an intrusive, omniscient third-person narrator who not only has privileged access to the characters' thoughts, feelings, and motives but also makes frequent comments in his own words. Whereas the first-person narrators of Qiu Dongping's other reportage pieces, with all their personal opinions, necessarily live within the boundaries of the worlds of their stories, the third-person narrator in this piece, as he shifts at will from character to character and freely reports and evaluates their actions and states of consciousness, moves above and beyond the world of the story and, in so doing, manipulates his story to such a degree that a problem is created as to its categorization. First published in *Qiyue* as fiction, it was acclaimed by Qiu's fellow writers as the best specimen of wartime reportage, perhaps on account of its verifiable setting of the Shanghai Campaign, and so classified by later critics and anthologists of wartime literature.[20]

The problem of classification stems from the crucial feature that, by intervening in an explicit manner under the guise of an omniscient narrator, the author presents not just a referable story but his own creative performance as well. As a result, "A Company Commander's War Experience" impresses the reader as a verbal artifact more than Qiu Dongping's other reportage works. What is more important than the enhanced artistry, however, is the author's critical viewpoint in all respects, especially with regard to the Chinese army's conduct of the war and its treatment of the heroes in its ranks. To begin with, the author regards the military operation on the Chinese side as incompetent and confusing. Consequently, the fourth company, the focus of the story, becomes

> an ill-fated, unfortunate and baffled contingent. It often receives new mysterious orders, only to abandon them halfway and, in their place, gets even newer and more mysterious orders.
> No one knows why.[21]

Tired of building emplacements they know they are soon going to give up, the Chinese soldiers become cynics and vent their frustration by demolishing and looting an old house as they prepare the battleground. Animal imagery is generously used in description of the soldiers that reminds the reader, for one thing, of Lu Xun's fiction such as "A Madman's Diary" and "The True Story of Ah Q." However, once the fighting has started, these soldiers become eager, determined warriors in spite of their inadequate training, heavy casualties, and the order from their headquarters against any unauthorized attack on the enemy. As the author highlights and praises the soldiers' spontaneous heroism that reaches into the instinctive and irrational realms of human psychology, he unambiguously demonstrates that the upper echelon of the Chinese army, martinetishly clinging to its original battle plan, is completely out of touch with the happenings on the battlefield.

Heroism is demonstrated on a different plane by Lin Qingshi, the title character in "A Company Commander's War Experience." Unlike the action-oriented characterization of the secondary characters in the piece, the portrayal of Lin is largely psychology-centered, a feature that definitely moves the story away from reportage and toward fiction. Lin's psychological complexity, rarely seen in the plot-oriented wartime heroics, is shown in his self-questioning as he is touched by his soldiers' determination to fight, in his musing over whether he should launch his troops into a battle with a well-equipped Japanese contingent, and in his decision, after winning the battle, to surrender himself to his battalion commander to take responsibility for disobeying the order to keep his men from fighting the enemy, knowing full well that he will be executed. As the author details these decision-makings, especially the last one, from inside the character's mind, he makes it clear that Lin is motivated not by patriotism but by his personal willpower. To a large extent the emphasis on willpower is derived from a fusion of the author with his character, since Qiu Dongping himself was a strong advocate of moral courage and self-discipline in real life. While heeding Hu Feng's persistent calls for the writer's intellectual and emotional engagement with his characters, the author/character fusion here presages an important feature of *Qiyue* fiction that we will discuss in later chapters.

The most direct authorial intervention in "A Company Commander's War Experience" lies in the comments the author/narrator makes in his own voice. The following homage in the story, paid to a Chinese soldier's dead body as it is carried past other Chinese soldiers standing at the salute, is an example:

> The cruel god of war has snatched away the heroic warrior's life. He looks so young as he lies silently on a make-shift stretcher made out of a bamboo reclining chair. Blood-covered hair, blood-covered ears, and blood-covered nose. Those soldiers still alive will always remember his looks and always remember his soul and will. . . .
>
> Comrade, rest in peace! You will live in our memory. As long as you can get some peace, whatever you need we will give it to you unconditionally! We will toughen our steely shoulders in these fierce battles to carry you and all other fallen soldiers![22]

Unlike the factual lexicon of Qiu Dongping's earlier reportage works, the emotive language employed here refers, not to the inner world of the story, but to the author's mental state as he sees the body of the fallen hero in his mind's eye. Its function is expressive rather than

Antidote to Wartime Heroics

referential. As the author waxes poetic, his perspective changes from that of a hard-nosed professional army officer to that of a passionate man of letters. However, Qiu Dongping soon distinguishes himself from the practitioners of wartime heroics with his plot arrangement and other comments. At the end of the story, the fourth company is wiped out by a Chinese regiment as "suspicious" troops and its commander Lin Qingshi is executed for disobeying orders. "Unfortunately," the author/narrator laments, "they are not defeated by the fierce fire of the Japanese army but are destroyed at the hands of their fellow soldiers."[23] With the undeserved ending of the heroes and the authorial comment, a critical message is conveyed both at the story level and at the discourse level.

When it comes to the depiction of the war against Japan, the reportage by Qiu Dongping, like that by his *Qiyue* colleague Cao Bai, is characterized by the absence of any consideration for political expediency. Its aim apparently is set higher than patriotic agitation. As it moves away from fact-bound first-person recollections of specific battlefield experiences to third-person panoramic, omniscient narration, its focus shifts from the revelation of the truth of war to the reflection on longstanding problems in Chinese society reappearing in a different form under changed circumstances. In the meantime, its mimetic function also gives way to its verisimilar function, with the norms of verisimilitude derived from previous texts of critical realism. In choosing the Chinese army as a representative segment of a problematic society, Qiu Dongping in effect transplants a basic May Fourth assumption about Chinese society from realist fiction to reportage, an assumption reinforced by the increasing authorial intervention in his reportage. As we shall see in the following analysis of A Long, authorial intervention will be further intensified and, while bridging what is left of the formal gap between reportage and fiction, it will leave a distinct *Qiyue* imprint on works written in both genres.

THREE

FROM REFLECTION TO LYRICISM: THE TRANSITION FROM *Qiyue* Reportage to *Qiyue* Fiction

In October 1937, after publishing three weekly issues of *Qiyue,* Hu Feng moved his journal to Wuhan as the war approached Shanghai. Publication was soon resumed and *Qiyue,* now a biweekly, kept its schedule rather punctually during its nine-month sojourn in Wuhan.[1] When Wuhan came under the threat of Japanese invasion Hu Feng had to relocate his journal once again. After an interregnum of a year, *Qiyue* came out in Chongqing in July 1939. As the worsened circumstances for the publishing industry added to its financial problems, the journal now could hardly keep its schedule as a monthly. In spite of all the odds, however, it managed to stay alive till September 1941, when its registration expired after Hu Feng left Chongqing in the wake of the New Fourth Army Incident. During these few years, under Hu Feng's tireless sponsorship, *Qiyue* ushered in a group of newcomers to the literary scene and strengthened its ranks.

As the war went into protraction and patriotic fervor calmed down, *Qiyue* reportage began to incorporate more literary techniques and engage itself in deeper reflection on the war before it gave way to fiction. The transition can be most clearly seen in the works by A Long, especially in his 1939 prize-winning work *Nanjing.* An important motor force for the transition was the increasing authorial intervention, which eventually became a hallmark of *Qiyue* fiction. As he blurred the boundaries between reportage and fiction with the injection of authorial subjectivity, A Long would soon find kindred spirits among his *Qiyue* colleagues who, like him, were under Hu Feng's influence. In consideration of the importance of this transition and of authorial intervention in the practices of *Qiyue* writers in general, I will devote the present chapter to three topics: A Long's deepening understanding of the war and the self in his battlefield reportage, the ramifications of authorial subjectivity in his *Nanjing*, and his *Qiyue* colleague Jia Zhifang's reworking of Lu Xun's first-person stories.

A LONG'S DEEPENING REFLECTIONS ON THE WAR

Besides Qiu Dongping, another important *Qiyue* practitioner of battlefield reportage was A Long (real name Chen Shoumei). Born into a poor family in Hangzhou in February 1907, A Long began to contribute short articles and traditional poems to local newspapers in the late 1920s, before he enrolled himself in an engineering school in Shanghai. Unable to find a job upon graduation from the engineering school, he went to a military academy and later joined the Guomindang army. In the 1930s he started to publish his works in Shanghai literary journals under the pen name S.M. Under the same pen name he made his debut in *Qiyue* with a feature story "Coughing" (Kesou) in March 1938. From then on he regularly sent to the journal various forms of works, including reportage, prose, poetry, prose poetry, and essays. As he got closer to Hu Feng and other *Qiyue* writers, he participated in their activities while remaining a low-ranking officer in the Guomindang army.

In the area of battlefield reportage, A Long's first significant contribution is "Fighting Started at Zhabei" (Zhabei dale qilai), serialized in the fifteenth and sixteenth issues of *Qiyue* in June 1938. Strictly based on his personal experience as a platoon leader in the Shanghai Campaign of August 13, 1937, and narrated in the first person throughout, "Fighting Started at Zhabei" records the Chinese army's maneuvers while registering A Long's reactions to what he saw in the events that finally led to fighting at the Zhabei district in Shanghai. Thus situating himself in the center of his story, A Long remains doubly active as a crucial player in the story and, more significantly, as a sounding board that evaluates his army's performance while propagating his own ideas. A Long himself was highly aware of the paramount importance of his personal perspective in his work, as is made clear in the following remarks in his article "How I Wrote 'Fighting Started at Zhabei'" (Wo xie "zhabei dale qilai"):

> Taking a certain angle in the selection of scenes enlivens description. Herein lies "truthfulness." To achieve "truthfulness," and heart-felt "truthfulness" at that, not some misguided approximations of "truthfulness," the writing has to be performed by someone like me.[2]

As a structuring force, A Long's personal perspective is, first and foremost, characterized by his dissatisfaction with the Chinese army in general and with its apathy to Japanese invasion in particular. The first half of "Fighting Started at Zhabei" is largely taken up by the description of the Chinese army's journey to Shanghai on the eve of the Shanghai Campaign. Since commanders at all levels shrink the actual sizes of their units well below reported numbers to embezzle the allowances allocated for the nonexistent troops, soldiers, sick or well, have to carry more than their share of weapons and ammunition at the order of their often abusive superiors. A short trip to the train station, therefore, becomes very exhausting:

> Each infantry man had to carry a rifle, two hundred rounds of bullets, four grenades, a bayonet, a helmet, tools, a canteen, a haversack stuffed with miscellaneous objects, a backpack, and eating and cleaning utensils. Some also carried gas masks. For exhausted soldiers these things were not that easy to carry, so before they covered one kilometer they could no longer keep their file. Some started to moan while others started to fall behind. My feet felt like two pieces of wood with only half of their sensation left, and a strange, uncomfortable sensation at that. More and more sand got into my shoes.[3]

Here the individual details are incorporated not just to create what Roland Barthes might call the "reality effect"[4] but to convey a critical message about the rampant corruption in the Chinese army. No longer sufficient in and of themselves, these functionalized realistic details point outward to the narrator's moral stand as the governing system of his work.

Chapter Three

In contrast to the corrupt, indifferent army and government leadership, ordinary Chinese soldiers and civilians in "Fighting Started at Zhabei" form a groundswell of resistance. On their way to Shanghai on a train, the soldiers in A Long's platoon talk about courage in combat at great length and vow to fight the Japanese heroically. Once in Shanghai, they are warmly welcomed by civilians and street vendors who give them food and water for free. Unlike the wartime heroics of the time, however, A Long's depiction of the groundswell of resistance contains an implicit critical edge. "Fighting Started at Zhabei" was written eight months after the event and during the interval A Long learned that more soldiers in his platoon had since deserted the army than had been wounded or killed in combat—something he would have never expected when he was with them at Zhabei. Had the army headquarters adopted a smarter strategy, had the company commander and the deputy company commander not run away one after the other with embezzled money, A Long concluded in his article "How I Wrote 'Fighting Started at Zhabei,' " desertion would have never occurred.[5] Sympathetic toward the enthusiasts-turned-deserters, he tries in his reportage piece to portray them as he perceived them at the time of the Shanghai Campaign. Nevertheless, his portrayal of his soldiers is to a certain extent swayed by his hindsight and by a critical purpose. The above-quoted passage on the trying trip to the train station, for instance, provides a clue to the soldiers' later desertion. Subtly controlled by hindsight, narration in A Long's hands becomes a reflection on history rather than a merely factual record.

At the level of commentary, A Long's reflections come out in a much more spontaneous and straightforward manner. In his own voice he forcefully expresses his discontent with the Chinese military establishment and his appreciation of Chinese soldiers' and civilians' desire for resistance. After his superiors reject his suggestion to mount a surprise attack on the enemy headquarters, which he found, on an unauthorized reconnaissance trip, to be inadequately fortified at first, he thinks aloud as he hears the Japanese strengthening their defense, "we no longer have the opportunity to attack the enemy. The Hengbang River is under enemy control now. If we apply an inflexible strategy to changing circumstances and deal with a real situation with a fanciful military plan, how can we not be defeated?"[6] Judgmental in nature and rhetorical in style, the authorial comment reveals most unambiguously the critical perspective that governs the development of A Long's story from the outside.

A Long's next reportage piece published in *Qiyue*, "From the Offensive to the Defensive" (Cong gongji dao fangyu), can be regarded as a sequel to "Fighting Started at Zhabei," since it picks up the story at a point where the latter leaves off. This time, however, instead of using a single narrative point of view consistently, A Long employs a multiplicity of viewpoints in narrating his story and in depicting the psychology of the characters. While the characters' opinions are still presented, comments from the omniscient third-person narrator are withheld and the reader is left with more room to reach his own conclusions. As different spatial and temporal viewpoints come into contact with each other and modify each other, a mixture of juxtaposed views on the Shanghai Campaign is offered that amounts to, in effect, a critique of the emotional attitude in "Fighting Started at Zhabei."

The coexistence of different viewpoints can be seen right from the beginning of "From the Offensive to the Defensive" in a description of a battle over a bridge. As an order comes from the Chinese army headquarters for a battalion to seize the bridge, the restrained third-person narrator agrees from a tactical viewpoint, believing that once the bridge is secured the Chinese troops will not only stop enemy encroachment but also cut into the heart of the enemy defense. The commander of the battalion, on the other hand, knows it is impossible to carry out the order with a small force and without any artillery support, since the bridge is very close to the enemy headquarters and the enemy are already on the alert. To him the attack is nothing but a posture of resistance with no substantial military consequences. After the battle starts, the combat situation is seen from the perspective of the fighting soldiers who, unable to make any headway under heavy enemy fire for all their bravery, begin to complain about the army headquarters' suicidal strategy. Finally, as the Chinese troops retreat from the battle after a stalemate, the third-person narrator, without making any explicit comment, subtly changes his view on the attack and sides with the soldiers with a list of casualties suffered in the fruitless battle.

With the battle as an example, A Long demonstrates that military operation is a multifaceted, dynamic event on which those involved, due to their different positions and functions in it, will have different views that remain qualifiable in combat. The change in the omniscient narrator's view is especially significant in that it demonstrates that no military blueprint, however sound it appears in the abstract, can be carried out to the letter when confronted with the concrete, often unpredictable, circumstances in the battlefield. As it overcomes the emotional, naive conviction in resistance that dominates "Fighting Started at Zhabei," the awareness of the complicated, changeful situation in combat also discredits the partial views of theoreticians, including the narrator himself. The cognitive balance is certainly tipped in favor of the participants when the narrator finally moves to the side of the soldiers and, in so doing, invests heavily in first-hand experience.

Added to the juxtaposition of spatially differentiated views is the protagonist's temporal initiation into the reality of war. Unhappy with the way the Chinese military establishment conducts the campaign and burning with eagerness to fight the Japanese at first, the platoon leader Mei Mofa, the main character around whom almost three fourths of the story's total space centers, resembles in many ways the platoon leader Chen, the "I" narrator in "Fighting Started at Zhabei" and A Long's impassioned alter ego. Yet A Long's very act of giving Mei an identity, a mind, and a voice of his own creates a distance, emotional as well as intellectual, over which the author examines the character from a more or less objective angle. Young, intelligent, sensible, and enthusiastic, Mei is, at the start of the story, affected by the patriotic optimism and impatience of the time, but, unlike his self-confident counterpart in "Fighting Started at Zhabei," he is haunted by serious doubts about his ability as an army officer once the war is under way. Whereas his counterpart, in spite of his low rank, appears to be an excellent tactician capable of finding the most opportune moment for crucial military operations, Mei offers no clearly defined corrective plan with all his criticism of the defensive strategy of his army. Frustrated by the unreasonable assignment of building defense works under difficult conditions and caught between inconsiderate commanders and rightfully grouchy soldiers most of the time, he can only resort to patriotic sermons that sound hollow and unconvincing even to himself. Greatly overshadowed by these doubts, frustrations, and dilemmas, the sanguine views Mei holds before the reality of war sets in now appear naive and groundless in retrospect.

The center of consciousness in the work and a reflector of sorts,

Mei learns the most serious lesson as he watches the changes over time in the behavior of his soldiers, of whom he harbors high expectations at the start of the campaign. When the campaign goes into a lull in the second half of the story, Chinese soldiers begin to act sadistically toward civilians. Prompted by a paranoid order from the army headquarters, they go overboard to arrest and even randomly shoot at the civilians in the battle zone on the unfounded assumption that they are all traitors and spies. On several occasions Mei also discovers that his soldiers still have the habit of looting. Finally, as Zhabei streets become dotted with defense works,

> [Chinese] soldiers either gambled, quarrelled in crowds or, having eaten their fill and dressed in civilian clothes, slept for several hours at a stretch, usually surrounded by seven, eight or, in extreme cases, seventeen coils of the Moon-Goddess brand mosquito-repellent incense that they took from the Yonghe Department Store and burned wastefully. With the rooms filled with winding smoke, even the loudest artillery fire outside could not wake them up and the trembling houses just became cradles in their dreams.[7]

Emphatically placed at the end of the work to leave a lingering impression, this disappointing scene, while calling attention to the demoralizing consequences of the Chinese army's erroneous strategy, completely shatters Mei's dreams about his soldiers. As he witnesses all the misconduct, he is apparently confronted with issues other than the incompetence of the army upper echelon, issues with their cultural roots struck deeply in society.

A Long's understanding of war entered a new phase in "Tangential Encounter" (Xiejiao zaoyuzhan), a piece published in *Qiyue* in May 1940 under the rubric of "Battle Reports." Starting out with a theoretical definition of the highly technical title, the topic of an ongoing discussion among military experts, A Long, however, quickly changes direction with an embedded story—a specific example of "tangential encounter" in all its circumstantiality—as the main body of his work. As the embedded story proceeds, we see a remnant of a routed Chinese regiment, led by a company commander, march at night to join its main forces. The extremely fatigued and drowsy soldiers unexpectedly cross paths with a column of Japanese troops. With no other option at his disposal, the company commander launches a surprise attack. When the enemy fights back with heavy fire, he decides that he himself should slip behind the enemy line and strike from the back. His heroic assault turns out to be a smashing success that completely breaks the deadlock and enables the Chinese soldiers to resume their march. Referring back to the theoretical discussion without offering a conclusion, the story ends with a deliberate revelation of the gap between experience and theorization.

"Tangential Encounter" signals an important change in A Long's attitude toward the issue of military strategy. The embedded story about a specified tangential encounter, fleshed out with all its realistic details, is intended as an answer to the theoretical discussion. Instead of providing a set of rules as a theoretical conclusion, it highlights the incommensurability between predetermined strategies and contingent factors on the battlefield. Located in particular circumstances and subject to the intrusion of accidental, random elements at any time, a battle becomes a situation of uncertainty and indeterminacy, a series of unpredictable, and often unrelated, moments. The only way to change such a volatile situation to one's favor is to remain constantly alert and courageously seize opportunity as soon as it appears. The message of courage is forcefully conveyed by the heroic company commander in a conversation with the storyteller before he leaves for the final attack. As a compulsive gambler, he draws an analogy between gambling and combat and argues that a good fighter, like a good gambler, has to be willing to wager everything to win the stake. That this daredevil comes out of the battle with flying colors demonstrates the worthlessness of any preconceived strategies. As the embedded story in the end refuses to respond to the discussion at the theoretical level, it drives home the irrelevance of theory in the battlefield.

As we have seen, in the works he had published thus far, A Long frequently adopts a macroscopical approach to the war against Japan, especially in his criticism of the Chinese army's overall military strategy. His quarrels with the Chinese military establishment from this macroscopical standpoint are theoretical rather than practical. In "Tangential Encounter," however, theorization is implicitly faulted as impertinent as war, now perceived as a multitude of specific battles under specific circumstances, becomes a practical matter in which what counts is willpower and courage rather than careful planning. A further confirmation for this significant change in A Long's view on war can be found in an article about war reportage that he wrote in May 1940, three months after he finished "Tangential Encounter":

> What military genius means is not just calculated scheming. More often than not it is courage and recklessness. Napoleon is a good example. He won his heroic achievements, glorious successes, and incomparable victories only because he had an iron will and acted so recklessly that he overcame the changeful circumstances in a very accidental way.[8]

The guarded attitude toward theory, already discernible at the end of "Tangential Encounter" and clearly articulated here, signals a self-criticism on A Long's part as he comes to a new perception of war. If we compare his battlefield reportage works, we realize that he has repeatedly subjected his views and perspectives to questioning and modification. The subject matter, as a result, has as much to do with what goes on in his mind as with what happens in the battlefield. In the meantime, his battlefield reportage shows the importance of his perspectives as structuring principles. Incessantly pushing toward fiction at the expense of factual neutrality, the structuring activities in A Long's reportage culminate in *Nanjing*, a work that, in spite of its classification as reportage, shares striking similarities with *Qiyue* fiction. In order to understand the transition from *Qiyue* reportage to *Qiyue* fiction, the next section will turn to this unduly overlooked work.

THE AUTHORIAL IMPACT IN *NANJING*

In April 1939, after a stay of six months in Yan'an where he attended the Resistance University, A Long went to Xi'an for medical care. In July he began to write *Nanjing*, a work about the fall of Nanjing in 1937 and, having finished it in October, he submitted it to a literary contest organized by the Chinese Writers' National Anti-Aggression Association in early 1940. It made the short list of prize-winning entries. When a judge violated the condition of anonymity by accidentally revealing A Long's name, the contest came to an abortive end. As a result, *Nanjing* did not win any title except a sum of money and was not published as stipulated in the terms of the contest. Unable to publish a revised version the next year, A Long kept the original manuscript for the rest of his life. It only came out in print in 1987 with an altered title *Nanjing Blood Sacrifice* (Nanjing xueji) and some slight editorial changes in the text.

Consisting of nine chapters and an epilogue, *Nanjing Blood Sacrifice* covers the disastrous fall of Nanjing both panoramically and in detail, describing in an episodic manner the defense strategy of the Chinese government, the military and civilian preparations against the anticipated Japanese onslaught, the horrors of Japanese atrocities, and the heroism of the Chinese soldiers on the battlefield. Faced with an event of great historical magnitude, *Nanjing Blood Sacrifice*, however, refuses to be bogged down in historical factuality. Instead, it interiorizes history by paying special attention to its participants' psychological reactions to the traumatic loss of the Chinese capital. In addition, the author uses such an emotional discourse that it prompts both Hu Feng and the *Qiyue* poet Lü Yuan to claim that, because A Long wrote as an angry poet, his passions more or less repressed the realist spirit of his work.[9]

Underlying the emotional effusion in *Nanjing Blood Sacrifice* is a pervasive authorial sensibility that determines both the introjection of the ravaging images of war and the projection of feelings, thoughts, and attitudes onto the characters. In this regard the third chapter of the book provides important clues to the constituents of the authorial sensibility. Beginning with detailed descriptions of the terrains, historical legends, local products, and folkways of the lower Yangtze valley, the first half of the chapter is written in the mode of the traditional travelogue. Through a host of geographical, historical information comes an image of the author not only as a military strategist who knows the best way to deploy troops for the defense of Nanjing but also as a highly cultured man of letters who is, almost like a traditional literatus, marked by his intelligence, historical knowledge, literary talent, decency, and probity. For the rest of the book these two aspects of the authorial image work in alternation as the standards for either the professional evaluation of the Chinese army's performance or the humanitarian judgment of the devastating impact of the war on Chinese society as a whole.

At the story level, the author in *Nanjing Blood Sacrifice* functions as a controlling consciousness that selects significant data and weaves them into a dramatic pattern. Beginning with a Japanese air raid upon

Nanjing on September 5, 1937, and ending with a Chinese army unit's recovery of the nearby city Wuhu on December 20 after the fall of Nanjing, A Long organizes his story in a roughly chronological order and incorporates many verifiable historical facts. The ultimate purpose of the story, however, lies beyond the realm of factuality, for facts serve as nothing more than a means to give veracity and density to the author's interpretation of reality. Take the aftermath of the Japanese air raid as an example. After the air raid, the busiest street in downtown Nanjing becomes "a hell, filled with such horrors and suffering and covered by dead bodies, blood, broken planks, debris, twisted iron posts, deformed iron gates, a spotted kitten without its hind legs, electric wire, and so on. A whole row of buildings has been completely destroyed. A car has been burned into a pile of dark ashes and iron. At one place the road is destroyed and near the Shanghai Bank embers are still smoldering."[10] Here the concatenation of images reminds one of the imagistic style employed by the New Perceptionists (Xin ganjuepai), particularly Liu Na'ou and Mu Shiying, in some of their stories about the fast-moving urban life in Shanghai. But what distinguishes A Long is not just the chronotope of a fallen city but his approach to the subject matter. Whereas Liu Na'ou and Mu Shiying are not unattracted to modernity, in their case exemplified by the bewildering pace of life in a contemporary metropolis, A Long here shows the most barbaric aspect of modernity. Through the above-quoted chaotic sensory impressions the reader can clearly detect a humane sensibility horrified by the bestiality of the Japanese atrocities. With these ghastly details the author highlights the catastrophic consequences of Japanese savagery and prepares the reader for his peace-loving characters' subsequent patriotic, heroic actions against the Japanese on and off the battlefields. Obviously these details are included for their potential impact on both the characters and the reader. Their function, therefore, is less informational than affective.

Behind the refraction of the details as they pass through the author's patterning sensibility is a moral confrontation between a personal mind and external events. One of the worst atrocities of the Second World War, the fall of Nanjing, or otherwise known in the West as the "Rape of Nanjing," was such a morally charged subject for a patriotic Chinese writer that he simply could not write about it in a disinterested fashion when the war was still going on. With an important moral mission on his mind, A Long often goes a step beyond refraction and applies his intelligence and emotions directly to his subject. Consequently, he comes through his work as a vividly experiencing "I" with an undisguised personal voice, an "I" that impresses the reader with his proximity to his materials in spite of the historical scope and the impressive cast of characters in his story. An eyewitness at all times, not a mere gatherer of secondhand accounts, A Long mixes public events with his personal reactions in an uninhibited manner. As he freely cuts across the boundaries between different genres with an intensified narratorial voice, he sets an important precedent for *Qiyue* fiction writers, especially Lu Ling.

At the level of characterization, A Long's effort to grapple with his characters at close quarters, the majority of them being soldiers, low-ranking officers, and ordinary civilians, results in a striking similarity between the characters and the authorial image. Like the authorial image, the soldiers and low-ranking officers are endowed with an excellent command of military tactics, patriotism, and love for peace. Confronted with a largely impersonal and invisible enemy and with incomprehensible violence, their conduct conveys a clear message about the reactions of responsible moral beings to a world hideously dehumanized. Heroic and yet self-possessed, they never lose their intelligence or decency even in the heat of combat. In short, they constitute a sharp contrast to the rapacity, cruelty, and sheer absurdity of the war imposed by Japanese fascists on the one hand and to the incompetence of the Chinese political and military establishment on the other. Thus conceived, they become composite figures with only negligible differences between each other.

The projection of the authorial image onto the characters is often psychological rather than behavioral. A large part of *Nanjing Blood Sacrifice* is taken up by the characters' thoughts and emotions. Since only the imaginative fiction writer, not the fact-bound historian, can look into the characters' minds, this realm of interiority will be inevitably colored by the author's personal predispositions. As the author thinks and reacts *through* his characters, the characters' psychological patterns increasingly cohere around authorial values and reinforce what the author expresses in his own words.

In addition to the projection of authorial values onto Chinese soldiers and low-ranking officers, mainly from the viewpoint of a professional officer, psychological identification between the author and the characters can be seen in the mental pictures of the civilians as well, this time mainly drawn from the perspective of a cultured man of letters. In *Nanjing Blood Sacrifice* Chinese civilians are portrayed as people strongly attached to their peacetime lifestyles and homes, so much so that, when thrust into the nightmare of war, they are simply unable to comprehend the reason behind the atrocities in any customary terms. Confronted with intolerable brutalities that completely cut them off from everything their former lives and homes represented, these civilians experience total mental collapse in the war. The trauma of war, thus highlighted, works in tandem with the idealization of peace to emphasize the incompatibility between war and civilized behavior.

One of the examples with which A Long shows the psychological impact of the war on civilians is the Buddhist Zhong Yulong. At first this devout pacifist, who has never killed anything even as small as an insect, considers the war an ordeal of bloodshed prophesied by the Buddha and spends much of his time chanting Buddhist scriptures in hopes of avoiding the ordeal. However, Buddhist myth crumbles under the weight of a horrifying reality as he witnesses a Japanese air raid. Seeing a civilian with a foot severed and a wounded young woman die leaving her baby behind, he cannot help but ask himself questions about the design of the world and about Buddha's purpose in inflicting all this suffering on innocent people. Finally, a bomb explodes near him and splashes something soft into his mouth. Realizing it is a piece of human flesh, he immediately starts to vomit and scream before he goes completely insane shortly afterwards.

Though presented as a character with his own belief system, Zhong Yulong shares the authorial attribute of humaneness in his reaction to the brutality of war and, more significantly, the reliance on the notions of causality and rationality for the understanding of the world. By interjecting his own intellectual beliefs into characters of all stripes and hues, as the example of Zhong Yulong shows, the author manages to imbue his characters with a consistent, unified outlook. As the author moves away from the reproduction of the characters' actual thoughts and toward the projection of his own values and mentality into his characters, the characters' mental processes become increasingly homogenized in spite of the differences in their personal backgrounds.

As in characterization, the authorial presence is equally pervasive in the language A Long employs in his work. Alternating between military terminology and an introspective discourse, his idiolect in *Nanjing Blood Sacrifice* reflects the two sides of the authorial image. As a professional officer with formal military training, he cares a great deal about the terminological accuracy in his work.[11] Yet more important is the subjective side of his idiolect, an aspect that demonstrates a mind reaching out to *create* meaning out of external facts. With an emotional tone and an expressive style, A Long's introspective discourse conveys to the reader the essential "mental" impressions events have made either upon the author or upon the characters created in the image of the author. As realistic details recede into a dreamlike background, the experience of war eventually becomes a series of mental images and sentiments resulted from the active interplay between interior consciousness and external actuality.

The following description of the Chinese army's breaking through the Japanese encirclement after the fall of Nanjing offers a sample of A Long's subjective discourse:

> Like a 12th-force typhoon from the south, they [the Chinese army] irresistibly swoop down on the surrounding enemy. In front of them the enemy are dwarfed and blown away like dust. . . .
>
> Like a prairie fire in December, they blaze a path for themselves in brambles and in inaccessible places with their passion and fierceness. As for the things in their path, the brambles and the undergrowth are burned into ashes and charcoal and the stones are scorched out of shape.[12]

Figurative as well as hyperbolic, A Long's language here reveals the pathos of the speaker more than anything else. It is dominated by what Roman Jakobson calls the "emotive" function, a linguistic function that, with its focus on the addresser, aims at a direct expression of the speaker's attitude toward what he is speaking about.[13] Instead of representing an objective, empirical order of actual events, this passage, while greatly downplaying the referential function of language, presents an outpouring of strong, personal emotions from an artificer intent on leaving his distinct mark on the events he describes.

With its pronounced turn toward internality, *Nanjing Blood Sacrifice* serves as an important link between *Qiyue* reportage and *Qiyue* fiction. Generally speaking, reportage, with its generic ties to the news report, usually deals with public events while leaving mental processes for fiction to handle. Although loosely placed in a historical frame, *Nanjing Blood Sacrifice* presents its material as the author imaginatively experiences and recollects it. In doing so, the author openly demonstrates his mental participation in the psychologization of the material. On the other hand, if we agree with Kate Hamburger that the portrayal of the subjectivity of a third-person *qua* third-person is the hallmark of fiction,[14] we can find abundant proofs of fictionality in A Long's work since his characters are not portrayed as objects but as thinking subjects. Acknowledging the various sources for his work, including his own imagination, A Long admits in his postface that it is difficult even for himself to tell whether his work is reportage or fiction.[15]

The most important similarity between *Nanjing Blood Sacrifice* and *Qiyue* fiction, especially Lu Ling's fiction, lies in the overarching presence of the author as the intellectual and moral nucleus of the text. The pervasive psychologization in *Nanjing Blood Sacrifice* all centers around the image of the author/narrator. As he approaches his characters' psyches, the third-person narrator injects his own opinions, emotions, and stylistic features into their thoughts and speeches. With the functions of seeing and feeling firmly in his grasp, his characters reinforce from various perspectives what he sets out to express. Bent on communicating to the reader his messages about the horrors of Japanese atrocities and the incompetence of the Guomindang establishment, he uninhibitedly projects his ordering and interpretive abilities upon the world he describes. In view of the direct, active engagement of the author's consciousness with his subject matter that we constantly see in *Nanjing Blood Sacrifice*, we might even argue that to a certain extent this work already embodies Hu Feng's notion of the "subjective fighting spirit."

JIA ZHIFANG'S APPROACHES TO LU XUN

Commenting on Lu Xun's first-person stories, Theodore Huters notes that Lu Xun counterposes self and society in a deliberately balanced manner

> by setting the narrator in the story, but at the same time holding this character up to scrutiny in such a way as to withdraw gradually

the sympathy and identification that the reader initially feels for him. To the extent that the reader has come to accept the narrator as a reliable moral guide, the process of withdrawing faith has the effect of causing the reader to look to himself for those flaws that elicited the identification in the first place.[16]

As many critics, including Theodore Huters himself, have observed, the result of Lu Xun's self-scrutiny is the realization of his complicity with a rapacious social system that he initially sets out to reject. Caught up in such a dilemma, Lu Xun has to abandon the modern short story form and move on to a less problematic genre—*zawen*. In the meantime his fiction, with its inquiry into the subtle relationship between self and society as a *locus classicus*, leaves behind inspiration as well as provocative questions and unsolved problems for later writers. In a way much of the Chinese fiction of the 1920s and 1930s can be regarded as different responses to Lu Xun's initial exploration.

As far as *Qiyue* reportage is concerned, the responses to the issue of the relationship between self and society are mixed: for instance, whereas Cao Bai, to deflate wartime heroics, deliberately emphasizes the human fallibility he shares with society while denouncing more perverted social forces, A Long, especially in *Nanjing Blood Sacrifice*, sets up self as an intellectual and moral center largely uncontaminated by the evils in society, although he still leaves room for its further expansion and improvement, including self-correction. As *Qiyue* writers begin to free themselves further from reportage's generic reliance on historicity and factuality as they shift their creative energy to fiction writing and, more importantly, as they begin to implement Hu Feng's "subjective fighting spirit," the issue of self becomes the central question in their works for which they keep trying to find different solutions.

The centrality of the issue of self in *Qiyue* fiction was first seen in the short stories by Jia Zhifang. A writer who started his career under Lu Xun's influence, Jia continued to write the majority of his short stories in the first person à la Lu Xun, therefore his stories could not help but direct the reader's attention to their specific models in Lu Xun's fictional corpus. Yet as he came increasingly under Hu Feng's influence in the 1940s, his stories struck out in a direction markedly different from the one Lu Xun had chosen. These departures from Lu Xun, as we shall see below, had resulted from Jia's rethinking of the

From Reflection to Lyricism

role of self and revealed a seminal position on which later *Qiyue* writers would expand.

The first story in Jia's career as a writer, "Human Sadness" (Ren de bei'ai), comes closest to Lu Xun in spirit. Written at the end of 1936 in Tokyo and published in *Work and Study* (*Gongzuo yu xuexi*), a series Hu Feng edited in 1937, this first-person story about a recently released political prisoner's depression, anguish, and vacillation incorporates a considerable amount of autobiographical elements. The scene of activities in "Human Sadness" is a sluggish gunnysack store, where the young "I" narrator, a relative of the store owner, tarries after his release from jail. Like the teahouse in Lu Xun's story "Medicine," the gunnysack store is a window to a cross-section of Chinese society. As the "I" narrator listlessly watches the world and chats with the idled store clerks, he assimilates to the depressed surroundings mentally. "Gloom, loneliness, boredom and frustration get tangled and crawl slowly in everyone's heart. The continuation of life seems troublesome and unnecessary here."[17]

Stranded from his hometown by war and haunted by nightmares of prison and murder, the confused "I" narrator finally gets out of the unbearable gunnysack store, only to spend most of his days and the little money he has in cheap taverns. When he gets back from a tavern late one night, he is summoned by the manager of the store who, out of suspicion that he is once again involved in revolutionary activities, politely but unequivocally asks him to leave. As he is forced to go, the narrator ends his story with a self-reflection that is immediately enveloped by the uncertainty hanging over the course of his future action.

> Indeed, I should take a path and that should be my old path. The painful and nervous life I have had for nearly two months has proven that my enemy is no longer those terrible detectives of the old days but the present cowardice that has come as I have found a refuge for myself. It is easy for people to be content with temporary peace and comfort, but now even this humiliating refuge is gone.
>
> I don't know how I passed the following day and night. The next thing I can recall is that I was already in a third-class car on a train one evening.[18]

To the extent that the self-reflection is offered more or less in the spirit of the positive endings or "distortions" in Lu Xun's early stories,

81

it is significant that the "I" narrator snuffs out the only glimpse of hope when he points out the coerced nature of his departure and stresses his continued confusion and lack of a destination. In view of the highlighted irresolution on the narrator's part and the weakening of his plea for the future, I would like to argue that Jia Zhifang in this story tries to subject the self to an examination similar to what we see in some of Lu Xun's stories in *Wandering*. Through introspection the "I" narrator in "Human Sadness" reveals not only his complicity and powerlessness in a repressive social system but also the discrepancy between his words and deeds. As we have seen, his avowal, extrinsic to his actions and weakened by the feeling of uncertainty, ends up being engulfed by the pessimism of his behavior. Thus the little intellectual and moral influence he might have through the use of language is completely compromised.

As Jia Zhifang depletes the "I" narrator of intellectual and moral authority, a certain ironical distance is created between the "I" narrator and the implied author in his story. We should note that, while it demonstrates a complexity in the author's handling of narratorial unreliability, the ironical distance also prevents the implied author, reticent as he is, from an unmediated engagement with his subject matter, thus cutting the ground from under him by arousing skepticism as to where he stands in this drama of hesitation. This ambiguity, in a way, is what Hu Feng's "subjective fighting spirit" sets out to remedy. So as Jia Zhifang further came under Hu Feng's influence in the early 1940s, when the formulation of Hu Feng's notion was in progress, his first-person stories began to undergo a significant transformation marked by the conflation of the "I" narrator with the implied author and, along the way, the restitution of perceptive adequacy and moral authority to the "I" narrator.

"Surplus Value" (Shenyu jiazhilun), written in the summer of 1942, is an example of this transformation. Though roughly framed after Lu Xun's "In the Tavern," Jia's story departs significantly from its model in its treatment of the relationship between the narrator and the protagonist. In Lu Xun's story, as Leo Ou-fan Lee points out, the "I" narrator and the protagonist Lü Weifu both have so much in common with Lu Xun that "in a sense both men are projections of Lu Xun's self; their dialogue a fictional dramatization of an inner monologue conducted by the author."[19] Jia's story, in contrast, is characterized by the polarization between the spirited "I" narrator and the dejected protagonist. The "I" narrator's enmity toward the protagonist Yu Zigu starts right at their chance meeting in a small town after years of separation, as he feels uncomfortable and excuses himself from his old friend who appears to him a prematurely aged young man. More important than the inimical first impression is the narrator's recounting of his old friend's backsliding. The information about Yu is conveyed in three blocks, the first two being the "I" narrator's recollections of Yu's vigorous youth and his later hedonistic lifestyle and the last one an anecdote about his present depression, told to amuse the "I" narrator by a fellow passenger on a truck as they leave the small town. Instead of letting the protagonist tell his own story, as Lu Xun does in "In the Tavern," Jia Zhifang deprives his protagonist of his own voice and reduces him to an object for comments from others. As the "I" narrator spends much of his time reflecting on the protagonist, he makes sure that his own superior moral position constantly stands in sharp opposition to the retrogression of his old friend.

The shifting of attention to comments and reflections results in the diminution of narrative elements in "Surplus Value." Much of the accounts of the protagonist is offered in the expositional mode. Moreover, engrossed in cerebration, the "I" narrator largely remains a voice with very few dramatizing elements such as physical appearance, age, or personality. Urged by his emotions and desire for expression, he often steps out of the bounds of the story at hand and directly, spontaneously appeals to the world at large. As he takes over the discursive and narrative ground, the protagonist's lyrical confession of uncertainty, hesitation, and disillusionment in Lu Xun's "In the Tavern" is replaced by his lyrical outbursts of conviction and hope, as the ending of "Surplus Value" shows:

> My agitated emotions once again turn toward fighting. Let us express our boundless gratitude to those real heroes in the world and wish them good health.[20]

Standing for the dynamism of the time, the "I" narrator finally dismisses Yu Zigu out of hand as a superfluous loner inappropriate for the age.

It is a commonplace among scholars of Chinese literature that Lu Xun's first-person stories invariably highlight the inadequacy of perception, a characteristic achieved through his subtle manipulation of the compromised narrators. Such an awareness is dispersed in Jia Zhifang's first-person stories of the 1940s as his "I" narrator gathers more and more cognitive power while merging with the implied author. The "I" narrator's conviction in his own opinions, already present in "Surplus Value," is further intensified in Jia's next story, "My Hometown" (Woxiang, written in September 1942), modeled on Lu Xun's "My Old Home" (Guxiang). With the issue of perception as his central concern, the "I" narrator in Lu Xun's story repeatedly displays his failure to reconcile a beautified past conjured up in his mind with the grim present he faces as he undercuts his half-hearted statements. In contrast, the narrator in Jia's story is not haunted by such self-doubts. Confident in his ability to feel the pulse of the times, he simply cannot help but revel in rhapsodic moments of self-expression.

To begin with, Jia's story mostly deals with what the "I" narrator sees and hears in the present on his homecoming trip and the briefly mentioned or remembered past is presented as a factual contrast to the hopeful present. Affected by the war against Japan, the hometown image in "My Hometown" goes through a dramatic change in comparison with that in Lu Xun's story. People participate in resistance activities and treat each other as equals, no longer hierarchized like their counterparts in Lu Xun's story. For the "I" narrator his family in particular becomes such a haven of love that he wants to escape from it for fear he might be intoxicated should he stay too long. On the other hand, he never hesitates to condemn the residues of old society, a superstitious relative for instance, as moribund elements on the verge of extinction.

As he offers such an upbeat hometown image, the "I" narrator harbors no doubts about the transparency of his perception and is unaware of the workings of his optimistic outlook. The willed nature of the hometown image is unambiguously revealed in the emotional crescendo at the end of the story:

> Like those herdsmen standing in the vast wilderness, we should not feel confused or gloomy in our thoughts about life. We should stand up and sing loudly of the delight and greatness of life; instead of living a life like animals, we should try to enrich life and enhance its true value.
> Yes, that is life. Struggle, creation, conquest.

> Our hometown, the war-torn hometown, is what provides us with the courage to live and fight. It is a harbor for a new life.[21]

To a large extent it is the "I" narrator's strong desire to impose a positive view on life, displayed in the discursive ending, that determines the narrative content, structure, as well as the commentary in the story. Without realizing the refraction of reality by this upbeat outlook, Jia Zhifang's "I" narrator assumes the ultimate intellectual power as he disqualifies perceptions other than his own in the process of seeking determinate meanings of life. Unable to brook indeterminacy or conflict, he unknowingly exhibits a weakness in certain *Qiyue* fiction—the susceptibility to exclusive interpretations. The exclusive view on self, not unrelated to the still lingering patriotic optimism during the wartime, will have to wait to be overcome by Jia Zhifang's *Qiyue* successors Lu Ling and Ji Pang.

Four

Image Making, Legacy Clarification, and Agenda Formulation: Hu Feng's Interpretations of Lu Xun, May Fourth, and the "Subjective Fighting Spirit"

During the wartime Hu Feng's charisma mainly came from his reputation as the only bona fide heir to Lu Xun, who was by now a lionized cultural hero. As he began to assume this position in and after the debate over the "Two Slogans," Hu Feng spent much of his energy interpreting the legacies of Lu Xun and the revolutionary tradition of May Fourth literature that, in his opinion, Lu Xun epitomized. For him the significance of both Lu Xun and May Fourth lay exclusively in the insightful understanding and relentless criticism of China's feudal tradition, a task that should be carried on under the wartime circumstances. At a time when any criticism of China or its tradition could be easily deemed unpatriotic, he refused to join the majority of Chinese writers and, instead, became one of the few completely unreserved advocates of internal cultural criticism. A crucial component of his efforts to justify his exceptional and controversial program, the set of radicalized clarifications of Lu Xun and May Fourth he offered over the years also underpinned the agenda of his school. In view of their importance, I will devote the present chapter first to his interpretations of the legacies of Lu Xun and May Fourth and then to his development of the legacies into the notion of the "subjective fighting spirit," unquestionably the cornerstone of his literary theory.

The obvious danger that during the war the cause of national defense could easily overwhelm the domestic agenda of internal criticism gave rise to the urgency and sonority in the clarion calls Hu Feng made while trying to keep alive the critical spirit of Lu Xun and May Fourth. As the war dragged on and writers in the Nationalist interior gradually grew accustomed to the routinized wartime conditions, an impetus was added to Hu Feng's advocacy of persistent cultural criticism. Meanwhile, in the wake of the Rectification Campaign in Yan'an, the CCP stepped up its thought reform of leftist writers in Chongqing by propagating Mao Zedong's "Talks at the Yan'an Forum on Literature and Art." Alarmed by the routinization of the war on the one hand and the Communist ideological regimentation on the other, Hu Feng elaborated on the notion of the "subjective fighting spirit" as a countermeasure in the last years of the war. As strategies necessitated by his position as a dominated player who needed to make his mark in the field of leftist literature, his explications of Lu Xun, May Fourth, and the "subjective fighting spirit," while remaining constant and consistent, underwent some modifications in their objectives and emphases alongside the changes in historical circumstances. To avoid the danger of abstraction, I will, in the following analysis of Hu Feng's views in these areas, keep making references to their historical conditions. Without such references our understanding would be incomplete and inadequate.

HU FENG'S RADICALIZED IMAGE OF LU XUN

Upon Lu Xun's death on October 19, 1936, as a close disciple in the last few years of Lu Xun's life, Hu Feng became an important member of Lu Xun's funeral committee. He was entrusted with the composition of an obituary and, then, the supervision of the funeral. Shortly after the funeral he contributed to the lionization of his mentor by working as an exegete for the voluminous *Collected Works of Lu Xun* in Japanese and as an editor of a journal, *Work and Study Series (Gongzuo yu xuexi congkan)*, mainly dedicated to bringing out Lu Xun's unpublished works and commemorative articles on Lu Xun. With his authority as a Lu Xun expert confirmed by these exegetical and editorial projects, he began to write and speak about the "spirit of Lu Xun" in later years, often on the anniversaries of Lu Xun's death, as he set out to assume Lu Xun's mantle.

The process of image making was set afoot right after Lu Xun's death. In a commemorative article "A Grievous Good-bye" (Beitong de gaobie) written ten days after Lu Xun's death, Hu Feng cited numerous anecdotes of the last days of Lu Xun's life to highlight Lu Xun's steely will to fight till the last moment of his life. In his description, Lu Xun, while dying, ignored the repeated exhortations from his wife, his doctor, and friends and continued his fight against the darkness of society. Never making light of his enemies' strength or showing any facile optimism, Lu Xun, in Hu Feng's view, had been a determined fighter for thirty years who had refused to concede to or compromise with his adversaries. At the end of the article, Hu Feng called on his readers to carry on Lu Xun's heritage and fight Lu Xun's still existing foes with Lu Xun's intrepid spirit.[1]

Hu Feng's depiction of Lu Xun as a resolute fighter against the old society—while disregarding Lu Xun's involvement with traditional China to which Lu Xun himself had freely admitted—focused on the last, radicalized stage in Lu Xun's career. For Hu Feng, a close associate of Lu Xun during this stage, as the personal anecdotes in the article indicate, this radicalized image of a high-principled fighter served as a polestar for himself and his readers more than anything else. In view of the still echoing debate over the "Two Slogans," to erect such a role model displayed Hu Feng's own determination to persist in the uncompromising spirit of the Lu Xun camp against the likes of Zhou Yang and other advocates of "National Defense Literature," who definitely fell into the category of Lu Xun's still present foes.

On October 17, 1937, Hu Feng wrote an article "On a Few Fundamentals of the Spirit of Lu Xun" (Guanyu Lu Xun jingshen de ersan jidian) for the first anniversary of Lu Xun's death. After accepting the charge, made by Lu Xun's detractors, that Lu Xun had not created an intellectual system of his own, Hu Feng turned the argument around and attributed Lu Xun's greatness, not to his espousal of Darwinian evolutionism or Marxist class analysis, but to his thorough, realistic understanding of Chinese society and the resolution Lu Xun derived from this understanding to fight at close quarters with both his heart and mind.[2] Hu Feng's defense of his mentor was an effort to kill two birds with one stone: while warding off Lu Xun's critics, it also controverted the attempts, made by the Communists, to assimilate Lu Xun into the fold of Marxism. While emphasizing Lu Xun's personal experience and his nondogmatic understanding of reality, Hu Feng further argued that, as he spent his life fighting for national "liberation," Lu Xun had never lost sight of domestic "progress" as a goal, without which liberation would be impossible. Faced with the dissipation of strength by the darkness and ignorance Lu Xun had attacked, Hu Feng held it necessary for intellectuals to carry on Lu Xun's domestic agenda.[3]

Hu Feng's article was written in Wuhan, a political and cultural center where a large number of intellectuals congregated in the first phase of the war. In spite of the numerous military setbacks China had already suffered, the atmosphere in Wuhan was marked by patriotic fervor and optimism at the time. The participants of the commemorative meeting held on the first anniversary of Lu Xun's death were enthusiastic about the triumphant outcome of the war. One poet, for example, wrote a poem for the occasion claiming that the next year a wreath of victory would be offered to Lu Xun's tomb in Shanghai, devastated by a raging war then and about to fall shortly. Confronted with the propagandist clamor for national salvation that all but silenced any internal criticism, Hu Feng invoked Lu Xun as an inspiration and a justification for his efforts to keep alive the agenda of internal emancipation from native tradition. Written nine days after the inaugural statement of *Qiyue,* Hu Feng's article on Lu Xun further clarified the direction his journal would take in the future.

Talking about Hu Feng's interpretations of Lu Xun, we have to agree with David Holm that during the war years Lu Xun's legacy was not only an oeuvre of recognized size and shape—an object of aesthetic appreciation and of scholarly devotion—but also a battleground, an ideological terrain that various contestants sought to occupy.[4] In view of the exegetical battle, the explications of Lu Xun by Hu Feng, one of the tireless claimants to Lu Xun's legacy, should be considered in connection with the CCP's official discourse on Lu Xun. Interestingly, an important specimen of the Communist discourse on Lu Xun, a transcript of a speech delivered by the Party chairman Mao Zedong at a commemorative meeting held in Yan'an on the first anniversary of Lu Xun's death, was first published in *Qiyue* in March 1938. In his speech Mao Zedong aligned Lu Xun with Marxism ideologically and with the CCP politically, setting him up as an example for the audience of educated youths whom the Party wanted to train to be its vanguards. In a pragmatic approach, Mao enlisted what he considered the three components of the spirit of Lu Xun—Lu Xun's political foresight (Mao used Lu Xun's 1936 prediction of the danger of Chinese Trotskyites as a proof), his persevering "fighting spirit" (Mao contrasted him with the Russian renegades Kautsky and Plekhanov), and his fearless "spirit of sacrifice" in the face of threats from his enemies[5]—into the service of the Party's cause.

In contrast to the CCP's utilitarian approach that tried to fit Lu Xun's legacy to its tasks of the moment, Hu Feng's expositions refused to subsume Lu Xun under any ideological system, political force, or historical exigency. Instead, he zeroed in on Lu Xun's voluntarist approach to reality, thus making Lu Xun's legacy self-perpetuating in the direction of cultural criticism. His emphasis on Lu Xun's voluntarism was typified by his article "A Brief Explanation of 'The Passerby'" (Guoke xiaoshi), written in October 1939 for the performance of Lu Xun's poetic drama by the Playwrights' Association as part of the commemorative activities of the third anniversary of Lu Xun's death. Interpreting Lu Xun's title character as Lu Xun's personal allegory rather than a dramatic persona, Hu Feng, with numerous quotations, highlighted Lu Xun's commitment and perseverance in a most difficult time of his life in spite of his despairing awareness of the power of conservatives and the betrayal by some of his fellow advocates of the New Culture.[6] Once again Hu Feng's exegesis of the protagonist/author in Lu Xun's piece was entirely focused on the domestic agenda of antifeudalism and, by endowing the perseverance of Lu Xun's Sisyphus-like character with tragic dignity, Hu Feng accentuated Lu Xun's personal choices in his fight against the old society.

In Hu Feng's view, Lu Xun's unswerving combative spirit demonstrated his keen awareness of the tenacity of tradition in Chinese society. Constantly vigilant against the recrudescence of tradition in contemporary society, especially in the revolutionary ranks, he repeatedly invoked Lu Xun as a farsighted social critic and prophet during the war when any attack on tradition could be easily seen as an assault on the nation and on the cause of national survival. In an article "If He Were Still Alive" (Ruguo ta hai huozhe), written for the fifth anniversary of Lu Xun's death in Hong Kong in October 1941, Hu Feng showed that the war did very little to change his social perception inherited from Lu Xun. Thumbing through Kuriyagawa Hakuson's

Outside the Ivory Tower, a work Lu Xun translated in 1924–25 as a mirror of the apathy, fence-sitting, hypocrisy, narrow-mindedness, megalomania, and conservatism of the Chinese nation, Hu Feng speculated on the reception of Lu Xun, had he not died, in the wartime atmosphere. Since in this atmosphere "it is only permitted to sing the praises of victory, to sing the praises of China's old, glorious culture and of the freedom and happiness of the Chinese nation," how could Lu Xun, Hu Feng concluded, not be placed in the category of "new-style traitors" or "fifth columnists" or even labelled as their ringleader?[7] Yet in Hu Feng's opinion it was Lu Xun, not the complacent wartime apologists for tradition, that had fully grasped the social reality of China. By envisioning, in Lu Xun's vein, China as an unchanging society, Hu Feng once again insisted on the necessity and the protracted nature of internal criticism.

In October 1943, Hu Feng wrote an article "Arising from 'Emanating a Ray of Light As Long As There Is an Ounce of Heat'" (Cong "you yifen re, fa yifen guang" shengzhang qilai de) to commemorate the seventh anniversary of Lu Xun's death. In this relatively long essay, five of the seven sections were devoted to an account of Lu Xun's life to stress the thesis that Lu Xun's beliefs, foresight, and vigilance had all come from his life experience. Hence, while acknowledging that one could draw on Lu Xun's ideas, Hu Feng argued that one could learn even more from Lu Xun's attitude toward life.[8] He summarized his article by saying that the lesson one could learn from Lu Xun consisted of directing one's battles against concrete targets, the ethic of loving the oppressed masses and hating the enemies, and the conscientious, down-to-earth work style.[9]

Standing in sharp contrast to the CCP's utilitarian interpretations of Lu Xun, the actual content of which, as David Holm shows, varied each year with the prevailing ideological climate,[10] Hu Feng's expositions of Lu Xun were consistently based on intellectual and cultural principles with little consideration of political expediency. He created an image of Lu Xun as a resolute critic of Chinese tradition who had derived his insight solely from his personal experience with the society, and who, with his keen awareness of the tenacity of tradition, had pioneered and persisted in domestic cultural criticism. While avoiding or downplaying such factors as Lu Xun's adoption of a Marxist-Leninist worldview in the last years of his life, Hu Feng turned Lu Xun's experience from a simplified ideological journey to Marxism, as the CCP claimed, into a legacy imitable only through practice. In short, Lu Xun, with his saintly status, became for him an inspiration for relentless criticism of a Chinese society still in thrall to its feudalist tradition. With Lu Xun as a role model, internal criticism of Chinese society never lost its appeal to Hu Feng even when it was deemed detrimental to the collective spirit of the nation.

HU FENG'S DEFENSE OF MAY FOURTH

Hu Feng's exposition of Lu Xun was closely tied to his understanding of May Fourth, since in his opinion Lu Xun not only represented the combative spirit at the time of the May Fourth movement but remained the only May Fourth veteran who had adhered to its revolutionary legacy throughout his life. Like his radicalized image of Lu Xun, Hu Feng's espousal of May Fourth values was by no means indiscriminate, for he consistently opted for cultural criticism, not nationalism, as the epitome of the spirit of May Fourth that deserved to be kept alive under any circumstances and against all odds. Defiant of the wartime nationalist atmosphere, Hu Feng's career was a conscious furtherance of the May Fourth tradition of intellectual enlightenment and, as such, it adopted what Lin Yü-sheng calls the "cultural-intellectualistic" approach of May Fourth participants, an approach that stressed the necessary priority of intellectual and cultural change over political, social, and economic changes.[11]

From the inception of his career Hu Feng made clear his stress on cultural criticism as the quintessence of May Fourth. In March 1935, not long after he appeared on the literary scene in Shanghai, in a review of a collection of essays by the May Fourth veteran Liu Bannong, Hu Feng argued that the anti-imperialism that sparked off the May Fourth movement had inevitably led to its antifeudalism. To him, despite the different routes May Fourth participants followed afterwards, the uncompromising criticism of the apathy, vileness, and chaos in Chinese society was the mainstream of May Fourth, a mainstream that further developed into critical realism on the literary front.[12] By calling attention to May Fourth's "down-to-earth fighting spirit" as being exemplified in the early writings of a linguist whose most significant achievements, as Hu Feng admitted, had been made in the area of language reform, Hu Feng's opinion differed from other discussions of May Fourth literature in the mid-1930s that remained mainly concerned with literary consumption, especially the creation of a literary language accessible to the broad masses. As he bypassed the thorny issue of linguistic accessibility in his emphasis on combative spirit, he seemed to suggest that nothing short of a complete transformation of Chinese culture and mentality, including the Chinese language, would rejuvenate China, a totalistic antitraditionalist approach he shared with many May Fourth radicals.

Subject to continuous strictures since the late 1920s, the legacy of May Fourth literature was in an even more perilous situation after the war with Japan started. Many Chinese writers abandoned Western-style narrative fiction, the mainstay of May Fourth literature, and took up popular forms of folk literature as more expedient means for national mobilization. At the same time, the reevaluations of the New Literature grew more and more divergent. Finally, a heated debate over "national forms" broke out in Chongqing and Yan'an from 1939 to 1940 in which not only questions were once again raised about the corpus of the New Literature produced after May Fourth but efforts were also made to attribute the little merit it still had to the influence of traditional literature.[13] Faced with the escalated criticisms and revisions of the tradition of the New Literature, Hu Feng stood firm during the debate and wholeheartedly defended May Fourth literature on its own terms.

The origin of the debate over "national forms" could be traced to some remarks by the CCP chairman Mao Zedong, made in October 1938 at the Sixth Plenum of the Sixth Party Congress of the CCP, about the integration of Marxism with Chinese circumstances so that foreign stereotypes and dogmatism could be replaced by the "fresh, lively Chinese style and spirit which the common people of China love."[14] Prompted by Mao's call, leftist writers in the Nationalist interior began to discuss the issue of "national forms" in September 1939. In March 1940 Xiang Linbing (Zhao Jibin) pushed the discussions to a dramatic height with his article "On the Main Sources of National Forms" (Lun minzu xingshi de zhongxin yuanquan). In his article Xiang regarded the forms of traditional folk literature as the fountainhead of national forms and insisted that writers, in their quest for the much desired national forms, should downplay the forms of the New Literature because they were only accessible to the petty bourgeoisie. Xiang's arguments and scathing criticism of the New Literature quickly drew fire from Hu Feng, who dubbed Xiang a "new nationalist essentialist" (xin guocui zhuyi zhe).

As Xiang Linbing's harshest critic, Hu Feng wrote an article entitled "May Fourth in Literature" (Wenxue shang de wusi) in April 1940 to refute Xiang's view that May Fourth literature was a literature of the petty bourgeoisie. With Lu Xun's famous character Ah Q as an example, Hu Feng argued that the "discovery of human beings"—the most significant historical achievement of May Fourth literature in his view—meant the humanitarian discovery of not only the bourgeoisie but also the proletariat and, as the May Fourth tradition developed, the issue of class affiliation was further transcended.[15] By expanding May Fourth literature into a humanitarian expression of the whole society, Hu Feng not only disputed the attribution of May Fourth literature to the petty bourgeoisie, a view popular among Chinese leftists since the late 1920s, but also pointed out the ineptitude of traditional literature, handicapped by feudal ideology, to reflect the humanitarian groundswell in Chinese society.

Hu Feng continued his defense of May Fourth literature and his criticism of traditional literature in two disquisitions "On the Origin of the Issue of National Forms and Its Points of Dispute" (Lun minzu xingshi wenti de tichu he zhengdian) and "On the Practical Significance of the Issue of National Forms" (Lun minzu xingshi wenti de shiji yiyi), later combined into a book *On the Issue of National Forms* (*Lun minzu xingshi wenti*) in December 1940 as his major contribution to the debate. In sharp contrast to the revisionists who, with their recourse to Marxist dialectics, argued that May Fourth literature had evolved from traditional literature, he emphasized the complete rupture between May Fourth literature and traditional literature. To him May Fourth literature was nothing but a new outgrowth of global progressive literature.[16] As such it sublimated the time-honored yet sporadic native tradition of antifeudalism, thereby carrying out a task traditional literature, confined by its feudal ideology, was unable to perform. Having thus dichotomized May Fourth literature and traditional literature, he gave the former his unreserved endorsement while criticizing the forms of the latter as doomed vehicles for feudal values.[17] The task for contemporary Chinese writers, he repeatedly argued in his articles, was to strive for further development of the May Fourth tradition.

The debate over "national forms," we should note, took place when China as a nation-state teetered on the verge of extinction and, out of consideration for mass mobilization, writers of all political persuasions moved toward an uncritical acceptance of popular culture. Under such circumstances, the utilization of popular forms of folk literature amounted to an ideological compromise with certain feudal values, of which some of Hu Feng's opponents were well aware.[18] In contrast to the majority of writers, including many May Fourth veterans, who made the expedient move to carry out the urgent task of patriotic mobilization, Hu Feng continued to set his sights on a long-term critique of native tradition in the manner of May Fourth intellectual enlightenment. He embraced this seemingly impractical, easily assailable position not only because he was alert to the harmful ideological implications of the adoption of traditional forms but also because he was firmly convinced of the deep-seated, if not apparent, populism of May Fourth. Unlike almost everyone else involved in the debate, Hu Feng was not at all bothered by the petty bourgeois origin of May Fourth literature or its foreign influence, since he did not take either of them as an issue. Free from the moral taint of insulation from the masses because of its un-Chineseness, May Fourth literature became in his opinion fully integrated into the Chinese nation's long struggle for emancipation from its feudal past.

Hu Feng's view on May Fourth literature, with the emphases on its spiritual roots in the native tradition of antifeudalist struggles, its spontaneity, and its broad social base, challenged the long-accepted evaluation of the New Literature among leftists in general and the recently formulated CCP official discourse on May Fourth in particular. On January 15, 1940, Mao Zedong published "On New Democracy," an important essay in which Mao gave, among other things, a list of the main features of the May Fourth movement that would become the CCP's official interpretation of May Fourth for the years to come. Describing it as a movement taking place at the summons of the Russian Revolution of 1917 and at the call of Lenin, Mao regarded May Fourth as a watershed between the "old democracy" in China led by the bourgeoisie and the "new democracy" led by the proletariat. Mao's definition obviously had in its view the self-legitimation of the CCP, the self-claimed vanguard of the Chinese proletariat. Mao also had in his view the enlistment of the progressive intelligentsia into the CCP's service. As he made clear in a previous commemorative article on the May Fourth movement, the progressive intelligentsia, in spite of their historical role as the first awakened element in the May Fourth movement, would achieve nothing if they did not unite with workers and peasants.[19] In other words, the progressive intelligentsia, no longer considered the vanguard of social reforms, would forfeit their revolutionary status altogether if they did not join the CCP's cause. In contrast, Hu Feng in his statements on May Fourth refused a categorical separation of the progressive intelligentsia from the proletariat. In his view the progressive intelligentsia during and after the May Fourth movement had been part and parcel of a revolutionary groundswell that permeated the whole Chinese society. From such a position it follows that they did not have to put themselves at the beck and call of the CCP to gain legitimacy for their own cause.

Hu Feng's efforts to identify the revolutionary intelligentsia with the awakening of the broad masses, in my view his most significant rehabilitation of May Fourth, were fully worked out in his interpretations of Lu Xun's fiction. Using Ah Q as an example, he argued in a February 1941 article "The National War and the Tradition of the New Literature" (Minzu zhanzheng yu xin wenyi chuantong) that with his ground-breaking creation of working-class characters Lu Xun had truthfully depicted the suffering of the working people as well as their awakened aspiration for freedom.[20] What makes his interpretation of Ah Q highly interesting is the complete elimination of the satirical distance between Lu Xun and his famous character. As he described in a speech written a month earlier, "when Ah Q, with a writing brush in his shaking hand, was trying to draw a perfect circle [as his signature on his execution warrant], the author Lu Xun himself was experiencing inexpressible sadness."[21] While identifying Lu Xun spiritually with his character and thereby granting Ah Q an interior self that most critics would argue that Ah Q fundamentally lacks,[22] Hu Feng entirely erased Lu Xun's intellectual and moral superiority to the butt of his scathing satire.

Behind this interesting interpretation of Ah Q lay the advocacy of Hu Feng's cherished way of writing, that is to say, in writing fiction a writer should grapple with the spiritual world of his characters from the inside. In 1941, when Hu Feng's articles were written, the war with Japan had entered a stage of protracted attrition. As Chinese writers' patriotic excitement had gradually calmed down, Hu Feng held it necessary that they should go beyond abstractions and delve deeper into reality to carry out the agenda of "internal reforms" (neibu gaizao) that had become increasingly urgent.[23] Aware that Chinese writers had fallen prey to blind beliefs or to the pressure of political conformity, Hu Feng's reiteration of the May Fourth agenda of "internal reforms" at this stage of the war took on an added meaning of self-emancipation for intellectuals. By associating Lu Xun, an epitome of the May Fourth combative spirit, with Ah Q, a commonly acknowledged member of the masses, Hu Feng illustrated an approach in which the writer grappled with his subject matter as well as himself. In effect Lu Xun was turned into a precursor of Hu Feng's "subjective fighting spirit," then in the making.

While augmenting the spectrum of meanings for the May Fourth agenda of "internal reforms," Hu Feng became increasingly bellicose in his advocacy of these reforms. His call on writers to take their own initiative reached a strident climax in "Taking 'A Madman's Diary' As a Starting Point" (Yi 'Kuangren riji' wei qidian), an article written in the form of a dialogue for the May Fourth anniversary of 1948. Quoting Lu Xun's remarks, made in one of his 1918 "Random Thoughts" (Suiganlu), that the potential of mankind could only be materialized in overcoming difficulties and that the road of life could only be blazed in bramble-covered places, Hu Feng vented his anger at the charge of idealism heaped on his "subjective fighting spirit." As for the contemporary continuation of the cultural struggle initiated by May Fourth, he contended that writers should start from reality so that they would not hang themselves on the steel rope of principles or drown themselves in the sea of a multifaceted reality.[24] At this moment of increasing ideological and political pressure from his orthodox detractors, Hu Feng obviously invoked the treasured down-to-earth combative spirit of May Fourth as a means to resist Communist dogmas.

Looking back at Hu Feng's interpretations of May Fourth literature, we note that he had always insisted on the importance of internal cultural criticism as its legacy. While globalizing it as part of world progressive literature, he broadened its social base by describing it as a humanitarian expression of the whole Chinese society, thus eliminating its distance from the broad masses. Poles apart from traditional literature, May Fourth literature in his opinion found the most concentrated expression of its uncompromising combative spirit in Lu Xun's fiction. While streamlining the legacy of May Fourth by leaving out the questions, the doubts, and the disillusionments of its participants, including Lu Xun, and, more importantly, by disregarding its

Image Making, Legacy Clarification, and Agenda Formulation

agenda of national salvation, Hu Feng's interpretation differed from the official views on May Fourth of the GMD and the CCP. Instead of using May Fourth pragmatically to justify a current political program, as both the GMD and the CCP did then and afterwards, Hu Feng emphasized the incompleteness of May Fourth and the need for further development of May Fourth–style internal reform. As he did with Lu Xun's legacy, he single-mindedly extracted a legacy of domestic cultural criticism from May Fourth literature, a legacy inheritable by practice. Moreover, as he injected a large dose of passion, resolve, and intellectual mediation into his revered mentor and May Fourth literature, what we see in his interpretations of both is to a large extent a manifestation of his own "subjective fighting spirit."

THE GENESIS OF THE "SUBJECTIVE FIGHTING SPIRIT"

Having discussed, in the previous sections, Hu Feng's interpretations of Lu Xun and May Fourth, we should realize that his explications were tailored to what he perceived to be the crucial contemporary issues and to his own theoretical and practical concerns. As Lu Xun's lone disciple and one of the few unreserved advocates of May Fourth, he eventually distilled what he considered the essence of both into his "subjective fighting spirit." Being a defiant stance as much as a program for literary creation, the notion of the "subjective fighting spirit" served for him and his *Qiyue* followers as an overriding guideline in their careers, accounting for the features of *Qiyue* works produced during and after its long gestation, especially the fiction by Lu Ling and Ji Pang. In view of its vital importance as a key to our understanding of Hu Feng's career and the works by his protégés, I will delineate the genesis of Hu Feng's notion in the remaining pages of this chapter.

To begin with, the notion of the "subjective fighting spirit" can be traced to the influence of the May Fourth radicalism on Hu Feng, particularly to Lu Xun's 1907 essay "On the Power of *Mara* Poetry" (Moluo shi li shuo) in which Lu Xun exalted a number of Western cultural figures as "warriors of the spirit" who had prophesied historical development as they struggled against society. An "idealist" consumed by the May Fourth spirit of emancipation, Hu Feng received further ingredients for his yet-to-be-articulated notion from

Hakuson's emphasis on the importance of struggle in life and in literary creativity. However, these early influences, received in the abstract, pale in significance when compared with Hu Feng's experience in the Japanese proletarian literature movement during his stay in Japan, from which he came out a maturated critic with his important views formulated in substance.

Hu Feng's stay in Japan, as I pointed out in chapter 1, coincided with the peak of the international leftist literary movement under the sway of the Soviet Union. Japanese proletarian literature of the late 1920s and early 1930s, like its counterparts elsewhere in the world, was dominated by the doctrinaire "method of dialectic materialism" that simplified the complex process of literary creativity into a rigid application of Marxist worldview. Advocated by the RAPP in the Soviet Union and promoted by its Japanese spokesmen such as Kurahara Korehito, this overly theorized and politicized approach, as noted by G. T. Shea, often became fetters to Japanese proletarian literature.[25] For that reason it was denounced by some Japanese proletarian writers soon after the RAPP was disbanded in April 1932 by the Soviet Communist Party as a scapegoat for the poor quality of Soviet literature. As a participant in the leftist literary movement, Hu Feng was at first influenced by the "method of dialectic materialism" to a certain degree and wrote several articles along that line in the 1932 debate over the "third-category" literature. However, as soon as he was prompted to the danger of excessive regimentation by, among other things, the discovery of Marx and Engels's letters on literature, he discarded the mechanistic approach once and for all. Unlike other leftist critics of his time who enthusiastically embraced "socialist realism," the successor to the "method of dialectic materialism" in the Soviet Union, without realizing the continued danger of rigidification, he remained indifferent to the new approach and opposed to any attempt that turned literature into a ready substantiation of Marxist outlook. His "subjective fighting spirit," with its emphasis squarely on the writer's individual initiative and personal understanding of life and society, could be said to have germinated from this antidogmatist stance.

After he returned to China and started a professional literary career, his antidogmatist viewpoint was brought into sharper focus. We find the following remarks in his May 1935 article "A Critique of Zhang Tianyi":

Image Making, Legacy Clarification, and Agenda Formulation

> The ultimate goal of artistic activities is to grasp the truth of human life and to create synthetic typical characters. That can only be reached in the writer's struggle with real life, when the writer himself looks into the depth of life with genuine feelings; if he only wanders, as he wishes, superficially among social phenomena with a plain materialist view, I am afraid it will be difficult for him to deepen his understanding and to develop his talent.[26]

While calling for the writer's active engagement with life for the sake of a truthful understanding of social reality, Hu Feng, at about the same time, also emphatically pointed out the indispensable function of the writer's subjective involvement in literary creativity. In an October 1935 article "A Discussion on Writing for Beginning Writers" (Wei chuzhibizhe de chuangzuotan), for instance, he argued that in the process of writing reality becomes mixed with the writer's creativity and, as the writer expands and modifies reality with the assistance of his imagination and intuition, he demonstrates his critique of reality and reflects the spirit of his times. Such a process, moreover, is an ongoing and ever-deepening one in which the writer's mind and his subject matter change each other through interaction.[27] In view of the above arguments, it seems apparent that the main components of the "subjective fighting spirit" were already in place at the beginning of Hu Feng's career as a leftist critic.

Interestingly, Hu Feng found a kindred spirit in Georg Lukács in the development of his "subjective fighting spirit." As I mentioned in chapter 1, according to Li Huoren, Hu Feng first came to know Lukács's *History and Class Consciousness* during his stay in Japan. In the 1930s, as Lukács embroiled himself in the debates in the Soviet Union and often ended up a target for criticism, Hu Feng obviously remained informed of Lukács's positions. One of the important debates that involved Lukács in the late 1930s was over the role of worldview in literary creativity and, as we shall see shortly, Lukács's reproach of the overreliance on the "correct" worldview—a codified Marxism in other words—would lend some support to Hu Feng's "subjective fighting spirit," then still in elaboration.

In December 1940 Hu Feng published his protégé Lü Ying's translation of Lukács's "Narrate or Describe?" in *Qiyue,* perhaps the first Chinese translation of Lukács. In an editor's note at the end of the issue he tried to clear the charge, levelled at Lukács in the Soviet Union at the time, that Lukács had overlooked the importance of worldview. Judging from Lukács's article, the question one should ask, he argued, was how to explain the functioning of worldview or how to understand, with specific examples from the history of literature, the functioning of worldview.[28] Soon afterwards, he gave a brief explanation for the working of worldview at a meeting of leftist writers in Chongqing on January 8, 1941, a spinoff of the debates that involved Lukács in the Soviet Union from 1939 to 1940. Contending over the role of worldview in Balzac's career, a favorite topic among leftist writers, he interpreted "worldview" as a cognitive process, not an unchanging political stand.[29] His emphasis on the expansibility of the cognitive process in effect greatly discounted the "correct" worldview to which other participants in the meeting attached so much weight.

At the meeting, he also insisted, as always, on the writer's active participation in the cognitive process. On this point his consistent position matched with Lukács's view expressed in "Narrate or Describe?" With his famous analysis of two horse races, one in Tolstoy's *Anna Karenina* and the other in Zola's *Nana*, Lukács argued in his article that active participation in the crises of bourgeois society enabled major European critical realists, including Balzac, Stendhal, Scott, Dickens, and Goethe, in addition to Tolstoy, to integrate their characters' experiences into socially significant events through *narration* in spite of the limitations of these writers' ideologies. In contrast, uninvolved observers of society such as Flaubert and Zola could only resort to *description* to turn out tableaux devoid of vitality. Maintaining the writer's active participation in the fundamental social processes of his time as the sine qua non for his productiveness, Lukács asserted that

> when a writer is isolated from the vital struggles of life and from varied experiences generally, all ideological questions in his work become abstractions, no matter whether abstractions of pseudoscientism, mysticism or of an indifference to vital issues; such abstraction results in the loss of the creative productiveness provided by questions of ideology in the earlier literature.[30]

In interpreting ideology as a derivative from life experience and giving priority to participation over belief system, Lukács appeared to have

Image Making, Legacy Clarification, and Agenda Formulation

mounted a covert attack, in this article written in the heyday of socialist realism, on the official approach to literary production in the Soviet Union that attached paramount importance to the mastery of the "correct" ideology—Marxist worldview.

Influenced by, among other things, the cultural-intellectualistic predisposition of May Fourth, Hu Feng went further than Lukács in interiorizing or cerebralizing the writer's participation in social experience, which resulted, after years of germination, in the clear expression and forceful advocacy of the "subjective fighting spirit" in 1944. The crystallization of this key notion in the last phase of the war against Japan was by no means an accident. With the routinization of the wartime conditions since the withdrawal from Wuhan in late 1938, Hu Feng felt, as he made clear in a speech he drafted for the board of directors of the Chinese Writers' National Anti-Aggression Association in April 1944, that more and more writers in the interior, trying to appeal to the unhealthy tastes of the public, had dissipated their fighting spirit and made compromises with harmful tendencies in society. As a remedy, he called on writers to cultivate their strength of character and to intensify their will to fight.[31]

Another cause for concern, a more important one, was the spread of Mao Zedong's "Yan'an Talks" to leftist circles in Chongqing and the attendant ideological rigidification. In the summer of 1943, leftist cultural circles in Chongqing began to hold meetings on Mao's talks. Invited to one of the first meetings, Hu Feng insisted on the differences between Guomindang areas and Communist base areas and argued that some of the tasks Mao laid down in his talks, particularly the task of training workers, peasants, and soldiers to be writers, were inapplicable in Guomindang areas. Having brought the meeting to an inconclusive and unhappy end, he was excluded from subsequent meetings on Mao's talks.[32] After the CCP sent He Qifang and Liu Baiyu, two participants in the Yan'an Forum, to Chongqing in spring 1944 to further indoctrinate leftist writers with Mao's ideas on literature and art, he became more recalcitrant, beginning to vent his anger and contempt in letters to his close associates. Apparently the intensification of the Communist thought reform campaign in Chongqing accounted for the urgency in Hu Feng's insistence on the "subjective fighting spirit," if not its content.

As he increasingly felt the need to combat spiritual flaccidity on the one hand and ideological regimentation on the other, Hu Feng issued a manifesto of the "subjective fighting spirit" with "Putting Ourselves into the Struggle for Democracy" (Zhishen zai wei minzhu de douzheng limian), an article, written on October 7, 1944, that later became the inaugural statement of his journal *Xiwang* (*Hope*). The task for the "subjective fighting spirit" is outlined in the following remarks:

> The assimilative process of representing the subject matter is, at the same time, a critical process of overcoming the subject matter. This requires, on the one hand, the fortification of subjective strength to the point that it can fight and criticize the subject matter from real life. Through this it creates an artistic world that contains deeper truth than any individual subject matter. On the other hand, it requires that the writer should delve into the sensuous subject matter to such a depth that he becomes one with the sensuosity of the subject matter and cannot tear himself away or stand aloof from the subject matter according to his wishes. Consequently, the artistic world he creates will be an accurate, lively and sensuous reflection of historical truth, not just a frigid illustration of an abstract concept.[33]

The "subjective fighting spirit," as specified above, contains several crucial points. First, it emphasizes the writer's individual initiative and activism in his dealing with social reality. Secondly, it prioritizes lived experience over preexisting theoretical abstractions. Thirdly, it acknowledges the reaction of the subject matter on the writer, hence a certain kind of malleability on the writer's part, by taking note of the tensional relationship between the two. In a nutshell, while emphasizing the cognitive and historical leeway in the development of truths, Hu Feng's notion amounts to a challenge to the monolithic, finalized "truth in itself" divorced from human agents and historical circumstances. Depending on the writer's personal approach and predilection, it can result in literary practices that stress either the function of human agency or the impact of external reality on the search for historical truths. Philosophically, as it calls attention to the interaction between the subjective and the objective in the cognitive process, it faults the basic Marxist conviction that there exists an objective reality totally independent of man's mind. In so doing it intends, in the realm of literary production, to change the complexion of a realism premised on the essential philosophical category of reflection. As we shall see in the following analyses of the works by Hu Feng's protégés Lu Ling and Ji Pang, realism in the hands of *Qiyue* writers is no longer content to be a transparent, inactive mirror to reality. While grappling with reality assertively, it can also question its own assumptions and conclusions about reality. Ultimately the explanation for both the acts of assertion and questioning lies in Hu Feng's "subjective fighting spirit."

Five

Different Modes of Intellectual Intervention: Lu Ling's Short Stories

After he resumed the publication of *Qiyue* in the wartime capital Chongqing in July 1939, Hu Feng, now geographically separated from most of his old contributors, tried hard to discover, train, and promote new writers, most of them young men with little experience or reputation. Like Lu Xun, he helped the newcomers with professional advice and supported them as their friend and mentor at a personal level. As they increased their ranks, developed their publication projects, and clarified their cultural agenda, Hu Feng and his young protégés consolidated the position of the *Qiyue* school and made it one of the most active forces in the literary scene in the Nationalist interior.

The practice of the *Qiyue* school, in this phase, was a double reaction to the escapist tendency in the interior and to the mechanistic application of Marxist beliefs in the leftist camp. As the war now entered a stage of attrition and many dislocated writers settled down willy-nilly in the interior, creative works, fiction in particular, experienced a boom in the early 1940s, partly due to the need of the public to assuage its angst. To meet the demand for entertainment, writers began to produce traditional regulated verse, familiar essays, humorous stories, exotic romances, and even erotic tales later in the war. Taking great alarm at what he saw as a trend of nonchalance and depravity, Hu Feng urgently and repeatedly called for an injection of moral intent into literary works. His followers answered his call by focusing on the tremendous wartime hardships as their subject matter. Somber and solemn, their works contrasted sharply with the lighthearted strain in wartime literature.

On the other hand, the reaction to Marxist doctrinaires was more important in determining the orientation of *Qiyue* works. Enmeshed in leftist politics and exposed to assaults from Hu Feng's old enemies almost from the start, *Qiyue* writers considered themselves Lu Xun–style "lone warriors" and adopted a pugnacious attitude toward the leftist cultural establishment. They believed some of the widely accepted Marxist doctrines, especially its millennialism, to be lifeless falsities under a scientific guise. As adherents of May Fourth critical realism, they counterposed their works against those written in the spirit, if not in the name, of socialist realism. Consequently, a host of old questions, such as the role of intellect and the intellectual vis-à-vis the spiritual deformities of the working people, were brought up again and answered in new ways.

In both its reaction to the recreational tendency in wartime literature and to leftist stereotypes, the fiction by Lu Ling, Hu Feng's favorite protégé, best illustrated the *Qiyue* group's disposition. Starting out his career with psychological explorations, in contradistinction to naturalistic representations of social reality, Lu Ling quickly began to question the belief in historical rationality and the act of sublimation, both of which were deeply embedded in revolutionary literature. Especially important in his case was the influence of Hu Feng's "subjective fighting spirit." In a sense all of his stories in this period, be they psychological or satirical, were efforts to carry out Hu Feng's directive from different angles. Yet perhaps due to either the space limit of the short story or the generic postulates of satire, his implementation of the "subjective fighting spirit" remained mainly concerned with the interactions between a rather stable authorial self and projected others. A further development, authorial self-transcendence, will have to await his novel *Children of Wealth*.

THE INTERVENTION OF THE MIND

Born on January 23, 1923, into a gentry family in Suzhou, Lu Ling (real name Xu Sixing) lost his biological father at the age of two. Soon afterwards his mother married a government clerk so that she could raise Lu Ling and his younger sister. After he started school at five in Nanjing, Lu Ling began to feel the social prejudices against his status as a stepchild. Years later he recalled that his childhood was spent in "depression, nervosity and the incomprehensible love and hatred for the world,"[1] an early experience that certainly contributed to the psychological orientation of his fiction. The only memorable events in his otherwise dull, depressing childhood were occasional visits to his mother's gentry relatives in Suzhou; these visits would eventually become source materials for his magnum opus *Children of Wealth*, a novel in which he included real names of his relatives and, possibly, real events in his life.[2] At the outbreak of the war in 1937 his stepfather took the family to Sichuan, where Lu Ling continued his high school education and started writing. In September 1939 he submitted a story "After Withdrawing from the 'Fortress'" ("Yaosai" tuichu yihou) to *Qiyue*. It was accepted and published in May 1940, thus becoming the beginning of Lu Ling's long, eventful association with Hu Feng that would not only spark off inspirations in the young writer but also bring about political tragedies to both the mentor and the disciple.

Focused on a shipper-turned-lieutenant's chaotic experience in the army shortly before and after the fall of a fortress where he is stationed, "After Withdrawing from the 'Fortress'" resembles Qiu Dongping's and A Long's battlefield reportage in its choice of subject matter, plot arrangement, and characterization, all premised on a novice's ill adaptation to army life. Yet there is a marked inclination toward psychological convolution. The main character Shen Sanbao, a total misfit in the army, constantly harbors thoughts of escape, but once on flight from the fallen fortress he provokes enemy fire with reckless shooting. When Shen, prodded by a welter of feelings and impulses, kills his superior for no good reason, even he himself cannot understand or justify his action. Precariously predicated on layers of motivations and a hair-trigger temper, the character's behavior becomes enigmatic and unpredictable, a feature that would develop into a staple of Lu Ling's fiction.

In the summer of 1940 Lu Ling got a clerical job at a mining research institute that involved frequent trips to mines in the suburbs of Chongqing. As he grew familiar with miners, Hu Feng, now a close friend and mentor, encouraged him to write about them, a suggestion that was soon carried out in a series of stories Lu Ling submitted to *Qiyue* in quick succession. With regard to these stories, which established Lu Ling as one of *Qiyue*'s major contributors, Hu Feng's advice on psychological focus far outweighed his suggestion of the subject matter. At his insistence on the relentless exposure of spiritual scars, Lu Ling parted company with the conventional plot-centered short story and took the mental worlds of his characters as the narrative locus of his stories. While waging a war in what Hu Feng called a "gray battlefield" with the contorted minds of his characters, the young writer staked out his personal space and developed his unique style.

When discussing Lu Ling's stories, we should first of all note that their pronounced psychological orientation is manifestly un-Chinese. Traditional Chinese fiction, action-centered, usually did not take mental experience as its main narrative concern. Even literati novels such as *The Scholars* (*Rulin waishi*) and *The Dream of the Red Chamber* (*Honglou meng*) were focused more on the depiction of a unifying, lyrical vision than on individual psyches of the characters.[3] Written in the wake of the debate over "national forms" and at a time when many Chinese writers still used techniques of folk literature to reach a broad audience, Lu Ling's psychology-centered stories answered Hu Feng's call for the further internationalization of Chinese literature in the manner of May Fourth cosmopolitanism. As it directly benefited from the translation boom of the early 1940s, Lu Ling's fiction was crucially inspired by European literature, particularly Russian literature, in many ways, including its use of a rather convoluted, Europeanized syntax.

Centered on marginal figures living at the bottom of society, Lu Ling's stories of the early 1940s undoubtedly reflect the influence of Maxim Gorky's works such as *In the World*, *The Lower Depths*, and "In the Steppe," to which Lu Ling was attracted at the time.[4] Like their predecessors in Gorky's works, Lu Ling's characters often reveal their intellectual personalities and concerns in spite of their nonintellectual facades. Regardless of their social backgrounds, they tend to think and emote similarly. A runaway soldier in "He Shaode Came under Arrest" (He Shaode beibu le) is equally absorbed in mulling over the frustrations in life as a fifteen-year-old sentimental petty clerk from a family in financial decline in "Grandfather's Job" (Zufu de zhiye). The local landlords in "Family" (Jia) and "The Coffins" (Guancai) remain as prone to ponder over the meanings of life and self-identity as the deracinated workers. Thoughtful, unhappy, and yet unable to take action to free themselves from the existential trap of life, many of the

Different Modes of Intellectual Intervention

characters in Lu Ling's stories are intellectually homogenized to a certain extent. After all, the Communist ideologist Hu Sheng is not totally unjustified in accusing Lu Ling of intellectualizing his working-class characters.[5]

Of course, the intellectual homogenization can be ascribed to Gorky's influence and, to a certain degree, to Lu Ling's inability to understand working-class people, as Hu Sheng argued, or to his inexperience as a young writer incapable of creating characters of many colors. A more crucial source for this important feature of his fiction, however, lies in Hu Feng's emphasis on the writer's psychological wrestling with his characters. In his close interrogations Lu Ling cannot help but inject certain intellectual concerns into his characters' psyches from time to time. As an example, let us take a look at the following narrated monologue in "Family," his first story about miners, that reveals the landlord Liu Yaoting's indefinable wistfulness on the eve of his wedding with a seventeen-year-old concubine:

> Such thick, confusing darkness and such quietude easily make one feel as if he were living in a different world. Liu Yaoting is in agony tonight! He has busied himself for forty years. But what has he gotten? What has he brought to this inscrutable, suffocating world?[6]

Though Liu's personal perspective and emotive modulations are preserved at the verbal level, the content of this miserly, industrious landlord's thoughts does not easily fit in with his customary behavior, his habitual mindset or the mode of consciousness conventionally associated with his type. Contrary to Dorrit Cohn's definition that a narrated monologue belongs to a character's, rather than to a narrator's, mental domain,[7] Lu Ling's above-quoted narrated monologue, like many other similar passages in his fiction, is inextricably tied up to the narrator's intellectual critique of the character. In comparison, plausibility in characterization becomes unimportant.

Obviously a moral enterprise, fiction writing for Lu Ling is inseparable from interpretation, which often overshadows the mimetic function of his stories. His main interpretive device is the reliable narrator, who always speaks vehemently for the norms of the implied author and constantly tells the reader where he should stand in the world of values. Yielding little room for ambiguity or irony, he tends to make ex cathedra pronouncements straightforwardly and copiously. As a result, we often encounter not only microcosmic mental examinations but also panoramic analyses in Lu Ling's stories, as can be seen in the following summary of Xu Xiaodong, a weakling miner and the main character in "Under the Loading Dock" (Xiemeitai xia):

> Like all those crushed by life, Xu Xiaodong is very good at self-deception. That is to say had no one found out about his theft of the wok nothing would have become so devastating. He would simply and stupidly find opportunities to tell his friends that he had been duped into buying the wok for thirty-five dollars. Although this innocent man would feel fears, reproaches and pains in private, his capability for self-deception would increase as long as he did not see the world had turned against him. To that extent such a soul will collapse irremediably when his transgression is exposed and the world changes its appearance in front of him; he will smash all the reasons for his existence and nakedly enter dark destruction.[8]

With the characters' psychic experiences firmly in his grasp, whether they are phenomenologically approached or discursively understood, Lu Ling's narrator often summarizes complex states of mind in analytical terms, without spending too much time to concretize their nuances. Although efforts are unquestionably made to find the appropriate scenes and situations as reflections of the wartime ethos of the Nationalist interior, the author, as a rule, does not leave them as "objective correlatives" that can speak for themselves. Rather, he treats them as stimuli that frequently draw comments either from the impressionable characters or from the reliable narrator himself on general questions about life. Thus extending their narrative attention across these mental reactions, Lu Ling's stories usually run much longer than the conventional short story concentrated on a "slice of life."

As Lu Ling contends with his characters at a psychological level, he pays much closer attention to characterization than to plot. Whereas the plot lines in his stories often consist of loosely strung small incidents in a stagnant world, the mental dramas of his characters, by no means calm, are played out in center stage. Though often initially sparked off by daily events, these mental dramas, once set in

Different Modes of Intellectual Intervention

motion, tend to follow their own trajectories without having to toe the line imposed by plot. In other words, they constitute an independent domain that merits attention in its own right. Having prioritized mental experiences over physical activities, Lu Ling often casts his characters as thinkers or talkers rather than doers. If his working-class characters already begin to display this propensity, then the intellectuals in his stories go a step further in this direction. In "Valley" (Gu), a story written in 1941 about two elementary school teachers tormented by the agony of love, the main character Lin Weiqi's tempestuous thoughts and orations all but drown out his attempts at action. Sensitive and disdainful of the corrupt environment around him, Lin spends most of his time and energy either looking into himself or perorating to his girlfriend. Yet instead of adding such a character so preoccupied with words to the long roster of "superfluous men" handicapped for deeds, Lu Ling appreciatively portrays Lin as a person who combines passion and intellect in his incessant, though inchoate, searches for the truths about the world and about himself. As they throw themselves into a battle of ideas and boldly confront the problems of their time, it is characters like Lin and his successors, including Jiang Chunzu, the cherished character in *Children of Wealth,* that are the real heroes of Lu Ling's fiction.

In Lu Ling's fiction the intellectual signifies a mode of life rather than a social class. An intellectual by profession, in other words, is not necessarily an intellectual in spirit, who has the mentality and, perhaps more importantly, the courage to confront his world and himself. Lu Ling's concentration on the function of the mind, in my view, signals an effort to restore the legitimacy of the intellectual mode of life. Instead of depicting intellect as a cause for political inaction and intellectuals as weaklings paralyzed by their self-consciousness and skepticism, as most of the contemporary leftists do, he tries his utmost to prove that the analytical mind has not outlived its usefulness. Moreover, as it refuses to be humbled into acquiescence and retains the capability of revolt, the mind only has to look into itself for sources of revolutionary consciousness. In other words, as a site for revolution, it does not have to be revitalized by any outside agent, be it the proletariat, Marxism, or the Communist Party. Though at moments burdened with gnawing self-doubts and keenly aware of its own limitations, it is rarely haunted by the specter of its divorce from the revolutionary causes to the point of abdication. Its power and nobility lie in its ability to regain the initiative in its battle with the world and with itself. In sharp contrast to the long anti-intellectual tradition in Marxism, a tradition further strengthened by the CCP and its literary henchmen, those intellectuals in Lu Ling's fiction that truly represent the analytical mind are never ashamed of being intellectuals and they never deny themselves the right to speak up. In that regard his narrator should be considered the true intellectual *par excellence*.

At the stylistic level, Lu Ling's emphasis on the vital function of the mind results in an increase in commentarial or discursive elements in his stories and, on the other hand, a decrease in narrative or story elements. Monologues, narrated monologues, speeches, and conversations take up a great deal of space and they are meant not so much for those living in the worlds of the stories as for an impersonal audience or the general public existing outside the purview of the stories, especially in the case of the narrator's comments. As both the narrator and the characters involve themselves in passionate mental and verbal pursuits, what gets highlighted is the enunciative act rather than the actual content of what is thought and said, which usually awaits further development. Nonetheless, the balance is certainly tipped in favor of what Émile Benveniste calls "discourse," or the intervention of the speaker to influence the listener.[9] As it moves away from mimesis and toward diegesis, and highly discursive diegesis at that, Lu Ling's is a dithyrambic style that keeps calling attention to the presences and expressions of speakers in the stories, particularly the narrator.

Why did Lu Ling write in a way so unique or, one is tempted to say, "unrealistic," since he keeps violating the norms of verisimilitude as regards character categorization, not to mention his narrator's stentorian voice that invariably disrupts the realist surface of the stories? The answer to this question, I believe, should be sought at least in part in his belligerent attitude toward the contemporary realist fiction of the leftist mainstream. In the 1930s and 1940s most left-leaning Chinese realists aspired to a Marxist revelation of the "objective" laws underlying historical movements as well as an epic representation of at least a certain segment of society in their works. In the eyes of the *Qiyue* school the paradigmatic and syntagmatic models the Marxist orthodoxy utilized to explain the instances and trajectories of meaning had sunken into models of predictability. To challenge the scientistic, universalist approach to a conceptually completed social reality,

Different Modes of Intellectual Intervention

Lu Ling shifts his attention to the volatile world of psychology, a world that does not follow any predetermined route or reach the point of completion. Without taking this challenge into consideration we will not be able to understand fully the features of unreadability in his stories, including the extensive intellectualization of his working-class characters. No longer stereotyped as un-self-conscious bearers of social energy educable by outside forces, workers and peasants in Lu Ling's stories, now endowed with their own minds and voices, join forces with the narrator to upset the prevalent Marxist social conception of how workers and peasants should be.

THE REVOLT OF THE ABJECT AND THE PRIMITIVE

In the 1930s the ascendancy of vulgar Marxism among Chinese leftist writers had put a parable in place, a parable consisting of, among other things, themes about the structures of society, the inevitability of historical progress and the revolutionary attributes of the working classes. When Hu Feng first called for a resistance to "formulism" in the mid-1930s, he was already aware of the danger in the widening tendency toward the mechanistic application of Marxist schemata in literary works and sought to curb it. Though overshadowed by patriotic concerns in the first phase of the war, the Marxist parable once again gained currency in the early 1940s as leftist writers gradually switched their attention from the war and the battlefield to society at large. Marxist social analysis was taken for granted, and so was its progressivist historical vision to a certain degree. It was against this built-in optimism in the Marxist tradition, especially the myth of the working classes, that Lu Ling, as a representative of the *Qiyue* school, wrote stories that focused on the spiritual injuries and stagnancy of the lower-class characters. Shrouded in gloom and peopled by either down-and-outers or rebels with neither clear causes nor group attachment, Lu Ling's stories called into question a host of basic assumptions in revolutionary literature, including, most importantly, the rationality of history and the sublimation of instincts into socially useful forces.

To begin with, many of Lu Ling's characters have blurred social backgrounds and the vicissitudes in their personal fortunes disqualify them as clearly bounded signs of large, impersonal historical forces.

Instead, they are presented as embodiments of moods and psyches that display emotional and psychological abnormalities across the social spectrum. As symptoms of a sick society, they fit in quite well with Julia Kristeva's following characterization of abjection: "It is . . . not lack of cleanliness or health that causes abjection but what disturbs identity, system, order. What does not respect borders, positions, rules. The in-between, the ambiguous, the composite."[10] In the case of the insulted and injured, the foci of Lu Ling's stories, many are depleted of their revolutionary potential by prolonged spiritual subjugation while the rebels among them misdirect their defiance because of their inappropriate compensatory strategies. As Lu Ling puts in the limelight the neuroses suffered by his characters, he dissolves the sociological notion of the autonomous individual or ego-personality into sub-individual and pre-individual components that stop the characters from becoming effective political agents.

For Lu Ling the etiology of his characters' neuroses is certainly social, cultural rather than biological or generic. Therefore his critical attitude toward the social environment is obvious. Living in a dismal society devoid of material or spiritual welfare and detrimental to the actualization of human potential, his vulnerable, fearful, and illusionary characters develop neurotic trends to cope with their hostile world and to gain a false sense of safety and security. To make things worse, many of them adopt incompatible neurotic strategies that result in unavoidable clashes, impasses, and disintegration of personality. Thus torn between conflicting motives, impulses, and feelings, they lack a psychological unity as well as an understanding of what they really want, feel, and value. They are, in short, unable to put their lives in perspective and hence dissipate whatever psychic energy they have before it can become socially productive.

To greater or lesser degrees the characters in Lu Ling's stories are invariably weighed down with anxiety, the essential factor common to all neuroses. Helpless and isolated, they tend to catapult their personal problems to an existential level and respond with intense and yet inappropriate psychological reactions. The following compensatory strategies are usually adopted to assuage anxiety. The first is to project bafflement onto irrelevant factors in life, as shown in "Under the Loading Dock" when the maudlin miner Xu Xiaodong blames his marriage for all his troubles while his wife finds it impossible to go on

Different Modes of Intellectual Intervention

with life when Xu breaks an old wok by accident. The second is to escape the harsh reality through dreams and fantasies, as, for instance, the maidservant Li Sao in "The Coffins" does so often in her daydreams about an afterlife in which justice will be meted out. The third is to gain a sense of power through sadism, as the chained laborer He Dexiang in "In Iron Chains" (Zai tielian zhong) does when he hits his wife with a tile as she begs a local despot for his release. Frequently the characters resort to different, often incongruent, strategies in quick succession, as illustrated by "Old Woman Wang and Her Piglet" (Wangjia laotaipo he ta de xiaozhu) in which the title character, abandoned by her family, first dotes on her piglet, the only hope for her funeral expenses, then whips it hysterically as it refuses to obey her. She then collapses and dreams about a reunion with her granddaughter in a trance. Psychologically fragmented, Lu Ling's characters usually can only experience themselves in a piecemeal way and, as a result, their inconsistent words, gestures, and acts become signals of confused minds.

While describing his characters' neurotic defense strategies, Lu Ling displays a unique grasp of the subconscious. Introduced into China in the 1920s, Freudian psychoanalysis attracted the attention of an impressive array of Chinese writers, among them Lu Xun, Zhou Zuoren, Guo Moruo, Yu Dafu, Xu Jie, and many others. As far as Lu Ling is concerned, the fictional works by the New Perceptionists—Shi Zhicun, Mu Shiying, and Liu Na'ou—and by Eileen Chang offer particularly interesting comparisons. Like these writers, Lu Ling tries hard to explore the power of the irrational as a force in human life. In doing so he, again like these writers, depends on intuition and shifting narrative perspectives to project the subjective into the objective and to create characters with multiple personalities. But he does not concern himself with the depiction of the fast-moving life in a modern metropolis, as the New Perceptionists do, or with the meticulous searches for the "objective correlatives" of a melancholic historical vision, as Eileen Chang does. Unlike these writers who are directly influenced by Freud and who often consciously flesh out Freudian ideas in their fiction, Lu Ling remains oblivious to many important Freudian notions. For instance, nowhere in his fiction can we find any trace of pan-sexualism, which figures so prominently in Shi Zhicun's historical stories. Given Lu Ling's interrupted education and the unlikelihood of direct exposure to Freud, we may argue that Freud's influence on him, if there is any, is heavily mediated by Hu Feng's insistence on the disclosure of working-people's spiritual scars.

What distinguishes Lu Ling's presentation of the subconscious is that he is not merely interested in the subconscious per se but in the unpredictable interference of this depository of hidden discord with purposeful social action. In an age when the notion of causality is firmly entrenched in literary realism, his rendition of the unrestrained subconscious breaks ranks with the rationalist approach that, as it unifies the human psyche, grants a continuity to exterior events that leads to a logical conclusion. The rationalist approach, as Herbert Marcuse notes in a different context, is essentially aggressive and offensive since it is perpetually bent on fighting, conquering, and even violating the "lower" faculties of the individual as it does to external nature.[11] Seen in this light, Lu Ling's invocation of the neurotic instincts in his characters amounts to a return of the repressed that strives to speak in the name of the real against the unity, continuity, and harmony that historical rationality tries to impose on the human psyche.

Lu Ling's recuperation of the subconscious can also be viewed as a revolt against the discourse of the revolutionary sublime. Recently Ban Wang has brilliantly analyzed the workings of the revolutionary sublime in modern Chinese literature to transform the instinctual, libidinal, bodily, and feminine elements into "higher," culturally and politically sanctioned and valued activities, and the subversion of this discourse in the post-Mao literature of the 1980s.[12] Following Wang's lead, I would stress that the discourse of the revolutionary sublime constitutes the core of socialist realism and the revolt against this discourse could be found in Lu Ling's fiction, written at a time when socialist realism was emerging as the dominant paradigm in leftist literature. However, unlike the 1980s insurgents such as Yu Hua and Can Xue who, as Wang demonstrates, tend to mask their attempts at desublimation behind the fantastic, the schizophrenic, and the grotesque, an ambivalent strategy to me because it bypasses the issues of everyday life, Lu Ling largely grounds his efforts in the realm of the real, thus indicating that reality is much richer than what the discourse of the revolutionary sublime denotes and connotes through its explanatory apparatuses.

Behind Lu Ling's attempts at desublimation we could find a

paradigm contest. In an article "Realism Today" (Xianshi zhuyi zai jintian) written in December 1943, Hu Feng remarked that wartime literature was in a state of crisis as the tendencies toward theorization and idealization of life threatened the spirit of realism. The redress, in his opinion, lay in the revival of the fundamental orientation of China's New Literature, epitomized by Lu Xun's famous statement "I selected most of my subject matter from the unfortunate people in a sick society, with the intention of exposing the diseases and calling for treatment."[13] Here what Hu Feng meant by the two erroneous tendencies, a highly schematic description of the literary scene, can be interpreted as a covert reference to the idealistic model of socialist realism. On the other hand, his remedy came from the model of May Fourth critical realism. Essentially derived from Lu Xun, the critical paradigm in Lu Ling's stories intensified itself as it competed against the influence of socialist realism for interpretive authority.

In socialist realism, as Régine Robin points out, one of the nodal vectors is that the social being takes precedence over the psychological being and, as a fundamental given of the social contract, the hero of socialist realism will never let himself be weakened by the vagaries of the psychological being.[14] Contrary to the positive hero in socialist realism, who only lives in the public sphere and embodies a clear political and existential message, Lu Ling's characters live in the psychic sphere and are marked by indeterminacy and uncertainty. Their experiences, in other words, do not prophesy a rosy future reachable through social action since they remain weighed down by the heavy burden of a nightmarish past and present. Disabled by the illogicalities and discontinuities in their psyches and wandering in the lower reaches of history, these wayward individuals stand in sharp contrast to the parabolic characters in socialist realism that invariably demonstrate the forward movement of history at an allegorical level.[15] The anticlimactic endings Lu Ling customarily gives to his stories further drive home his subversive message.

Lu Ling's antagonistic attitude toward the paradigm of socialist realism leads to the disappearance of a fundamental theme of socialist realism from his fiction: working-class characters' spiritual journey from spontaneous action to political consciousness. In contrast to the heroes of socialist realism, Lu Ling's characters are perpetually marked by the absences of a clearly defined sociopolitical goal, of the knowledge of their historical mission and of the competence to over-

Chapter Five

come their opponents for the actualization of their goals. The most poignant examples in this respect are not so much the down-and-outers as the rebels who, though sporadically and impulsively striking back at oppression and injustice individually, remain deeply rooted in unconsciousness. Bearers of what Hu Feng calls the "primitive vitality," they represent instincts in defiance of not just social repression but also Marxist sublimation intent on naming their significance. In the latter regard, as they keep seeking and losing their self-identities, they end up turning into fluid signs of heterogeneity.

While one can draw a long list of rebels in Lu Ling's stories, credit for the most detailed presentation of the "primitive vitality" certainly goes to his well-known novella *Hungry Guo Su'e* (*Ji'e de Guo Su'e*), a work that shocked the Chongqing literary circles with its explicit description of sex and violence when it came out in 1942. As pointed out by Hu Feng in his preface to the work, what Lu Ling searches for in the novella is the blood-stained truth of life rather than abstract, lifeless conclusions.[16] In view of Lu Ling's open polemics against leftist stereotypes, any reading of this work that does not fully take its political intent into account, for instance Kirk Denton's interpretation of the title character as an emblem of a cosmological force analogous to that embodied by the mythological goddess Chang E,[17] would run the risk of overlooking the most fundamental thrust of the work. Hence I will concentrate on sorting out the political implications of the novella in the following reading.

Centered on the rebellion of a young woman, driven by a famine from her hometown, abandoned by her father and later picked up by an opium addict to be his common-law wife, *Hungry Guo Su'e* impresses the reader, first and foremost, with its creation of a female character whose stormy temper, uninhibited sensual indulgence, and undaunted willpower in the face of brutal punishments have few parallels in modern Chinese fiction. According to Zhu Hengqing, Lu Ling modeled his eponymous heroine on a cigarette vendor he came to know in his high school days,[18] but he certainly projected his understanding of "primitive vitality" as the essence of the character, as his following admission proves:

> Guo Su'e is not a woman crushed in the old society. What I tried "romantically" to look for is people's primitive vitality and the active liberation of individuality.[19]

Different Modes of Intellectual Intervention

As a result, this character stands out as an antipode to certain values traditionally associated with femininity, passivity in particular. Significantly, Guo Su'e demonstrates her strength not through her higher faculties but through sexual insurgence and bodily endurance of violent tortures. Fed up with her wretched husband, she seduces the mechanic Zhang Zhenshan in the hope that Zhang might take her away, only to be disappointed by Zhang's reluctance and eventual desertion. When her husband finds out about her affair he has her detained and tortured, and tries to sell her in collusion with the village headman and a local thug. But nothing could force her to give in. Finally, she is burned with a hot iron and raped by the thug before she dies a few days later.

Throughout the story the drama of rebellion and repression is staged on Guo Su'e's body, not in her mind. Unable to find a way out of her misery or to win any promise from her lover determined to keep himself away from any social tie, she can only seek momentary ecstasies through sex, ecstasies preceded and followed by worries, fears, resentment, dejection, and despair. When she feels, at the climax of her sexual intercourse with Zhang Zhenshan, "as if she were only alive at this moment and as if her life in the past had been a dull, deep slumber and in the future would be unavoidable fragmentation and extinction,"[20] we see her confusion as well as pessimism. However, her sexual insurgence is undeniably liberating in its own ways. Situated in an undifferentiated state in which pleasure is mixed with unpleasure, hers is a revolt that, while refusing to be converted into politically useful energy, expresses itself through excess rather than limit, thus beckoning to a plenitude of future possibilities. It is precisely this historical plenitude Lu Ling wants to keep in his story, so much so that we find few traces of his narrator's overt analyses that we usually encounter in his other stories. In the end Guo Su'e becomes memorable because of her story, a story that, in Hu Feng's words, resembles not a drawing or a sketch but an oil painting in which a motley of colors and lines are overlaid to indicate the depth and multidimensionality of the characters.[21]

At a more conscious level Lu Ling's effort to keep the particularity, spontaneity, and plenitude in working people's historical struggles is coordinated with his portrayal of Guo's lover Zhang Zhenshan. One of the most impressive industrial workers in modern Chinese fiction, Zhang nonetheless has a personal history, character traits, and even facial features so complicated that one would feel hard put to label him as a typical proletarian. In turn he has been a newsboy, orphaned tramp, petty informer, soldier, and apprentice before he becomes a mechanic. As a worker, he enjoys his work as much as he enjoys sex and, in the latter regard, his attitude to Guo Su'e is a mixture of lust, indifference, and awed respect. Obsessively concerned with his self-identity and determined to keep experimenting with himself to safeguard his individuality, he deliberately refuses to fall into the stereotype of the proletarian worker, knowing by heart the latter's attributes such as the knowledge about the worker's social status and the importance of solidarity in collective causes. A hard-core individualist, he functions, at the syntagmatic level, as a wayward sign that always consciously declines the role expected of an industrial worker by Marxist dogmatists. His life experience, therefore, like Guo Su'e's, rejects the schematic harness that tries to make life yield revolutionary meaning.

Again we may argue that what both Guo Su'e and Zhang Zhenshan contrive to impart, though in different ways, is the message of desublimation or, more exactly, antisublimation. Orthodox Marxism, under the influence of the Hegelian notion of the absolute subject, conceives of the proletariat as a class of conscious actors who understand where they collectively stand in history and rationalize their actions, purifying, in the meantime, their instinctual and libidinal energies into sociopolitically progressive forces of revolution. Julia Kristeva's following words about sublimation help us understand, from a psychoanalytical perspective, this Marxist conception of proletarians as historical actors: "sublimation is nothing else than the possibility of naming the pre-nominal, the pre-objectal, which are in fact only a trans-nominal, a trans-objectal."[22] Lu Ling, in contrast, sees the working people as saturated with a political unconsciousness and to him the political unconsciousness is a locus of "truth" and "authenticity," not a lower realm to be transcended or discarded. His emphasis on the bodily and the individual further undercuts Marxist sublimation by rejecting the Marxist objectification of the proletariat into a set of characteristics. While stressing the trans-nominal and the transobjectal through Guo Su'e's unconscious and Zhang Zhenshan's conscious efforts to escape the trap of objectification, Lu Ling clearly indicates that the Marxist sublimation of the proletariat is nothing but a totalizing attempt that fails to grasp the human subject in all his or her complexity. In that sense Liu Kang is certainly right in regarding, from a Bakhtinian standpoint, Guo Su'e as a carnival body whose violent movement of participation, transgression, and transformation constantly undermines the attempt to represent desire, body, and class consciousness from the perspective of the sublime.[23]

With his detailed portrayals of the psychological abnormalities among his lower-class characters, the issue of violence looms very large in Lu Ling's fiction. Working-class violence, we should note, is usually a form of political sublimation in Chinese leftist fiction. First treated by Ding Ling in a description of a peasant uprising in her 1931 story "Flood" (Shui) and soon further elaborated by writers such as Zhang Tianyi, Ye Zi, Sha Ting, and Wu Zuxiang, it is customarily depicted as the consummate action of a revolutionary crowd that signals both the elevation of the crowd's political consciousness and its collective power. Its destructive force, celebrated as a historically and morally justified means, is directed outward toward a defective social order and its demonized representatives. In contrast, the violence exhibited by Lu Ling's working-class characters is individualized rather than collectivized, neuroticized rather than normalized, and implosive rather than explosive. In a word, stemming from the protracted oppression of the working people in Chinese society and mainly displaying itself through sadistic or masochistic behavior, the dispersed and directionless violence remains a roadblock to historical rationality rather than its crystallization. Meanwhile, with their psychic energy decimated by such internal violence before it could be sublimated, the working-class characters in Lu Ling's fiction become a far cry from their progressive counterparts in the mainstream leftist fiction.

THE LIMITS OF SATIRE

As the war against Japan drew to an end, Lu Ling began to write satiric stories, a mode he had so far not used consistently. Satire, to be sure, had been an important strain in wartime fiction. Projected into prominence by Zhang Tianyi's "Mr. Huawei" early in the war, satire had enjoyed a certain popularity in GMD areas and, as government corruption worsened and living conditions continued to deteriorate, a wave of satires in different genres appeared in the last years of the war, to which Lu Ling's satiric stories were in a way related. There was, however, a difference between him and most of the satiric practitioners of the time. Whereas the latter singled out for their condemnation the inept GMD government, its corrupt bureaucrats, and the evil gentry, Lu Ling vented his scorn on the society as a whole without stratifying it into different segments. Focusing on the widespread degeneration of either a miniature or a cross-section of China, he distinguished himself particularly from those leftist satirists who, motivated by their political ideology, implicitly harbored a progressivist vision of the future as they denounced the status quo. His satiric scalpel spared no one, and working classes were no exception, since in his satiric stories characters of all social backgrounds contributed equally to the spiritual languor of society.

With class distinction thus rendered irrelevant, the crowd and its individual members loom very large as the targets of Lu Ling's satiric stories. Unlike the crowd in much of the contemporary leftist fiction, which is increasingly depicted as a revolutionary force to which the intellectual narrator, diminished in importance, feels attracted,[24] the conception of the crowd in Lu Ling is influenced by Chekhov, whose short stories and plays inspired his satires, as his *Qiyue* colleague Ji Pang tells us.[25] An equally crucial source of influence, it seems to me, might be Lu Xun's Nietzschean view on the herd. Content with life as it is without making any effort to improve it, the crowd represents for Lu Ling, as for Lu Xun, an ahistorical inertia incapable of self-perfection. It, in other words, lives in a world without historical possibilities. Thus depleted of historical potential, it is completely disqualified as an innovative social force. Dynamism, instead, is solely invested in the narrator who, antagonized by the crowd's inertia, stands out as its absolute opposite while incessantly denouncing its various deformities.

It is small wonder that Lu Ling's satiric stories, so polemically disposed, impress us most with their presentation of a dystopia contaminated at the grass roots. Set either in the countryside or in small towns enveloped in a timeless quiescence, these vignettes of life in the GMD interior depict their characters as either clowns devoid of interiority or hypocrites who do not practice what they preach. As the characters are flattened into caricatures to highlight the apathy, servility, vainglory, and pettiness of a degraded community, the narrative tone is sharpened toward ridicule. In order for his direct attacks on the vices to be effective, Lu Ling the satirist makes absolute the moral

Different Modes of Intellectual Intervention

distance between himself and the evils he condemns. As he calls attention to the behavior of fools and knaves without telling the reader anything about himself, he becomes a point of view that organizes a group of symbols—situations, scenes, and figures—to express a particular vision of the world.

Besides Chekhov, a specific influence on Lu Ling's satirical social vision might be sought in "Public Display" (Shizhong), a story Lu Xun wrote in March 1925 and collected in *Wandering*. Taking as its ostensible subject an exhortative public display of a group of prisoners on a drowsy summer day in Beijing, Lu Xun's story aims its attacks at the callous onlookers, referring to them by synecdoches such as "Fatty," "Skinny," "Baldy," and "Red-nose" to indicate their physical as well as mental deformities. A similar scene is depicted in Lu Ling's story "A Well-Matched Chess Game" (Qifeng dishou), with the difference that the ambiance of Lu Ling's story is even more lethargic:

> Around noon on a sultry summer day, almost the whole street in the small town has fallen asleep, dominated by a vast stupor and silence. At any slightly shaded place, whether it is behind dilapidated walls, under bare trees, on the ground or on benches, people are lying on their backs, half naked.[26]

After a panoramic view of the squalid town, the story closes in on a chess game between two clownish local residents. Their squabble over each other's moves and the subsequent invectives only momentarily rouse the slumbering townspeople and in the end, with the two main characters going back to their chess game, the whole town falls back into stupor.

If we take the small town as a miniature of Chinese society, what we see in high relief in "A Well-Matched Chess Game," as well as in Lu Ling's other similar vignettes, is a vision of a hopelessly languid nation. In order to highlight the stasis characteristic of the community, Lu Ling resorts to bold, swift strokes. As a result, realistic details give way to exaggeration. Devoid of wit, humor, playfulness, irony, or fantasy, it is exaggeration with moral seriousness, unity, and intensity. Austere and angry, the satirist always lashes out at the evils in society from an elevated position and in a dignified manner. Since for him the moral standards and boundaries are crystal clear, he harbors few ambiguities with respect to his own standpoint and to the evils he attacks. However, as I will discuss in more detail later, behind the moral distance and certitude lurks an awareness of solipsism, a ghost that throws a monkey wrench into Lu Ling's satiric machinery and botches its social functioning.

Paying scanty attention to their social backgrounds, Lu Ling makes sure that his caricaturized characters remain easily extendable to cover a wide range of similar figures. In "Novel Amusement" (Xinqi de yule), he describes the total lack of compassion shown by a cross-section of society—office workers, well-dressed young women, blue-collar workers, and tramps, all of them waiting for a bus at a Chongqing bus stop—as the line of passengers shamelessly play a practical joke on a blind beggar by not letting him go through. Putting his characters physically and mentally into a metonymic relationship, Lu Ling in effect launches a totalistic attack on the crowd. A similar attack is mounted in the story "The Night China Won the Victory" (Zhongguo shengli zhiye), a satiric depiction of the celebration of Japan's unconditional surrender in an interior town on the evening of August 10, 1945. Consisting of several unrelated scenes of foolish revelry, wild fantasies and schemes that involve people from various walks of life, the story presents the celebration in the small town as a senseless farce that bodes ill for the future, now that history has supposedly turned over a new leaf. As Lu Ling foregrounds the irremovability of his characters' spiritual deformities, repetition and stasis become the hallmarks of the historical vision in his satiric stories.

Marked primarily by their repulsive outward behaviors and mannerisms, Lu Ling's caricaturized characters are shown to lack in spirituality. As an avowed moralist, the author is rather unwilling to give sustained presentations of the thoughts of his depraved characters, since, as Wayne Booth puts it, "any sustained inside view, of whatever depth, temporally turns the character whose mind is shown into a narrator,"[27] which would mean to give up the moral battleground to the enemy, the last thing Lu Ling the satirist wants to do. What we see in the stories, then, is the pervasive, prominent presence of the satirist on the one hand and, on the other, the erasure of the characters' viewpoints. These two sides of the same coin work together to ensure that in the end the satirist always prevails in the moral battles.

Even when Lu Ling does give the floor to his degenerate characters, he makes sure what they think and say can be easily judged by the reader as shallow and frivolous. Thus the characters, in spite of their mental and verbal activities, are still marked by the lack of an interior self. In "A Blind Man" (Xiazi) the more scurrilous guesses the self-important ticket collector Gao Guohua makes about his passengers, the more he reveals his vulgar mind. As he gets carried away by his highfalutin lecture to a blind passenger, this self-deceiving *alazon* draws not laughter but ridicule from the satirist, who quietly and yet unambiguously serves as his foil in the background. In "Autumn Night" (Qiuye) Lu Ling achieves a satiric effect by juxtaposing the county government clerk Zhang Boyao's grandiose late-night planning for the future with the delight Zhang takes in inflicting excessive tortures on a rat he catches under the door. The gaping discrepancy between the character's interiority and his exteriority reveals that, unbeknown to the character himself, his "solemn" decisions are nothing but illusions he conjures up as he continues his frivolous existence. Like the pompous ticket collector in "A Blind Man," Zhang ends up an *alazon* who deceives nobody except himself.

Through the depletion of interiority from his characters, the flattening of their minds or the accentuation of the gap between their thoughts and deeds, Lu Ling achieves a kind of satiric pleasure that strongly asserts the satirist's moral and intellectual superiority, a pleasure accompanied by a sense of mastery over a world he can fully understand and assess. Behind the confidence, however, lurks the feeling of inefficacy on the author's part. Elitist and disdainful in attitude, Lu Ling the satirist polarizes himself from the rabble of his characters and, in so doing, renders himself irrelevant in terms of any influence upon the latter. In other words, the separate realms in which the satirist and his targets remain locked respectively become static rather than interactive and, as a result, their conflicts stay unresolved to the end.

The lack of resolution is best illustrated by "An Important Letter" (Yifeng zhongyao de laixin), a rare example in which Lu Ling endows his satiric character with an interiority. Excited about an impending visit from his former boss, the philistine clerk Wu Qishi, the main character of the story, is fully aware of his sycophancy and feels exasperated with himself for being so fawning. Wu's self-accusation, displayed in mental dialogues he conducts with himself, should be viewed, like many psychological excursions in Lu Ling's stories, as an instance of authorial intrusion, since this apparently righteous attitude is incompatible with Wu's character and has no bearing on his obsequious behavior. As Wu sits down and composes a long welcome letter to his old boss at the end of the story, he remains what he is in spite of his intermittent realizations of what he ought to be. The final triumph of the character's deeply ingrained behavioral pattern over his interiority, injected by the author from the outside, shows the irreconcilability between Lu Ling's caricaturist design and his psychological approach, for the former requires demarcation and distance while the latter calls for empathy and interaction. With its implicitly static conception of both the satirist and his targets, satire finally proves not to be an entirely appropriate mode for the "subjective fighting spirit." To overcome this stasis Lu Ling has to move to a different ground.

Six

Manifestations of Self-Transcendence: Lu Ling's *Children of Wealth*

In 1940, soon after he started his literary career with *Qiyue,* Lu Ling began to write his magnum opus, the novel *Children of Wealth* (*Caizhu de ernumen*), inspired in part by what he had seen and heard about his mother's gentry relatives in his childhood. He finished the first version of the novel in 1941 and mailed it to Hong Kong, where Hu Feng was staying at the time, but the manuscript got lost in the chaos caused by the Japanese occupation of Hong Kong. After Hu Feng made a safe escape to Guilin in early 1942, he encouraged Lu Ling to rewrite the novel. With amazing speed Lu Ling completed the first half of the novel, in its present form, in November 1943 and the second half in May 1944. As the two volumes came out in print in November 1945 and February 1948 respectively, the novel, more than 1,300 pages in length, was acclaimed by Hu Feng as the most magnificent epic in the history of China's New Literature.[1]

Designed as an exploration of various aspects of the material and spiritual world of Chinese intellectuals,[2] *Children of Wealth* impresses the reader with its tremendous psychological energy that upstages everything else in the novel. Whereas the first volume is heavily punctuated by reflections on different members of the powerful Jiang family, the second volume closes in on the spiritual peregrinations of Jiang Chunzu, the youngest Jiang brother. The dynamic psychological processes in the novel are clearly motivated by a polemic intention, crystallized in Lu Ling's following remarks in his preface to the novel:

> Human life is a process of struggle. In the world there are no permanent palaces, not to mention that the palaces surrounding us are made of pasted paper. There are no permanent prisons, not to mention that the prisons surrounding us are hidden in secrecy. Young people dare to despise, unsettle, and destroy them and this contempt and attack amount to creativity from our point of view. . . . But if the young people, after taking a few steps, hope to save the future from trouble once for all and begin to admire the paper-pasted palaces and the dark prisons, they will certainly be knocked down heavily by their successors in the name of life, no matter what kind of smile or tears they wear on their faces.[3]

The consequences of such a strong polemic intention are manifold. Discursive rather than narrative, the novel pays little attention to typicality in subject matter, natural causality in plot development, coherence in characterization, or consistency in point of view. In other words, being a novel of its own kind, it can hardly be judged by such standards as mimesis or verisimilitude that one usually employs in evaluating a novel, especially a realist novel. We should also bear in mind some important facts about the author: young (Lu Ling finished the lengthy novel at the age of twenty-one); not formally well educated, especially on the subject of traditional Chinese literature or thought;[4] writing at a strikingly fast pace that made it virtually impossible for him to attend to the niceties of his novel, allegorical or otherwise.[5] In view of the actual production of the novel, we might want to raise some questions about the meticulous attempts in Kirk Denton's recent book to dovetail certain scenes in the novel with the often abstruse symbols and themes in Daoist cosmology.[6] One could even go so far as to argue that the above-mentioned biographical factors significantly contributed to what would be conventionally regarded as technical flaws in a hastily written work by a young writer. However, the way Lu Ling wrote his novel did have an advantage: it enabled him to pour out what was on his mind without any hesitation or reservation. Straightforward, forceful, and emotionally charged, Lu Ling's novel calls for a political reading that takes account of the author's burning concerns at the time of writing. To approach the novel in its own terms, I will, in the following pages, explain its unique features in connection with Hu Feng's "subjective fighting spirit" and other intellectual influences.

NARRATORIAL SELF-TRANSCENDENCE

As an anomaly in its time, *Children of Wealth* has attracted a certain amount of attention since its publication. Yet apart from the encomiums from fellow *Qiyue* writers on the one hand and the strictures from Communist ideologists on the other, few critiques of the novel have satisfactorily accounted for its unique characteristics. The recent research on the novel by Kirk Denton and Kang Liu, two literary scholars in the United States, ameliorates the situation, but there is still room for further debate. While Denton, besides spending much of his energy unearthing what he considers the novel's parallel with Daoist cosmology, mainly focuses on the major character Jiang Chunzu as a figural emblem of the tension between romantic individualism and revolutionary collectivism and while Liu considers the novel a dyad of "family saga" and *Bildungsroman* torn between the "outer form" of critical realism and the "inner form" of subjectivity,[7] neither of them explains the overall features of the novel, which include the prominence of the narrator, the discursive preoccupation, the fast-shifting viewpoints, the zigzagging plot arrangement, the jagged characterization, and the high-strung style. All these features, I would like to argue, stem from the antisystematic thinking Lu Ling tries to promote in various ways as a remedy for spiritual stagnancy and degeneration. They are, in other words, the outgrowths of Lu Ling's fundamental compositional approach, a glimpse of which could be obtained from the passage quoted at the beginning of this chapter. As the author wrestles with his subject matter from different angles and constantly modifies everything, including his own previously expressed opinions, the novel becomes an expanding field of energy that keeps rupturing a host of basic assumptions about reality, realism, and the novel as a genre.

Lu Ling's following confession about his novel, made in his preface, indicates his awareness of the consequences of his compositional approach:

It is still somewhat disorderly and unavoidably shallow at certain places. What I felt especially frustrated about was: when I entered

> a world I pursued, I tried my best to grapple with it, assisted by my spiritual demands and enthusiasm for the world. But my efforts seemed to have ended in exaggeration, confusion, bewilderment and gloom. As a result my weaknesses were exposed. These weaknesses, however, can be shown as painful endeavors and I did not feel ashamed at all that I had made these endeavors, since they were intended only as attempts. Never willing to give up these attempts and with some practical difficulties in view as well, I have made no correction of them.[8]

That Hu Feng's "subjective fighting spirit" serves as the guideline for the writing of the novel, broadly implied here, results at the discursive level in the complete convergence of the narrator with the implied author, since the messages in the novel will not be conveyed directly and forcefully if a gap is created between them. Thus created in the implied author's image and invested with omniscience and reliability, the narrator stands for authorial norms at all times. Furthermore, the narrator is characterized by his eagerness to communicate his opinions and thereby build an immediate rapport with the reader. In short, the narrator is a plain-speaking spokesman for the author who means to have his words taken faithfully and seriously.

At the story level, the narrator in *Children of Wealth* usually stands outside and above the *histoire* he narrates, and is often prone to give brief outlines with broad strokes, dotting the novel with summaries like the following one about the powerful Jiang family:

> Basking in the glory of wealth are the admirable life experience and personality of the patriarch, Jin Suhen's feminine heroism or ambition, Jiang Weizu's frailty and Jiang Shaozu's silence, constantly and strongly hinting at the future of the Jiang family. But the Jiang sisters' sentimental strivings amidst all this remain the most moving.[9]

With the story pushed into a subordinate position, the narrator's real interest lies in his psychological interactions with the characters. Like many characters in Lu Ling's short stories, most of the characters in the novel never hesitate to express their views and feelings at great length, but with the narrator elevated to a position of moral and cognitive superiority the interpretative balance is unquestionably tipped in his favor as he penetrates and evaluates the innermost recesses of the characters' minds. In view of this imbalance in cognitive power between the narrator and the characters, we would be hard put to take *Children of Wealth* as the kind of Dostoevskian "polyphonic" novel defined by Mikhail Bakhtin, as Kang Liu would like us to do.[10]

Literary scholars have repeatedly pointed out that Lu Ling's novel was heavily indebted to Romain Rolland's *Jean Christophe,* a novel about which Lu Ling in fact knew nothing even in October 1942, when the composition of the first volume of his novel, in its final version, was well under way.[11] In structural terms, a more important influence, at least as far as the first volume is concerned, is Leo Tolstoy's *War and Peace.* In his preface to Lu Ling's novel, Hu Feng singles out Tolstoy as the master Lu Ling took great pains to learn from and the literary historian Yang Yi, in his biographical sketch of Lu Ling, also tells us that Lu Ling was profoundly moved by Tolstoy's masterpiece in the course of rewriting his own novel.[12] In the fashion of the Russian masterpiece, Lu Ling constantly changes the perspectives in his novel to reflect the polymorphism of life and the multiplicity of viewpoints on life. With its attention focused more on the discursive than on the narrative, *Children of Wealth,* especially the first volume, presents a dynamic interweaving of views that all lay claim to validity as they are directly and, more often than not, vehemently articulated.

Amidst the welter of viewpoints stands out the narrator's perspective, a perspective that tends to override those of the characters when they come into contact. The narrator is accustomed to expressing himself, in a Tolstoyan voice, with categorical statements, often pontifications on such big issues as history, social reality, individuality, and, most importantly, philosophy of living, so much so that sometimes he appears to claim a kind of philosophical knowledge not ordinarily the province of novelists, thus stretching the limits of conventional "omniscience" far beyond the fictional world. Yet there is a crucial difference between his persona and that of the Tolstoyan narrator. Whereas the narrator in *War and Peace,* on which the middle-aged Tolstoy spent years painstakingly writing and revising, impresses the reader as a philosopher who has derived encyclopedic knowledge and a profound understanding of history and human life from his extensive reading and thinking, the narrator in *Children of Wealth* comes out as a young man eager to voice his opinions before they are fully crystallized and polished. Unlike Tolstoy's narrator who serenely makes indisputable, Homeric theoretical digressions, Lu Ling's narrator is not afraid to change, modify, or even contradict his own views as he impatiently searches for the truths of life. For him, neither the searcher nor the searched stands still and therefore the ongoing process of searching is far more important than its results.

As an example, let us take a look at the characterization of Jin Suhen, the daughter-in-law who almost single-handedly brings down the Jiang family with her machinations to grab its wealth. One of the fully delineated characters in the novel, Jin, partly modeled on Wang Xifeng in *The Dream of the Red Chamber*, is at first depicted as a shameless, relentless femme fatale with self-confidence and many tricks up her sleeve. However, after she drives her husband Jiang Weizu insane and her father-in-law Jiang Jiesan, the family patriarch, to the verge of mental collapse, she develops a kind of sentimental affection for her husband and son. The narrator summarizes the change as follows:

> In certain harsh, difficult situations people resort to their frank, modest souls as their willpower becomes useless; they all have candor and modesty in their heart. Now this woman known for her ruthlessness begins to seek this kind of help. Staying awake late at night as she quietly lies in bed, she feels that her damaged conscience is coming back.[13]

After Jiang Jiesan dies with a broken heart, a further development in Jin is introduced as she relapses into money-grabbing maneuvers. Before other family members get to the Jiang residence in Suzhou, she searches every room, selects the best of the family's jewelry, fur coats, and antique furniture and transports them to Nanjing, where she lives with her husband. An ensuing lawsuit against her launched by her in-laws, however, exhausts and disconcerts her. In the end her deranged husband, no longer a mere pawn in her financial schemes, turns out to be a tormenter of her sickly mind and totally subdues this shrew for the rest of her life.

The twists and turns in Jin Suhen's psyche and personality display Lu Ling's intention of creating a multifaceted and unfinalizable character. Without a clearly mapped out developmental blueprint, Lu Ling's sensitive and sentimental characters, Jin Suhen being the least typical of them, remain susceptible to psychological sidetracking and mood swings. As the characters are caught in multidirectional processes of ceaseless becoming, the narrator has to keep changing his views on them. Made sometimes in proximity and sometimes in distance, the narratorial comments in the novel, ex cathedra as they often are, constitute a variable movement of their own. As a result of the implicitly yet constantly raised questions about the cognitive and rhetorical authority invested in the narratorial discourse, the inquiries initiated in the novel become continuous and open-ended. In this sense the narratorial discourse, for all its prominence in the novel, operates differently from the absolute, totalizing social understanding of the contemporary leftist orthodoxy. Whereas the latter exhibits a world already fully comprehended from a "scientific," and static, point of view, the former shows not just a fictional world in the making but the maker and judge of the fictional world in the process of revising his own opinions.

The strong interest in directly expressed ideas, the obvious didactic intent and the intensified presence of the narrator in *Children of Wealth* might easily lead one to take the novel as a *roman à thèse*. Yet if we adopt Susan Rubin Suleiman's definition of the *roman à thèse*, that is, a novel based on the realistic aesthetic of verisimilitude and representation that signals itself to the reader as primarily didactic in intent, seeking to demonstrate the validity of a political, philosophical, or religious doctrine,[14] we will find that Lu Ling's novel does not quite fit in. Not only does it largely discard the realistic aesthetic of verisimilitude and representation but it gives the lie to any self-enclosed doctrine that exists before and outside the ever-changing social and psychological realities. Whereas the *roman à thèse*, again in Susan Rubin Suleiman's words, remains essentially an authoritarian genre with its appeal to the need for certainty, stability, and unity and its affirmation of absolute truths and absolute values,[15] Lu Ling's novel is anti-authoritarian in the sense that it subjects everything to revision and, as a novel of ideas, it ultimately reveals the inadequacy and insufficiency of ideas, including its own.

In addition to the perpetual revision of his own opinions, another strategy the narrator in *Children of Wealth* adopts to put the fictional world in flux is frequent changes in his relation with his characters. I have pointed out that he often tends to evaluate his characters categorically from an Olympian vantage point, but that does not prevent him from identifying with them ideationally, psychologically, and emotionally at other times. The characters with whom he identifies range from the spirited fighter Jiang Chunzu to the femme fatale Jin Suhen and the renegade Jiang Shaozu. Instead of reducing the culpable characters to mere targets for denunciation stripped of their own defense, the narrator often thinks with, for and against them in quick succession while keeping their verbal, psychological, and emotional effusion largely intact. Created in the wake of the frequent changes in perspective and relationship is a mercurial distance between the narrator and the characters that keeps raising implicit questions about the former's absolute pronouncements on the latter.

One of the reprobated characters in *Children of Wealth*, arguably the target of Lu Ling's most severe criticism, is Jiang Shaozu, the second son of the Jiang family. In the course of the novel this onetime rebel eventually turns away from the troubled times and ensconces himself in traditional quietism for solace, thus becoming, in Hu Feng's words, a sad reminder of a certain type of modern Chinese intellectual.[16] In spite of all the explicit narratorial reproaches on his retrogression, Jiang Shaozu is portrayed as an eloquent orator and a considerable amount of space in the novel is spent on his thoughts, often as feverish as those of Jiang Chunzu. His beliefs, tinged with escapism as they frequently are, sometimes do have a ring of truth as lessons painfully learned by a middle-aged man from his experience with Chinese society. For example, when he points out to Jiang Chunzu in a debate near the end of the first volume that the abstract concept of the "people" (renmin), upon which his impetuous younger brother pins his faith, has been and will be manipulated by all kinds of political forces for their own purposes,[17] what comes out is an almost indisputable truism. At moments like this the narrator, for all his censures, implicitly makes allowance for Jiang Shaozu by granting validity to his opinions.

As he takes Jiang Shaozu's views into account from the character's own perspective, the narrator cannot but tone down his criticism. Therefore some of his statements on Jiang Shaozu, like the following one, border on equivocations:

> People are often negligent when they are young, since to them everything in life is easily accessible. But after their souls have experienced enough suffering and worries, they will encounter

something that they realize they had missed in the past. Singing an elegy over a world full of errors, they begin to look for what they have missed in the past and will not exist in the future in order to inspire candid confessions and examinations of their character. It seems to them that they have to take a close look at their errors and evaluate themselves in front of their errors before they could gather enough strength to stand up once again from evil and cowardice and start their journey in the world.[18]

Here the patently sympathetic, if not entirely exculpatory, tone reveals a certain elasticity in the narrator's attitude towards Jiang Shaozu. I have pointed out the eagerness for communication as an important feature of the narrator in Lu Ling's novel. Another important characteristic of the narrator, related to his eagerness to communicate his ideas before smoothing out their rough edges, is his strong desire to tackle his subject matter from as many angles as he can. As indicated by his mixed opinions on Jiang Shaozu, what he pursues is an interpretive openness that perpetually tries to ward off any self-imposed confinement of its own evaluative system.

As the narrator strikes out in all directions in his explorations of the characters' spiritual worlds, *Children of Wealth* bears some resemblance to what Roland Barthes calls the "text." An activity or production rather than a defined object, the "text," in Barthes's view, is governed not by a comprehensive logic but by a metonymic logic. As the "text" practices the infinite deferral of the signified, textual associations, contiguities, and cross-references coincide with a liberation of symbolic energy.[19] In Lu Ling's novel—a field of discursive energy bursting at the seams—the narrator constantly arouses and releases textual energy without trying to put it back into a well-framed plenum. This practice, I would like to argue, ultimately comes from Lu Ling's awareness of the heterogeneity, multivalence, and inexhaustibility of reality. Unfinalizable and incommensurable with any distilled systems, reality as conceived in his novel can only be approached by means of a pyrotechnics of expandable ideas from a wide spectrum of perspectives. As we shall see in the following section, the impact of such a conceptualization of reality is pervasive, spilling over from the narratorial comments to the plot arrangement and characterization in *Children of Wealth*.

Chapter Six

WAR AND PEACE DOMESTICATED AND PSYCHOLOGIZED

In spite of its extraordinary length, *Children of Wealth* pays scanty attention to the epoch-making events that happened during the historical period it covers. Setting his novel in a turbulent time between the Japanese attack on Shanghai on January 28, 1932, and Nazi Germany's blitzkrieg on the Soviet Union in June 1941, Lu Ling, however, often brushes historical events aside with brief, incidental references to concentrate on the stories of his characters, as typified by the following passage:

> In January 1934, the young Puyi, the last progeny of the dynasty, formed the Manchukuo Empire and ascended the throne. At the same time Japan closed in on eastern Hebei and invaded eastern Chahar.
> All this was put into the archives and written in the annals. But the residents of Nanjing still spent their lives playing mahjongg games, gossiping about Madame Hu Die, engaging in adultery, love murder, dividing family fortunes, hanging themselves, and drowning themselves in wells. Each lived with his own troubles.
> Life is troublesome and meaningless, but it is real. Life in Nanjing entails a complex variety of tricks and everyone is stuck in his own game. Most people practice professions they inherited from their ancestors—high-interest loans, quarrels over real estate ownership, petty rivalries in the officialdom and in hyperactive law firms. People show no concern for the change in the country's situation.[20]

An aggregate of happenings, big and small, history, as adumbrated in the above passage, takes place at different levels and along different, often unrelated, trajectories. In view of Leo Tolstoy's influence on *Children of Wealth,* we may argue that Lu Ling's atomization of history pushes the Tolstoyan thesis a step further: history should be viewed as an infinitely large number of infinitesimally small actions by ordinary people. However, while the Russian master still manages to create a grand epic with his panoramic view of a whole country in an entire era, not to mention the loving description and acceptance of a way of life in its totality, Lu Ling channels his novel almost exclusively into the domestic and personal realms. As it upstages the macrocosmic movements of history, *Children of Wealth* remains a partial imitation of *War and Peace*, that is to say, it imitates the Russian masterpiece only at the level of the family chronicle and not at the level of the military-historical novel.

Lu Ling's focus on the domestic and the personal at the expense of the epochal should be viewed as a reaction to the entrenchment of Marxist historical schemata in Chinese literary realism. In the 1940s, as it continued to strive for an unimpeded understanding of not only social phenomena but the main forces and mechanisms underlying social existence, a search initiated by writers such as Mao Dun and Wu Zuxiang in the 1930s, Chinese literary realism had given rise to a doxic mode that comprehended "objective" social phenomena while concealing its own subjective structuring principles. Realism's clarity and appeal to verisimilitude, having covered over its schematism, kept reproducing its patterns of perception in its unsuspecting audience. For all its critical attitude toward a world it sets out to portray, this mode contains certain conservative cognitive elements as it renders the world "natural," self-evident, and, hence, in no need of further inquiry. Furthermore, compounded by the Marxist subsumption of human beings under the power of social formations, these conservative cognitive elements, while stressing the inevitability of historical movement, ironically deprive human subjects of the initiative to bring about historical changes as individuals.

As shapers of their own destinies, Lu Ling's characters stand in sharp contrast to Marxist human subjects overshadowed by the absolute categories of social structure and historical development. The personal trajectories of the seventy-odd characters in his novel are multitudinous, variable, and thus difficult to classify or summarize. Instead of tying up his characters' experiences into a forward-moving plot, Lu Ling fills the first volume of his novel with digressive incidents in an extended family—love affairs, intrigues, squabbles, matchmakings, marriages, and so on—and the second with loose episodes in Jiang Chunzu's personal life, thus fully demonstrating his unwillingness to impose a finalized, tight-knit general structure onto the characters' lives. As a result, in his hands the characters are no longer narrative functions glued together by realist conventions to move the story toward a terminus. Instead, they become epicenters of their own activities that bear out an energetics rather than an economics of plot and plotting.

Chapter Six

Lying behind the sprawling plot and the roaming characters is an anti-universalist historical view. The Jiang family, for all its rich experience, is not depicted as a mirror to the nation at large. On the contrary, mostly cut off from historical events of national significance, it represents the fleeting, the incidental, the arbitrary, and the unnecessary elements of its time. The separation of the domestic from the public indicates Lu Ling's refusal to make the individual destinies of his characters flow into the titanic forces of history. Unlike Tolstoy, who emphasizes in *War and Peace* that popular life is the real basis of historical happenings, Lu Ling depicts popular life as constituting its own realm. With his attention concentrated on this rather self-enclosed realm, historical events, to Tolstoy the crowning peaks of the contradictory, vying forces in popular life, are rarely seen in *Children of Wealth*. In spite of its renown as an epic, Lu Ling's novel lacks the sweep, the grandeur and the national or even universal importance of the heroic figure that usually characterize the epic as a genre. Put in the cultural environment, these intentional lacks constitute a challenge to the literary realism premised on the philosophical concept of "totality," a mode best exemplified by Mao Dun.

The motor force of Mao Dun's literary realism, as Jaroslav Průšek notes, is the belief in natural causality.[21] In contrast to this philosophico-scientific conception that explains the phenomena in society with cause-effect reasoning, Lu Ling's is an antirationalist approach. Unfolding temporally rather than causally, the rapid alterations of a wide array of characters as the foci of attention in the first volume of his novel bear out a richness of life inexhaustible by ratiocination. In his clear unconcern about the structural unity of his novel, an unconcern that leaves so many loose ends untied, we further witness his refusal to subscribe to any comforting theory that synthesizes the world, by forging its inner connections, into a logically seamless whole. In sum, the fate of the world in his novel is not predetermined.

Ultimately, Lu Ling's subversion of rationalism culminates in the psychological peripeteia that so characterizes *Children of Wealth*, as it distinguishes his fiction in general. The richness of his novel does not lie in the scenes or the actions it tries to record, for these externals of life are usually only briefly sketched. Rather, the richness is exemplified by the details in feelings and thoughts, which certainly take precedence over the events. Far more complex, erratic, and unpredictable than actions, the psychological experiences of his characters

Manifestations of Self-Transcendence

preserve their irregularity, fortuity, and jerkiness as they come in quick succession to constitute a movement that, frequently interrupted as it already is, has no well-defined beginning or ending. Especially in the first volume in which characters constantly arrive and depart, none of their psychological experiences is dwelt upon at any great length. As a result, there is no obvious climax. What meets the reader's eyes is a series of highlighted moments that refuse to converge into a logical pattern.

To illustrate Lu Ling's interest in peripeteia, both actantial and psychological, let us now turn to a specific episode in his novel. The first section of chapter 10 in volume 1 of *Children of Wealth* covers a military review of a Japanese-made warship by a Japanese emissary in the company of Wang Jingwei, a real historical figure who later became the most infamous traitor of the war years. Although involving Wang Zuolun, a lieutenant in the naval ministry who has just married one of the daughters of the Jiang family, this interlude has little bearing on the vicissitudes of the Jiangs or, as it turns out, on the national history. As for Wang Zuolun, unhappy with the bureaucracy at the naval ministry, he at first cynically refers to the approaching review as a demonstration to show that the Japanese product has not been soiled in China. However, once the review gets started, as an officer standing at the salute,

> he immediately leaves behind the humdrum, detestable, enervating world in which he has stood and begins to feel a compelling solemnity created by the activities on the Yangtze River. Whatever significance this event might have in itself, it has a unique meaning for everyone of its participants. As they vanquish everything in their path, the glory and solemnity overwhelm Wang Zuolun's weak character. Therefore all the beliefs and mental activities he had just a moment ago are submerged by a new conviction. As the steamboat [that carries the Japanese emissary and Wang Jingwei] sails toward the frigate to the martial music on board, Wang Zuolun, his lips steadfastly sealed, warmly yet disconcertedly feels that the arrivals are marvelous human beings. The martial music once again appears expansive, mighty, and beautiful. Wang Zuolun takes a quick look to see whether anything has gone wrong. He feels that on the Yangtze River the Chinese nation is

Chapter Six

fighting with all its strength against its weaknesses and against an enormously tangible force.[22]

The first thing that strikes the reader here is the destabilization of the character's personality. Floating between incoherent impulses that keep changing the course of his thoughts, Wang Zuolun no longer retains his psychological unity or intelligibility. In other words, the discontinuities and inconsistencies in his personality make it impossible to contain him with conventional psychological categories. Meanwhile, as the train of his thoughts continually gets sidetracked, the narrative focus always falls on his fluid musings of the present moment rather than their enchainment to the past or the future. Freed from the chain of logic and pregnant with the potential of unpredictable changes, the present moment, no longer a mere parameter, is perpetually kept malleable and open as Lu Ling fills it with a multiplicity of psychological experiences.

In tandem with the psychologization of temporality in *Children of Wealth* is the psychologization of spatiality. At the start of chapter 2 in the second volume, as Jiang Chunzu flees across a plain with a group of new acquaintances early one morning, Lu Ling gives us a description that deserves to be quoted in its entirety because it typifies his approach to space:

> A thick fog is floating on this plain. Wheat and leguminous plants grow quite well in the fields; the ponds in the fields present a mysterious appearance of calmness. All this surrounds a quiet village hidden in the fog and densely dotted with houses. You could find villages of this kind anywhere on the fertile plains by the Yangtze River, as if they had been built one day when people, in their flight over the plains, suddenly agreed to descend on various places at will. Those who walk on the plains feel as if they were in a deep dream. They are so vast and so gloomy that they dwarf human life and, putting the lonely travellers into a trance, they carry them into a barren dreamland: people come to realize their ancestors' lives, accomplishments, and deaths; they feel that life, however heroic it was, has disappeared into the vastness in the same manner passengers disappeared over the horizon; what is left behind the soaring life is dilapidated houses, temples of trickery degraded from sanctuaries of the soul, and the somber,

Manifestations of Self-Transcendence

humdrum, numbed offspring. As they walk on the plains and pass by countless villages that have been transformed into dens of strange shapes, people cannot help but come to an awareness time and again in front of the scene of stubborn, repetitive human lives; in instantaneous phantoms people see the ancestors of China; they then begin to understand the emptiness and China. While touching off a callous philosophy of life, the plains have produced its apostles again and again.[23]

Part of the above passage is quoted by Kirk Denton to support his argument that the plains, which he interprets as "wilderness," suggest, on the one hand, "a genealogical lineage from the Daoist precivilized chaos condition, or *hundun*," and, on the other hand, stand out as an emblem of the discourse of revolutionary collectivism that posits the people as the motive force driving History.[24] My interpretation will, however, throw different light on the significance or, more exactly, the signification of the locale. Fertile, inhabited and cultivated for thousands of years, the plains help people understand life in China, its stagnancy and degeneration. Far more importantly, instead of presenting a static scene pregnant with inherent symbolic meaning, this passage fleshes out an active process of coming to grips with the plains, a process of psychological associations that tells us much more about the viewers' mental makeup and operation than about the intrinsic character of the scene itself. No longer a thing-in-itself, a mere container in which objects exist, space here becomes a humanized medium through which the mind tries to unlock the significance of the world.

Neither flattened nor homogenized into colorless, neutral, impersonal coordinates, time and space in *Children of Wealth* retain their "accents" by remaining fluid and elastic. Every moment, every location is a potential center pregnant with meanings waiting to be discovered and expanded by human agents. No longer securely premised on a causally conjoined framework of temporal succession and spatial configuration, the fictional world in the novel becomes a world of "becoming." In the end what we see is the dissolution of isolated entities into an interpenetration of the subject and the object.

Many important features of Lu Ling's novel dovetail with his conception of temporality and spatiality. For one thing, as I have discussed at length in the previous section, the narrator does not treat

Chapter Six

the world of the novel as an already constituted, objective world that, sufficient unto itself and separate from the narrator's subjectivity, can be apprehended by an equally self-sufficient consciousness from a distance. In terms of characterization, we should note that the characters in the novel have lost their hard edges as discrete, consistent beings sealed off from each other. Here I want to adduce one more example to illustrate Lu Ling's approach. One of the most captivating episodes in *Children of Wealth* is the moral struggle between Zhu Guliang, a typical drifter in Lu Ling's fiction, and Shi Huagui, a rabble soldier and rapist, that unfolds on the war-torn plains in front of Jiang Chunzu's eyes. Though presented as the conscience of mankind, Zhu is prevented time and again by his self-protective concerns from meting out punishments on his nemesis. On the other hand, Shi is shown to have no lack of moral justifications for his repeated offenses and even assumes the role of a law enforcer. So the final life-and-death struggle between the two is fought "on both sides for avenging the humiliations and injuries in their souls and for justice and survival."[25] The indication of the sameness in the opposites, an alternative to dualistic thinking, is further reinforced by the shifting responses from the witnesses. For instance, after he watches Zhu Guliang kill an officer for raping a peasant woman, Jiang Chunzu strongly feels that because of his pride and narrow-mindedness Zhu has ignored the significance of another life. As a variety of standpoints come into contact in quick succession, the drama on the plains, kaleidoscopic as it is, can hardly be streamlined into one single message.

In a sense the heavy psychologization in Lu Ling's novel can be regarded as the operation of what Roland Barthes in *S/Z* labels the "semic" code, a code indicative of the function of language and characterized by its instability and reversibility.[26] As it punctuates, disperses, and overshadows the Barthian "hermeneutic" code, which suggests, formulates, holds in suspense, and finally discloses and solves an enigma, and the Barthian "proairetic" code, which puts actions into a sequence, Lu Ling's psychologization constantly disrupts the logico-temporal order implicit in the plot of classical realism, showing that there is neither a final enigma to be solved nor a final truth to be told about the world. Taken as discourse, the pyrotechnics of psychological reflections in *Children of Wealth* demonstrates that truths, rather than standing in a relationship of correspondence to an inert, independent reality, have to take into account the flux in both reality and thinking as well as the interpenetration between the two realms. In the following pages, we shall see that this lesson is reiterated in the experience of Lu Ling's favorite character Jiang Chunzu, who represents the uncontainable searches for truths about the world and about the self.

CHARACTEROLOGICAL PROJECTION OF SELF-TRANSCENDENCE

While addressing his readers, Lu Ling is not at all shy about his partiality for Jiang Chunzu:

> I do not want to conceal that my targeted readers are people like Jiang Chunzu. For them Jiang Chunzu calls out with his whole life. I hope people will remember, as they criticize his weaknesses and detest his sinfulness, that his tragedy is caused by his honesty and bravery and that he is a noble person. The goal he sees is just what most of us have lost sight of due to our naive belief in dogmas and our toil in trivial schemes.[27]

As David Wang points out, the choice of Jiang Chunzu, a sentimental, artistic, temperamental, and slightly decadent social misfit, as the representative of students-in-exile during the war is in itself a challenge to the leftist formula according to which the degeneration of petty bourgeois intellectuals like Jiang Chunzu is necessitated by history.[28] By exalting Jiang Chunzu as an embodiment of passion, honesty, sincerity, and bravery, in short, a role model for his imagined readers in their pursuit of liberation, Lu Ling in effect attempts to exonerate intellectuals from the stigma Chinese Marxists indiscriminately brand on them.

It is not coincidental that Jiang Chunzu is the youngest son of the Jiang family. Like his counterparts in Ba Jin's *Family* (*Jia*) and in Lao She's *Four Generations under One Roof* (*Sishi tongtang*), he exemplifies dissatisfaction with the status quo, restlessness, and dynamism. Inspired by the eponymous hero in Romain Rolland's *Jean Christophe*, which Lu Ling read as he wrote the second volume of his novel, Jiang Chunzu continues to emphasize the message of *Kraft*—force—at the expense of the pacifist internationalism, the symbolic, allegorical, and musical elements in Romain Rolland's novel, a reception afforded to the French novel by Chinese literary circles as soon as its partial translation was serialized in *Fiction Monthly* (*Xiaoshuo yuebao*) in January 1926, as Leo Ou-fan Lee notes.[29] A twist, however, is added to the energy he carries as Lu Ling psychologizes and verbalizes it. Thus channelled into the discursive realm, Jiang Chunzu's youthful spirit refuses to rest content with any conclusions, including his own, as he keeps exploring a variety of issues. While introducing a new theme into the depiction of the radical youth, Lu Ling's choice of a psychological, verbal rather than actantial orientation for his favorite character also calls attention to the ossification of thought as one of the most serious obstacles to be overcome in the course of revolution.

Lu Ling's remarks about Jiang Chunzu that I quote at the beginning of this section show that his attitude toward the character is appreciative and empathetic, not doubled-sided and ironical as Kirk Denton interprets it.[30] A further, more pervasive indication of the authorial appreciation and empathy can be found in the character's mode of action in his explorations of the world, which, with its emphasis on dynamism and self-transcendence, is virtually the same as the mode adopted by the narrator in the novel. As far as their spiritual trajectories are concerned, the similarities between the narrator and the character are so strong that we should regard Jiang Chunzu as an intense characterological projection of authorial values, particularly the "subjective fighting spirit." As a writer, Lu Ling heeds quite well the advice Jean Christophe gives to his literary friend Olivier that a writer should say what he has to say, to think what he thinks, to feel what he feels and to express himself in his work without bothering too much about the purity of his style. The same frankness and boldness are bestowed on Jiang Chunzu from the outset as he makes one of his few appearances in volume 1 of the novel:

> Falling suddenly from intense rapture into burning despair, from excitement into gloom and then back into excitement, young life looks like waves. All this turbulence has no apparent reason, only because young people need it: in their heart they are having their first and most burning thoughts about the world, always feeling a voice ahead is calling them.[31]

Setting the primal tone for the character, the explosive emotions described here derive their force from an amorphous, spontaneous, and self-generative inner self that refuses to follow a fixed direction. Propelled by the intransigent force of the inner self, Jiang Chunzu's personal development always remains in the making.

The emphasis on the perpetual movement in Jiang Chunzu's spiritual experience leads to a number of conspicuous absences in his life—absences of a personal telos, a rite of passage, and a mentor who helps him reach a state of grace. Since these missing elements are, significantly, the basic ingredients of socialist realism,[32] we may take these absences as Lu Ling's challenge to the codified master plot in socialist realism rather than technical oversights of an immature writer. Unlike the hero in socialist realism who is guided by outside forces as he follows a predetermined route in his journey to a foreseeable destination, Jiang Chunzu remains a self-made character in that he is not inspired by others to assume their likeness. Keeping in sight Lu Ling's emphasis on internal strength rather than an external model, we will realize, after reading the second volume of *Children of Wealth,* that the process by which Jiang Chunzu tries to come to grips with society and with himself is rendered open-ended by the constant adjustments he has to make in his perceptions. In the end nothing remains inviolable.

In the previous section of this chapter, I already touched upon the multifacetedness and fluidity of the drama on the plains. The lessons Jiang Chunzu has learned on the plains, however memorable, soon prove to be in need of renewal and expansion. In the three important stages of his life covered in the second volume of the novel—his experience with the soldiers on the plains, as a travelling musician and as a school teacher in a small town in the countryside—the truths of life simply refuse to be grasped easily and conclusively. Here a developmental pattern can be discerned: Jiang Chunzu begins each stage with certain preconceptions that are eventually proven to be false as he accumulates more and more experience. Before the war comes he awaits destruction with a Nietzschean impatience, but the shocking drama on the plains opens his eyes to what destruction really means in human and moral terms. As a travelling musician, he falls in love several times with different types of women, only to have his romantic dreams shattered by either the indifference or worldly considerations on the women's part. In the last stage of his life, the utopia he makes of the small town Stonebridge (Shiqiaochang) turns out to be a dystopia that he cannot reform, however hard he tries. As reality gives the lie to his preconceptions, he comes closer and closer to different aspects of Chinese society, but at no point in his life does he rest completely satisfied with what he has discovered. He remains constantly on the move in his quest for more and further truths.

Interestingly, one of the highlighted discoveries Jiang Chunzu has made is about leftist politics. After joining a Communist-controlled theatrical troupe, he comes face to face with a clique of authoritarians and toadies who brandish high-sounding principles to attack their personal enemies, mostly their rivals in love triangles. As he starts a relationship with a young woman that the leader of the clique tries to approach, a meeting is organized by the clique to criticize him as an advocate of individualism. At the scene of criticism and self-criticism couched in leftist ideological jargon, Jiang Chunzu gains an insight into leftist politics and realizes his own integrity:

> A passionate, untamable force came to him [Jiang Chunzu]. Overwhelmed by the excitement in his heart, he felt that all of a sudden he had gained a thorough understanding of the whole situation he faced: he felt he understood his own sincerity and nobility as well as the ignominy of his enemies. For a long time he had somehow admired and envied the power wielded by the clique of his enemies. Now in the tempest of his passion he felt that only his soul was the paramount existence.[33]

Here Jiang Chunzu is presented in sharp contrast to the scheming, hypocritical users of leftist discourse. With his exposure of the operation of leftist discourse that conceals selfish motivations and brings about moral censorship and servility, Lu Ling makes sure that what Jiang Chunzu thinks and says, though rugged and inconsistent, outstrips the leftist lingo in terms of sincerity and honesty.

With regard to Jiang Chunzu's character, we should take note of the ever-existing juxtaposition of incongruous qualities in his personality. Alternately humble and haughty, he often harbors questions about himself as he takes immoderate measures in his dealings with the world. With all his youthful energy, he does not always live above the seduction of Daoist quietism. As he takes action, he is also frequently engaged in a self-observation that makes him hesitant. Instead of despairing of this state of irreconcilable internal contradictions as a state preventing the character from reaching a rounded totality of being, Lu Ling, however, endows it with certain positive values by viewing it as a rugged state of potentiality, a state with room for new, unexpected meanings. If taken as a spiritual biography, the second volume of *Children of Wealth* aspires not after Jiang Chunzu's eventual self-identity but after a provisionality that, as it gives temporary structures to his speeches and thoughts, makes movement a necessity under the weight of the character's internal contradictions.

With Jiang Chunzu as a multifaceted prism that refracts different aspects of an outside world through his now contemplative, now tempestuous subjectivity, the understanding he gains of society is poles apart from leftist clichés. As he in turn goes through the war-torn plains, the urban leftist artistic circles and the countryside with an increasing awareness of the vast gap between doctrine and reality, he feels more and more the importance of the individual's initiative in the quest for truths:

> Jiang Chunzu, as if looking back at the past, could see through the propaganda, exaggerations and idols of the age and get a glimpse of reality. He feels that, for a marching soldier, a deracinated peasant or a worker wandering from factory to factory, it is the first step to gain an awareness of his own fate from his involvement in collective life. Then follow a series of complicated movements, spiritual as well as material; some will stop, some will come to destruction and some will continue to develop. This is a gigantic process that needs boundless enthusiasm and creativity. Intellectuals should give up all propaganda, exaggerations, and idols to go into the depths of life.[34]

Always dissatisfied with not only leftist abstractions but his own past opinions, Jiang Chunzu stands as an incarnation of cognitive energy that knows no bounds as it tries to come to grips with a complicated world. As much an embodiment of the "subjective fighting spirit" as the narrator, he further contributes to the latter's disruption of literary conventions in the novel.

In discussing Jiang Chunzu the question of individualism seems unavoidable, for the character is generally depicted, not as a mere element that functions in a sociohistorical nexus, but as a privileged locus of meaning, an agent as well as a site of power at the discursive level. As Lydia Liu points out, the concept of individualism had already

Chapter Six

taken on a dubious reputation when it was first introduced into China at the turn of the twentieth century, easily susceptible to criticism and subordination by the notions of nation-state and society.[35] The death sentence passed on individualism as bourgeois ideology by the advocates of proletarian consciousness and revolutionary collectivism in the late 1920s continued to be widely accepted by leftist writers when Lu Ling was writing his novel in the 1940s. To take a cue from Lydia Liu that the notion of the individual should be studied as a historical category rather than assumed as a superior, transcendental value, I would argue that Lu Ling's prioritization of individual struggle in a generally anti-individualist environment takes over the May Fourth legacy of pitting the radicalized individual against a deadening tradition while replacing the content of what is meant by tradition. Sensing the tendency toward manipulation, disingenuousness, rigidification, and inertia in the forces that speak in the names of collectivities such as the proletariat, the masses, and the nation, Lu Ling tries to restore the individual, and the intellectualized individual at that, as an authentic source for internal as well as external revolution. While polarizing the individual from the limitations of its progressive-sounding Other(s) in the portrayal of Jiang Chunzu, Lu Ling in effect attempts to revoke the universal verdict on individualism.

Since most of its space is devoted to a single character's life experience, volume 2 of *Children of Wealth* is regarded by critics, among them Kirk Denton and Kang Liu, as a *Bildungsroman*. Indeed Jiang Chunzu resembles the hero in the *Bildungsroman* to a certain degree: his experience shares many typical *Bildungsroman* topois such as travel, ordeal by love, and search for a vocation. A careful reading of the volume, however, reveals that an essential component of the *Bildungsroman* is missing—the protagonist's eventual proper socialization achieved through self-cultivation and self-adjustment. The growth of the hero in the conventional *Bildungsroman* means little more than the acceptance of the values of his society. As Franco Moretti notes, "the legitimacy of a ruling class and through it of an entire social order: whatever its domain, this is always the distinctive framework of the *Bildungsroman*."[36] Constantly at odds with his social environment, and with himself at the same time, Jiang Chunzu apparently could not be any further away from the confirmation of social legitimacy we usually see in the *Bildungsroman*.

Ultimately, what distinguishes Jiang Chunzu from the hero of

Manifestations of Self-Transcendence

the *Bildungsroman* is the former's efforts to escape the ideological appropriation that characterizes the latter. Lu Ling sums up his character's constant intellectual struggles with the following words:

> He [Jiang Chunzu] gets confused every day. He seems to long for and seek after confusion, although he manages to dash out each time. The waves of darkness swallow everything and he can only fiercely hold on in the last ditch. . . . Apparently, due to his character and his unique candor, his standpoint for today and for now will collapse under his ruthless analysis tomorrow. His journey is especially dangerous and tortuous.[37]

As he tries to preserve the immediacy and contingency of his own ideas produced under the pressure of momentary experiences and impulses, Jiang Chunzu fully demonstrates the fundamental incommensurability between reality and totalizing thinking. That he continues to take great pains with his ideas despite all his awareness of their deficiencies is an index of his nobility, for his ceaseless endeavors enable his mind to surpass itself. In essence, as a concrete example, he enacts Lu Ling's effort to privilege praxis over "scientific truth" as the crux of human knowledge. The dynamic process he boldly represents as an alternative to the leftist ideological stranglehold is meant to produce repercussions beyond the fictional world.

Part of a coordinated assault on the rigidification of Marxist dogmas that includes, among other works by *Qiyue* writers, "On Subjectivity," a philosophical treatise by Lu Ling's then roommate and close friend Shu Wu, *Children of Wealth* displays in various ways its aspiration for freedom from the completed world of absolute principles. In tandem with its ideational focus on the as yet uncompleted, it demonstrates itself as a novel in the making by incorporating elements that are not strictly belletristic. Firmly lodged in the field of contemporary leftist cultural production, its symbolic content and its form define themselves socially and aesthetically against the dominant mainstream leftist works in antagonistic terms. It would be historically inaccurate, on our part, to take its messages and the way they are forcefully expressed and revised as fictional. Instead, we should understand them as patently political endeavors from a member of a dominated group to discredit the status quo in the leftist cultural field.

SEVEN

(RE)PRESENTATION OF HISTORICAL PARTICULARITIES: JI PANG'S *Night Travellers*

In an article on the authorial voice in modern Chinese literature, Theodore Huters puts the Bakhtinian notion of polyphony to creative use by calling attention to the centrality of univocality or authoritarian narration among Chinese writers.[1] These writers of a literature of resistance, Huters argues,

> perceived the burden of the past as being of almost stifling proportions. Their sense of tradition's monolithic weight served to push their writing toward a monological confrontation with it, as they saw the concentration of rhetorical power in one voice as the only effective means of gaining leverage against tradition's tenacious influence.[2]

The univocal mode, however, does not always reign unchallenged. In the narrator's and Jiang Chunzu's perpetual attempts at self-transcendence in *Children of Wealth,* for example, we can detect Lu Ling's implicit criticism of univocality as a totalized, stagnant, confining cognitive approach and his searches for a temporally more open replacement. A different challenge to univocality is mounted by his *Qiyue* colleague Ji Pang in the novel *Night Travellers* (*Zou yelu de renmen*), in which a spatially conceived confrontation with the tenacious hold of tradition on Chinese peasants eventually leads to the narrator's doubts about his own progressivist assumptions. Aware of the implicit danger of solipsism in univocality, Ji Pang's narrator ends up allowing the benighted characters to occupy the center stage while he himself only keeps a low profile in the background.

Ji Pang started *Night Travellers* in 1943, by then he, a frequent contributor to *Qiyue* since 1940, had already come under Hu Feng's influence through correspondence. The notion of the "subjective fighting spirit" undoubtedly played a crucial role in the composition of the novel, for Ji Pang informs the reader, in his postface, that as he wrote *Night Travellers* he had tried diligently to combat "objectivism" and "formulism,"[3] two harmful tendencies Hu Feng's notion set out to rectify. Crystallized in Hu Feng's notion was a strong desire for spiritual independence that Ji Pang thoroughly grasped, a glimpse of which could be obtained from his poem "Oath" (Shi), written in 1943 around the time he began his novel:

> I will stay with you forever
> Comrade
>
> I won't shout "Long live the emperor"
> Won't write a single word in praise of any mummy
> Won't compose a "Hero Symphony" to dedicate it to Napoleon
> Won't barter for position or glory
>
> I don't want the laurels
> Nor the welcome party
> Nor the sumptuous dinner banquet
> When I die
> I don't want any eulogy
> Nor any statue
>
> My good comrade
> You and I are the same type
> "Those who shed blood won't shed tears"
> What I want is also what you want![4]

Though unyielding to the Guomindang government censorship, Ji Pang, as a *Qiyue* member, mainly takes issue with Communist ideologists while highlighting in his novel the gap between multiplanar lived experience and a number of essentialist myths prevailing in the leftist camp: the myths of the centrality of the working class, of the unity and homogeneity of collective will, and of the inevitability of revolution. As we shall see in the following analysis, the plot arrangement, the characterization, and the narrator's infrequent quiet musings to himself and to the reader all strive to show that the "ought" of revolutionary change bears little intrinsic relation to the historical "is." In the meantime, the novel's focus on historical authenticity as a rebuttal to revolutionary utopianism embodies an aspect of the "subject fighting spirit" so far unseen in the works of the *Qiyue* school. As the last major work in the corpus of *Qiyue* fiction, *Night Travellers* enriches the practice of the school by adopting a comparatively restrained narrative strategy that nonetheless raises many provocative questions.

THE DESTABILIZATION OF PLOT

Before we start our analysis of *Night Travellers,* we should realize that the content of Hu Feng's "subjective fighting spirit" is more than simply an imperative call for the individual writer to take the initiative in combatting "formulism." Keeping in view the interaction between the writer and his subject matter in the process of writing, Hu Feng stresses the writer's active role on the one hand and, on the other, attaches great importance to the necessary modifications of the writer's subjective world vis-à-vis a social reality he should not manipulate at will. In "Putting Ourselves into the Struggle for Democracy," the manifesto of the "subjective fighting spirit," we read the following clarification:

> The process of representing or overcoming the subject matter is at the same time a process of continuous self-expansion and self-struggle for the writer as an agent. In the process of representing or overcoming the subject matter, the subject matter enters the writer's subjective world and enables the writer to expand himself. In this entrance, while the writer must actively play the roles of welcoming, selecting, or resisting the subject matter, the subject matter should, by means of its authenticity, actively promote, modify, or even overthrow the writer's efforts. That will

Chapter Seven

result in a fundamental self-struggle and only through this self-struggle will the writer be able to achieve self-expansion, the source of artistic creation, on the basis of historical authenticity.

Writers should sincerely acknowledge and undertake this self-struggle now.[5]

The key phrase in the above passage is "historical authenticity." Closely bound up with the concept of verisimilitude, which, as Tzvetan Todorov and Jonathan Culler both note, comes out of a cultural matrix,[6] what stands for "historical authenticity" in Hu Feng's opinion derives its intelligibility and credibility from the tradition of May Fourth critical realism, particularly Lu Xun's fiction. As far as Lu Xun's fiction is concerned, we should realize that it is characterized not only by its humanism and its critical view on Chinese society but also by its keen awareness of its own inefficacy, as a discursive practice, to bring about any social change in the face of an intransigent environment. When Hu Feng talks about the reaction of "historical authenticity" on the writer's subjective world, he, like his mentor, delimits the writer's sociopolitical power as he acknowledges the unamenability of subject matter. By interpreting it as a counterpoise to Marxist schematism, however, he adds a new meaning to "historical authenticity," therefore in his view the notion, with all its concern for particularity, peculiarity, and sensuality, acts as a force to rein in the writer's imagination lest it fall for facile optimism and overlook the zigzags of history.

In terms of the narrative structure in *Night Travellers*, the influence of Hu Feng's emphasis on "historical authenticity" is demonstrated by the novel's focus on individual stories rather than their configuration into a general pattern. In 1987 Ji Pang could still vividly recall that, during a visit in 1944, when the writing of his novel was still at an early stage, Hu Feng emphatically encouraged him to focus his novel on characters, not issues.[7] In reading his novel we see that Ji Pang understands characters as reflections of human beings in real life that, simultaneously situated in a multitude of relationships and contradictions, can hardly be adequately explained by linear analysis or syllogistic reasoning in political abstractions. As a result, he shuns simplistic, predetermined notions such as class attributes because they cannot account for his characters' complexities. The preference for characters over issues also results in Ji Pang's avoidance of formulaic approaches to contemporary concerns. For example, although his novel, started during the war, takes the wartime as its time frame, Japanese cruelties are relegated to a secondary position. Compounded by natural disasters and the local Chinese landlord's relentless exploitation among other things, they end up becoming just one of the many causes for the trials and tribulations of the peasant characters. The crisscross of different causal links in the development of the events covered in the novel, as a result, invites explanations from different perspectives without granting any of them exclusive, exhaustive interpretive power.

In addition to his refusal to attribute a single cause to the events in his novel, Ji Pang takes a further step to weaken the explanatory power of causality by including fortuitous conditions and aleatory incidents in his account of his characters' behaviors. Largely grounded in the domestic realm of two peasant households, many occurrences in his novel are touched off by contingent factors such as sexual impotence, drought, and a plague of locusts that propel the story line, intersected as it already is, along a rather unpredictable trajectory. Causality is further reduced in importance as Ji Pang links his characters' actions to the unexpected twists and turns in their moods and psyches. Because his characters act on the spur of the moment in response to their peculiar circumstances, their individuated personal developments constitute, from various angles, challenges to the revolutionary master plot that reduces the peasantry to their collective experience of suffering from exploitation/oppression and subsequent political awakening. Driven by a desire to include all the truths and details of reality, the narrative machine in *Night Travellers* not only offers diverse stories about the past and the present but also broadly suggests different scenarios for the future. The social realm, thus opened up, becomes a realm of multiformity that refuses to be apprehended by any system of necessary laws or principles since it is shot through with precarious identities, positions, occurrences, and relations.

With causality rendered unimportant, the novel presents a series of episodes related to each other only temporally. In turn we see a narrative juxtaposition of love relationships, domestic disputes, seductions, misunderstandings and rapprochements, a village supplication for rain, an engagement, harvesting, the moral dilemmas of a Chinese collaborator and a Chinese landlord in the face of Japanese occupation, a suicide in the wake of a scandalizing pregnancy, Japanese cruelties, a plague of locusts and the subsequent famine, a theft and its dire consequences, and so on. Instead of converging into a logically connected plot, these discrete, heterogeneous, and multidirectional episodes call attention to themselves as rather independent narrative units about individual characters. As he blurs the class distinctions of his characters on the one hand (both the Liu and He families, renting as well as owning lands, are economically situated between the rich and the poor) and devotes much of his novel's space to domestic events and personal relationships on the other, Ji Pang further removes his stories from the grand narrative of class struggle. Even when he does come to the subject of class conflict, he zeros in on the spontaneity, sporadicity, and chaos of the individual struggles put up by his peasant characters, characters who remain totally unaware of the large picture of history and society. Unchannelled and unsublimated, the energy carried by the peasants in the novel definitely falls into the category of what Hu Feng calls "primitive vitality."

Being embodiments of the blind "primitive vitality," the peasant characters in Ji Pang's novel all fail to reach the state of grace—to engage themselves *consciously* in political struggles. In his postface written in 1951 after the Communist takeover, Ji Pang mentions that originally he had planned to chronicle the progress from spontaneous struggle and individual revenge to guided social revolution in peasant movements, but, due to his own lack of spiritual strength and inability to further his explorations of the development of history, he had to stop before he could endow his characters with political consciousness.[8] In view of the endless polemics he launches in his novel against the Marxist progressivist historical vision, both the "original" plan and the excuse for failing to execute it sound somewhat disingenuous. It is obvious that, as Ji Pang resolutely keeps his characters—historical particularities in human forms—in the stage of spontaneity, he intends to undermine, not to confirm, the Marxist vision. The ultimate message that comes out of his tireless efforts to maintain the pliability and unpredictability of his characters is that any attempt to synthesize and channel these carriers of human potential distorts their truths and falls into the trap of reductionism.

Stemming from Ji Pang's firm refusal to convert individual experiences to the collective cause of revolution, the dispersal of the story lines culminates in the nonclosure at the end of his novel. The main characters end their experiences in different ways: Xiaoyu, the daughter-in-law of the Liu family, after a disastrous affair triggered by her desire to punish her husband for his sexual impotence, commits suicide; Jintang, the eldest son of the He family, is forced into hard labor by the Japanese army after his arrest for a drunken brawl with a local militiaman; Qiaoqiao, the daughter of the Liu family and Jintang's wife, is coerced to sell her body to the profligate Jian Runqing, the landlord Jian Fucheng's son, to save her husband and her brother-in-law Yintang; and Yintang, the second son of the He family and Xiaoyu's lover, is still searching for ways of revenge without taking any action after a failed attempt to steal food from Jian Fucheng's compound. Instead of laying disturbing issues to rest, as the narrative closure in realism, particularly socialist realism, invariably manages to do, the nonclosure of *Night Travellers* makes a host of questions about its characters' futures all the more poignant by leaving them unanswered. Behind the nonclosure one can detect a view that regards history not as an ascendant continuum of social progress but as a discontinuous, incoherent series of individual experiences that leave room for the viewer's imagination, among other things. Rather than co-opting the reader into an agreement on the inevitability that guides the plot to its logical end, Ji Pang invites the reader to confront the potentials and contradictions in his characters and to make his own conjectures about their futures.

Much of the Chinese fiction about peasants in the 1930s and 1940s is penned by leftist authors that, intent on revealing its characters' spiritual maturation from spontaneity to consciousness, can be regarded as a kind of political *Bildungsroman*. With its emphasis squarely on the diversity and latitude of lived experiences, *Night Travellers* unambiguously demonstrates its unease with the rigid providential scenario that pervades this kind of political *Bildungsroman*. Instead of establishing unequivocal certainties of purposes and goals or projecting an unproblematic route of growth for Chinese peasants, as the political *Bildungsroman* does, Ji Pang's novel focuses on the difficulties in the gestation and realization of revolutionary aspirations among peasants. As it determinedly withholds political consciousness from its characters and thus curtails their spiritual growth, it becomes a rather self-conscious anti-*Bildungsroman* that resists the socialization imposed by the logic of the revolutionary discourse.

The dispersed, multiplying story lines and, especially, the nonclosure at the end turn *Night Travellers* into an interrogative text. Keeping itself from complacently or servilely echoing the conventional, recognizable articulation of the vulgarized Marxist social vision or, in other words, from reinforcing the reader's position as a subject in a familiar ideological system, the novel encourages the reader to question his own political presumptions by highlighting the amorphism and irregularity of the real conditions of existence. Since the reader is not offered familiar political messages for passive consumption and has to ponder over the uncompleted stories on his own, he will inevitably come to realize, under the author's direction, the imaginary nature of the revolutionary millennium. Ultimately the effect of such an awareness is liberating.

Talking about the immense importance of narrative in human life, Peter Brooks writes: "Narrative is one of the large categories or systems of understanding that we use in our negotiations with reality, specifically, in the case of narrative, with the problem of temporality: man's time-boundedness, his consciousness of existence within the limits of mortality. And plot is the principal ordering force of those meanings that we try to wrest from human temporality."[9] Simply put, plot shows how human life and history are understood and organized. In the case of the revolutionary *Bildungsroman*, the driving force behind the plot is a fundamental assumption of history as a linear progression toward a millennial terminus, an assumption that provides the cause, the agent and the trajectory for holistic historical transformations. In contrast, what we see in *Night Travellers* is not a causally integrated plot but a group of individuated stories that move in different directions and often end up hampering each other. As a result, historical progress, if there is any, is slow in coming and tends to stop at the threshold, giving rise to all kinds of delays and detours. Furthermore, since the interfering stories are not hierarchized, the changes they bring to the fictional world become overdetermined to the point no general movement of history is suggested. In the end what can be inferred for the future is that history will continue to be erratic. Last but not the least, the historical forces depicted in *Night Travellers* are localized and concretized, implicitly raising questions about universalist assumptions. All these emphases on the complex workings of history dovetail with Ji Pang's understanding of human beings as variable agents of history, as we shall see in the next section. After all, for him as for his mentor Hu Feng, history without active human involvement is nothing but an empty shell.

THE NOMADIZATION OF CHARACTERS

In the final analysis the dispersed plot lines in *Night Travellers* are connected with its wayward characters. Situated simultaneously at different planes and in different sequences of events, causal as well as noncausal, in an inchoate world, these characters impress the reader as nomads without any fixed historical destination. The nomad, as Slavoj Žižek notes, is the "moment of discontinuity, of rupture, at which the linear 'flow of time' is suspended, arrested, 'coagulated,' because in it resounds directly—that is to say: bypassing the linear succession of continuous time—the past which was repressed, pushed out of the continuity established by prevailing history. It is literally the point of 'suspended dialectics,' of pure repetition where historical movement is placed within parentheses."[10] As such, the characters in Ji Pang's novel are no longer plain functions of a self-enclosed plot bent on revealing the underlying rationality in history. In other words, instead of being ideologically interpellated as historical "subjects," they become overdetermined nexuses through which the sensuousness, fullness, and contradictoriness of lived experience are preserved. As their erratic personalities undergo changes alongside the ceaseless alterations in their multilayered situations, they in effect challenge the revolutionary presuppositions in leftist fiction that sublimate human subjects into orderly sociohistorical forces.

In his recent book on the aesthetics of the sublime in modern China, Ban Wang correctly points out that revolutionary sublimation, as a process of cultural edification and elevation, purges whatever smacks too much of the human creature—appetite, sensuality, imagination, lust, self-interest, and the like.[11] In contrast to the works of the revolutionary sublime, for which precedents could certainly be found in the 1940s, *Night Travellers* remains determined to keep individuals as individuals, refusing to make them merge with or cohere into forces larger than themselves. Ji Pang's main strategy is to maintain the disorderly details in his characters' psyches. A considerable amount of space in his novel is devoted to the characters' shifting psychological, emotional reactions to the events in their lives and, in comparison, the sketchily described and loosely strung episodes that form the story lines of the novel only serve as stimuli setting the reactions in motion. The prioritization of psychological idiosyncrasies over general sociohistorical patterns is clearly offered as an alternative to the narrative matrix in Chinese realism that, while largely grounding human beings in socioeconomic relations, seeks to give a rational, universalistic explanation to historical changes. Chaotic and disruptive, the psyches of Ji Pang's peasant characters are composed of instinctual drives that refuse to be displaced upwards, as the title *Night Travellers* aptly indicates. Thus psychologized, the characters are marked not by their unities or transparency but by their fragmented and polysemous positions as social agents. Since the blind forces they represent are invested with truth value, it is clear that to the author the journey to eventual political consciousness, as envisioned by Marxist dogmatists with regard to Chinese peasantry, is nothing but a revolutionary myth conceived in macrocosmic terms.

In a way Ji Pang's interest in the instinctual could be interpreted as a revolt against what we might call a "Symbolic order" in Lacanian sense. To Jacques Lacan, the "Symbolic order" means the intersubjective mediation and socialization of the ego through language.[12] It is, as Malcolm Bowie puts it, "a *res publica* that does not allow any one of its members to be himself, keep himself to himself or recreate in his own image the things that lie beyond him."[13] In the Chinese context of the 1940s, a "Symbolic order" could be said to have existed among leftist writers as Marxist discourse appropriated the constitution of human beings as historical subjects and thereby imposed a "dictatorship of the signifier." As he tries to restore sensory plenitude to lived experiences by keeping his characters in the instinctual realm, Ji Pang exposes the modes of consciousness stipulated by Marxist discourse as reductionistic signification that leaves out much more than it includes in its account of human experience.

Let us take Xiaoyu, one of the major characters in *Night Travellers*, as an example of Ji Pang's transgression of the Marxist "Symbolic order." An unhappily married daughter-in-law in a peasant family, Xiaoyu could, in the hands of most leftist writers, easily become a candidate for the double victimization of the feminine gender and the peasants. Instead, by attributing her unhappiness exclusively to her husband's sexual impotence, Ji Pang locates her suffering and her subsequent rebellion against traditional morals at an elemental, biological level rather than a sociopolitical level. Often bullying and cursing her timorous husband for hours, Xiaoyu can neither vent all her grievances, loneliness and anger through such cursings nor take any comfort in the rude and unrestrained curses. Her highest and biggest goal is to change her situation entirely, although she is at a complete loss as to how she could bring about the change and what kind of effort she should make to reach the goal. However, a most primitive, simplest desire is burning in her intensely. She wants to pay back all her suffering to the person who imposes it upon her.[14]

Completely depoliticized, the malfunction in Xiaoyu's sexual relationship with her husband is not treated as a symptom of a dysfunctional society. Instead, sexuality becomes a respite from the social realm in which desires, frustrations, and energy circulate in the forms of myopic aggressivity and fantasy. It constitutes, in other words, a revolt of the low bodily stratum against the revolutionary sublime. Consumed by an impetuous desire for sexual gratification, Xiaoyu seduces Yintang, a boy of fifteen, and gets pregnant. After she fails to force her husband to acknowledge the unborn baby as his own and, then, to persuade Yintang to elope with her, she makes an attempt to run away one evening. Soon afterwards she is caught by members of her husband's clan and, realizing that she will be cruelly punished the next morning, she commits suicide by hanging herself.

Part of Xiaoyu's experience—the adulterous relationship and the betrayal by a fainthearted lover—reminds one of Shen Congwen's 1930 story "Xiaoxiao." However, whereas the eventual peaceful survival of the adulterous heroine in Shen Congwen's story presents, as David Wang points out, a pastoral triumph over actual hypocrisy and prudery from a romanticized viewpoint of childish innocence and simplicity,[15] Xiaoyu's gendered role highlights her subversiveness vis-à-vis the traditional morals and the revolutionary discourse. Conceived solely in sexual terms, Xiaoyu's presymbolic energy, or "primitive vitality" in other words, is shot through with a single-minded sensual desire, a desire that, while limited to the realm of bodily functions, defies any socialization, be it feudal, revolutionary, or otherwise. As a result, her rebellion becomes an individual affair that sheds little light on the general movement of society.

Of all the characters in *Night Travellers* Yintang is the only one who eventually resists the social order; the others succumb to their harsh circumstances. But Yintang, weighed down by painful, debilitating doubts, questions, and hesitations, can only be regarded as an uneasy rebel, not the kind of clear-headed, strong-willed rebel one usually sees in Chinese revolutionary literature. Starting out as a mischievous boy of fifteen who happens to be the unwitting object of Xiaoyu's desire, Yintang remains rather passive in his sexual liaison with Xiaoyu, incognizant of the consequences. When the pregnant Xiaoyu urges him to elope with her, his repeated refusals show lack of courage and reluctance to change his rutted way of life. After Xiaoyu's suicide he begins to mature, yet what he does is nothing more than helping his family out in dire times. In other words his growth is moral rather than political. When he finally decides to steal food from the landlord Jian Fucheng's compound to save himself and his sister-in-law Qiaoqiao from starvation, his decision is presented not as a conscious political act but as an act of desperation. What is noteworthy is that many factors, such as Japanese looting, the plague of locusts, and deaths in the family, contribute to his unbearable situation and, just as there is no single cause for his desperate act, the target and the course of action for his revenge remain unclear.

Compared with the hero in the revolutionary *Bildungsroman* that brings out, in an insistent manner, a rule of action intended for the audience, Yintang is marked by the absence of any "teleological" design. He is not treated as a mere cipher to illustrate a doctrine that exists "before" and "above" his story. Rather, the value of his story lies in its specificity and experiential richness, borne out by the numerous predicaments, vacillations, delays, and sidetracks in his young life. Consequently, his growth, if there is any, turns out to be anything but straightforward, as can be seen in the following description of him after he makes the decision to steal from the landlord:

> After a meager dinner Yintang went to bed. He had never gone to bed so early. "I should get some sleep first," he said to himself before he closed his eyes and tried to fall asleep. But he was so excited that he could not calm himself down as he hoped. He could not stop speculating in various ways and from various angles about the outcomes of his daring, adventurous decision. There were only two possible outcomes: a smooth success or a miserable failure. When he thought about the success, he felt he should pluck up his courage to carry out his attempt, but he was

immediately shrouded by the shadow of the miserable failure. Wavering, he felt confused and pained. From time to time he harshly condemned himself and could hardly believe that he could come up with such a decision.[16]

Instead of becoming a threshold of a new life, this important moment is fraught with qualms and doubts, bespeaking confusion rather than resolution to carry out a leap of faith. Finally, Yintang's disinclination to change the world and himself is brought home to the reader by his self-exhortation, after the act of theft: "'Yintang, you should not continue doing this kind of thing for the rest of your life. Yes, you will never do it again!'"[17] Perpetually wavering and backsliding, Yintang certainly cannot serve as an inspirational exemplar.

Faced with all the uncertainties in their situations and, more importantly, the twists and turns in their physical and mental experiences, the characters in *Night Travellers* have to create themselves at all times, continually making unavoidable existential choices according to their personalities, their moral values, and the possibilities provided by their circumstances. In this respect the portrayal of Ma Qishi, an initially reluctant Chinese collaborator, deserves our attention. Because of his position as the mayor of a small town occupied by Japanese troops, Ma is forced to deal with the enemy uncomfortably at first, remaining caught in the web of conflicting values, interests, goals, and impulses. To seek refuge from all his moral dilemmas, he goes home one night for a visit—an event on which Ji Pang spends a whole chapter—as an affectionate husband and father who keeps tormenting himself for serving the Japanese at the expense of the real joys of life. Right after the homecoming trip he falls into a bigger quandary, when an order comes from the Japanese for rice and comfort women.

> "Should I do what I am asked to do?" he [Ma Qishi] asked himself, clenching the order tightly. He knew he should not discard this proof, his hand shaking because of his nervousness. "I am going to hand over beautiful women to the Japanese to be raped!" That was indeed horrible! He felt it was manageable to collect a thousand piculs of rice but intolerable to collect women for the Japanese. In his subconsciousness there existed a deep-rooted belief: the pride and dignity of a nation should not be destroyed like

that! "Whose women am I supposed to send? Whose women can be sent?" he asked himself in anguish. "Can I send my wife? Can I send my thirteen-year-old daughter? . . ." He shook his head heavily, his eyes glistening with angry tears.[18]

The moralization of a collaborator here and elsewhere in the novel, an act bound to raise patriots' eyebrows, demonstrates that to Ji Pang even a villain should not be judged by neat and simple moral categories. Like other characters in the novel, Ma is endowed with developmental potential and the later changes in his behavior, including his increasing arrogance to the local gentry and obsequiousness to the Japanese, result from his interactions with his environment, not from his innate character.

Given Ji Pang's emphasis on his characters' developmental potential, history in his novel is regarded not as hypostatization of socioeconomic mechanisms but as creation by people who act to transform their world and themselves without a predetermined blueprint. Here the psychological makeup of the characters, with all its contradictory tendencies, not to mention the spiritual residues of the past, becomes a formidable material force in influencing the concrete processes of history. It is a force that has to be understood in its own terms. As he strives to describe the characters' minds as they are, unsublimated and unrefined, Ji Pang already shows respect for their autonomy. Since his respect for the characters as bearers of historical authenticity is best exemplified in the interactions between the reticent narrator and the unsuppressed characters in his novel, I will, in the following section, offer an analysis of these interactions and try to sort out their implications.

THE QUESTIONS FROM THE NARRATOR

Thus far I have argued that Ji Pang's emphasis on the amorphism of his characters and their stories should be regarded as his transgression of a Marxist Symbolic order bent on the appropriation and socialization of human subjects for the agenda of revolution. This transgression, I would like to further argue, ultimately displays itself in the relationship between the narrator and the characters in his novel. Unlike the highly vocal and visible narrator in Lu Ling's *Children of*

Wealth, the narrator in *Night Travellers* keeps a low profile by eavesdropping on the psyches of the characters without overtly offering his own comments. As he remains behind the scene most of the time and tries to reproduce the characters' thoughts, he grants a certain independence to their standpoints with all his awareness of their cognitive flaws. In other words, since their thoughts are not interfered with or merged into the narratorial consciousness, the characters become "subjects" who retain their own modes of thinking.

The strategy Ji Pang uses to maintain the integrity of his characters' mental worlds can be seen in the following description of Xiaoyu as she, after failing to coerce her husband into falsely admitting that he had made her pregnant, tries to run away to avoid a scandal:

> She feels that she is truly free now, like an animal that wants to rush right back to the wilderness after too long a confinement. But with neither direction nor destination she is just running along the road for all she is worth. She feels the coolness of the evening breeze, the quiet of the night and the vastness of the fields. With an insatiable appetite, she breathes avidly. The air, cool and fresh, is strange to her, but she feels that it has been waiting for her to breathe it for a long time. So she breathes avidly as she runs. What a rare feeling of happiness! . . . The night, such a gentle night! It is speaking and intimately greeting her: "Come, come. I want to embrace you and I will protect you. Trust me. I am spreading out my warm arms for you. Come and accept my incomparable caress and protection." . . . Getting unusual encouragement and temptation, she feels refreshed and happy. As she runs she gives herself to the vast night.[19]

Obviously the perceptions, feelings and thoughts in this passage come exclusively from Xiaoyu. Indulging herself in fantasy at this moment, she does not realize that, with many members of her husband's clan chasing at her heels, her freedom will certainly be short-lived. What is significant here is that, refraining from intruding into Xiaoyu's psyche and revealing her euphoric feeling as delusional, the narrator keeps himself out of the picture and yields the narrative ground to the imperceptive character. His approach is largely dramatic in that he tries to reproduce Xiaoyu's mental process as it occurs. Consequently, instead of being defined from the outside and being acted upon as an emblem, Xiaoyu obtains her own voice that, unsound it might be, nevertheless holds its ground in the face of the more perceptive narratorial voice. It is neither assimilated nor dismissed because of its perceptual deficiency.

In the above passage we can see that free indirect speech is used to render Xiaoyu's figural mind, a technique complex and, sometimes, oblique because of its lack of explicit linguistic markers. When he comes to topics prone to political interpretations, Ji Pang tends to resort to quoted speech, a more direct means, to challenge the revolutionary assumptions about peasants. Near the end of his novel we see He Baoshan, the head of the He household, goes to the landlord Jian Fucheng's compound to borrow rice to tide his family over the lean season before the summer harvest. Forced by Jian's steward to put down his rice seedlings as the security for the loan, He leaves the compound with two pecks of rice and a tormented mind. On his way home he witnesses a terrifying natural disaster, a swarm of locusts devouring all the rice shoots near the road in a matter of minutes before it spreads its destruction further and further. At this devastating moment we see the following representation of the character's mind:

> "Should I return the two pecks of rice?" he [He Baoshan] asked himself. "I have borrowed it with my rice seedlings as security! Now the rice seedlings are gone, all gone! . . . I have to live by my conscience. I must not carry home the rice!" His mind was totally occupied by his contractual relationship with the Jians. With his kindness and sincerity, he felt that under the current circumstances the contractual relationship no longer existed and he should return the two pecks of rice. If he did that, he would be very happy. "Send the rice back like that? Well, what should my family eat?" he started crying again, collapsing to the ground and putting his face against the rice emotionally.
>
> Puzzling over this question, he sadly realized how kind and how innocent he was. Yet he was still afflicted with such a harsh punishment. What if he harbored some slightly evil thoughts? Would he receive a harsher punishment? He was scared.
>
> "I have never let my own conscience down all my life! Now I am old and about to die, how can I go against my conscience? Even if I can deceive humans, I cannot deceive the Yama! Send it back, I

(Re)presentation of Historical Particularities

must send it back." He made up his mind, stood up, lifted the rice and stumbled back toward the Purple Pine Villa [the landlord's compound].[20]

In the hands of mainstream leftist writers—here one could readily recall a trend in Chinese revolutionary literature that dates back to Ding Ling's "Flood"—the crisis He faces would easily push him toward rebellion. In contrast, Ji Pang emphasizes the grip of feudal morality on the quixotic character, who could only lead himself to suicide and his family to starvation. As he describes He as the victim of his feudal values at this point, who later will also be partially responsible for his son Yintang's desperate act of theft and his daughter-in-law Qiaoqiao's surrender to Jian Runqing, the author/narrator, for all his knowledge about the "right" thing to do, stops short of making the character think thoughts incompatible with his entrenched mindset.

Ji Pang's refusal to align his characters' psyches with narratorial consciousness is part and parcel of his effort to maintain "historical authenticity," a sensory reality that gives the slip to any calcified theoretical viewpoint. In granting independence to his characters he lets them become masters of their own fates and commentators of their own actions. In contrast to Lu Ling's *Children of Wealth*, *Night Travellers* contains far less propositions, generalizations, and declamations that, when removed from their contexts, would still retain their messages or rhetorical force in an impersonal form. Even when the narrator does express his opinions, his tone is much more subdued and cautious, indicating an unwillingness to pour out generalities that appeal, not to the characters in question, but to the general reading public outside the fictional world. If we take Ji Pang's novel as a hegemonic act, as is demonstrated by the intentional contrast of its historico-narrative form to that of the mainstream leftist fiction, we see that, while anchoring himself firmly on the domain of the circumstantial and keeping in view the intransigence of his characters as social agents, Ji Pang also sets a limit to his own articulation as a hegemonic insertion and raises questions about its operation.

The following narratorial statement near the end of the novel, a rare example of the narrator's own voice, spells out the consequences of Ji Pang's reluctance to meddle with his characters. As Qiaoqiao, in order to save her husband Jintang and brother-in-law Yintang, is forced to surrender her body to Jian Runqing, the narrator laments:

> Alas, this poverty-stricken village, this desolate village, this suffering village, is poor Qiaoqiao about to leave you forever? Is she going to be forever appended to the rich and the powerful and to be toyed with as a maidservant? The humble girl, some day she will be abandoned like a worn-out shoe. Then, will she remain numbed in her humbleness? Will she wait endlessly, as she is doing now? These kind, innocent children of this old race are in possession of such resilience. But the most determined rebels also often come out of these most kind and most innocent people. This old race, this sorrowful race, we have heard too many of your sad songs, now you should loudly sing your declaration of war. . . . This old race, this sorrowful race, on the journey from hell to heaven there is already a most glorious road in front of us, you do not have to ask in hesitation: where should we go?[21]

What stands out in this passage is that, not knowing for sure the future of the character, as well as that of the whole Chinese nation, the narrator repeatedly raises questions about Marxist millennialism. With his keen awareness of all the possibilities for the future, the narrator ultimately directs his questioning toward his own assertive, predictive act as he overwhelms his feeble forecast with doubts and uncertainties. In the end, the concrete course of history and its reserved spokesman still hang in suspense.

The cluster of questions in the above passage indicates Ji Pang's hesitation to map out a course of action for his self-governing character. The same hesitation is displayed in the narrator's treatments of other characters in the novel as well. Ji Pang seems to understand that an excessively strong narratorial voice that does not allow the characters to be themselves will inevitably lead to a symbolic order in the world of the novel and that the best strategy to avoid establishing a new symbolic order while rejecting an old one is to maintain the characters' alternate voices and to restrain the authorial voice. Although one could hardly argue that a *heteroglossia* in the Bakhtinian sense—the coexistence of a variety of individual voices, including the authorial voice, on an equal footing—has come into being in *Night Travellers*, Ji Pang certainly moves in the direction of overcoming univocality. To put it in a different way, we may argue that, recognizing the characters as unassimilable nodal points of specificity, plurality, opacity as well as potentiality, Ji Pang's narrator realizes that he has to give up the Marxist totalistic claim to the universal knowledge about society. Unlike Marxist intellectuals who, while regarding themselves as inferior to the proletariat in revolutionary attributes, assume an a priori privileged cognitive position as spokesmen of the universal, he relinquishes this paradoxical position as he turns himself into an unsutured, floating entity capable of self-questioning.

The coexistence of the characters' problematic voices with the narrator's reticent, uncertain voice is, in a way, a development of a May Fourth legacy. Separated from the characters by an unbridgeable intellectual gap, the narrator in Ji Pang's novel strongly reminds us of the doubtful, self-questioning "I" narrator in Lu Xun's stories such as "My Old Home" and "New Year's Sacrifice." The novel further takes over the critical appraisal of the masses from Lu Xun and other May Fourth writers as it strives to reveal their "spiritual scars." In other words, its social and psychological perceptions are largely premised on the May Fourth schemata. In consideration of the optimistic prediction Chinese Marxist writers make for their country, *Night Travellers* can be said to involve itself in a competition for interpretive authority by seeking strength from the May Fourth perception. Yet a spin is put on the May Fourth heritage. By creating self-determining characters with their own minds and voices on the one hand and by keeping the narratorial intervention to a minimum on the other, Ji Pang reintroduces the active role of the human agent in the changing of reality. In contrast to the prevalent orthodox Marxist view that "objective conditions" are always the primary factor determining both the course of history and the desires of "historical subjects," Ji Pang's anthropocentric approach emphasizes the crucial importance of uncontained human praxis in the transformation of history and society. Bound up with its specific circumstances, the kind of uncontained human praxis described in *Night Travellers* takes to task the criteria of Marxist historical dialectics. In the end what is called into question is the scientistic, monist aspiration, deeply embedded in Marxism, to capture the underlying meaning of History from an external point of view. It is this refusal to impose any external standard on human praxis that eventually results in the effacement of the narrator from *Night Travellers*.

Chapter Seven

As Ji Pang tries hard to safeguard the integrity of his characters, he even adopts a more or less "detached" approach in his depiction of Jian Runqing, an approach that leads to the trap of naturalism, as he himself admits apologetically in his postface.[22] Instead of providing clear-cut norms for the judgment of the characters, the unintrusive narrator in *Night Travellers* often tends to first imply his opinions and then question them. I would like to argue, at this point, that the prioritization of autonomous characters over the reticent, weakened narrator amounts to an effort to restore the primacy of praxis over the act of cognition. Praxis, in this case the praxis of the characters, no longer means the verification of the narrator's preexisting knowledge. Rather, it becomes an essential constitutive force that, in the course of its development, inevitably changes the contour of narratorial knowledge. In other words, praxis, not the theoretical knowledge acquired prior to it, becomes the criterion of truth.

For all the doubts and questions demonstrated with or without the disconcerting presence of the narrator, *Night Travellers* harbors an ambivalent attitude toward theoretical knowledge. The historical authenticity Ji Pang tries so hard to preserve, we should realize, is by and large predicated on such fundamental May Fourth presuppositions as the passivity of peasants and the attendant difficulty in social reform. Though taken for granted and presented transparently and seamlessly, these presuppositions are far from being irrefutable facts of life, as Ji Pang would like us to believe. On the contrary, they are postulates Ji Pang utilizes to co-opt the reader, at a subliminal level, into an agreement with his social assessment. As such, they are by no means politically or ideologically neutral.

Related to the issue of presupposition is the use of language. In *Night Travellers* the language Ji Pang employs is largely descriptive rather than assertive or performative. At first glance the narrator, with all his reticence and questions, does not seem to grant himself much overt interpretive authority. The power component, however, still remains central in his use of language. As Pierre Bourdieu notes, utterances are not only signs to be understood and deciphered; they are also signs of wealth, intended to be evaluated and appreciated, and signs of authority, intended to be believed and obeyed.[23] Clearly an effort to secure the right to redefine life in the teeth of an orthodox interpretation, Ji Pang's descriptive language is meant to have a social influence as it tries to change the social perception of the informed

(Re)presentation of Historical Particularities

reader of revolutionary literature. It is, on this score, related to the argumentative mode in spite of its seemingly unassuming appearance. In its quiet ways *Night Travellers* serves as a complement to Lu Ling's *Children of Wealth* in their joint effort to embody the "subjective fighting spirit."

Epilogue

The founding of the People's Republic of China on October 1, 1949 marked the complete ascendancy of the CCP in all areas of public life. In the field of literature, the Communist takeover resulted in fundamental ideological and structural changes. On July 2, 1949, the First National Congress of Writers and Artists was convened. Shortly after the congress, a national association was formed. As an arm of the soon-to-be-established government, this association effectively put all the writers in the country under its supervision. With the monopoly of all social organizations by the Party-state and the eradication of openly expressed heretical views, an era of widespread censorship and self-censorship had set in. The tight control over communication by the Party-state, installed shortly after the establishment of the PRC in the form of the "public ownership" of the news media and publishing houses, not to mention the restrictions on educational institutions and artistic circles, assured the promulgation of the Party ideology among the general population. The most important ideological consequence of the Communist takeover in the literary field was, of course, the sanctification of Chairman Mao's "Yan'an Talks." Since Hu Feng had raised doubts in 1943–44 about the feasibility of Mao's mandates in Guomindang areas, his old adversaries in the leftist camp, now occupying important government positions and motivated, in part, by personal animosity, quickly launched attacks on Hu Feng and his *Qiyue* followers as part of the ideological rectification the CCP implemented soon after it came to power.

Epilogue

The attacks on Hu Feng and his followers, to be sure, dated back to the mid-1940s. After he questioned the applicability of Mao's directive of training writers from ordinary workers, peasants, and soldiers in 1943, Hu Feng and, later, his favorite protégés Shu Wu and Lu Ling became targets for criticism in a campaign waged by Communist ideologists in Chongqing. The assaults culminated in a spate of articles by a group of Communist critics, the so-called "Hong Kong talents," in 1948 that charged Hu Feng, Shu Wu and Lu Ling with, among other things, deviation from Marxist class analysis, defamation of working people, and flattery of petty bourgeois intellectuals. Hu Feng, however, was not completely silenced. He not only voiced his disagreement at some meetings but also wrote a booklet *On the Direction of Realism* (*Lun xianshi zhuyi de lu*) in September 1948 as a counterattack. Although in his booklet he could only argue his case under the cover of remarks by Marx, Engels, and Mao Zedong unnecessarily put in to enhance the legitimacy of his own views, as he admits in his postscript,[1] he still managed to hold onto his cherished ideas without making any substantial compromise.

After 1949, however, the ideological stranglehold of the Communist orthodoxy and the fundamental structural changes in the literary field made it much more difficult for him to strike back at his detractors. Recalcitrant yet powerless, Hu Feng was singled out as a negative example of an "incorrect" tendency in the first official assessment of the pre-1949 literary field in Guomindang areas. Between 1949 and 1950 he attempted to put himself in Mao's good graces with a long poem "Time Has Begun" (Shijian kaishile), in which he, while singing praises of Mao and his new regime, associated his own mother, an ordinary woman without any revolutionary experience in real life, with well-known female Communist role-models and himself with revolutionary martyrs and saints such as Kobayashi Takiji and Lu Xun. This public panegyric written out of necessity, however, only drew attacks from his adversaries for its format of modern free verse. In the end, a restriction was imposed on it and some of the printed copies had to be sold as waste paper.[2] Meanwhile, as Hu Feng refused to cooperate with the cultural authorities, he was left out in the cold without a job. Soon some of his protégés, A Long and Lu Ling in particular, came under fire from government apparatchiks and critics in the service of the Communist establishment. Hamstrung by the great difficulties in getting its rebuttals published in official newspapers even under the cover

Epilogue

of Marxist discourse and thus virtually stripped of its defense, the *Qiyue* group fell an easy prey to government ideologists.

On May 25, 1952, a bombshell exploded within the Hu Feng camp when Shu Wu published an article "Study Anew 'Talks at the Yan'an Forum on Literature and Art'" (Congtou xuexi 'Zai Yan'an wenyi zuotanhui shang de jianghua') in which he, besides pleading guilty to individualism, berated his fellow *Qiyue* writers for holding Mao's "Yan'an Talks" in contempt. When the article, originally carried by *Yangtze Daily* (*Changjiang ribao*) in Wuhan, was reprinted on June 8 in *People's Daily* (*Renmin ribao*), the official CCP propaganda organ, an editorial headnote condemnatorily labeled Hu Feng and his followers as a "small clique" that exaggerated the importance of subjectivity and denied the significance of revolutionary practice and thought reform. Still under the mistaken impression that the criticisms were heaped on him by his old enemies without the support from the highest CCP leadership, Hu Feng continued to defend his views and refused to denounce himself as leading Communist ideologists stepped up the campaign against him.

In February 1954 the CCP held the Fourth Plenum of the Seventh Party Congress to attack sectarianism and promote criticism and self-criticism within the Party. Without knowing its real target was the Gao Gang-Rao Shushi faction in the Party leadership, Hu Feng took this campaign as a good opportunity to settle accounts with his foes like Zhou Yang, who in his opinion had monopolized the cultural world as their personal territory after 1949. With the assistance of many of his followers, he spent more than three months from March to June writing a long report to the Party Central Committee on the post-1949 practice of art and literature, the famous "three-hundred-thousand-character petition." In his petition, couched in Marxist jargon, Hu Feng resorted to the approach of blaming the problems on government functionaries without faulting the emperor, a strategy widely used by critics of government in feudal times, yet he did fight back on the fundamental issue of ideological regimentation by denouncing the "five daggers": the imposition of a preordained Marxist worldview; the confinement of subject matter to the lives of the workers, peasants, and soldiers; the prerequisite of thought reform; the enforcement of traditional forms; and the absolute focus on "sunny subjects" to the exclusion of any criticism of the new society. The section on the "five daggers," the best known and most memor-

Epilogue

able section in an otherwise long-winded, sometimes tedious, disquisition, apparently went beyond personal enmity and turned into an urgent cry for freedom from the ideological suppression by the Party's literary policies.

By now, however, the Party's authority over cultural matters, consolidated by Mao's personal participation and the Party's efforts at the thought reform of intellectuals, had become unquestionable. As it turned out, Hu Feng's submission of the petition to the CCP Central Committee in July only sped up his downfall instead of persuading the Party to change its literary policies, as he had hoped. After he harshly denounced vulgar Marxism and the suppression of emerging writers such as A Long and Lu Ling by the status quo in two speeches he made at a conference jointly held by the presidiums of the All-China Federation of Literature and Art Circles and the All-China Union of Writers in November 1954, Chairman Mao and his henchmen decided to strike back. On December 8 Zhou Yang condemned Hu Feng as anti-Marxist in a speech "We Must Fight" (Women bixu zhandou) edited by Mao himself. Things became even worse when, in May 1955, Mao saw over a hundred private letters from Hu Feng to Shu Wu, requested by the Party's cultural authorities to support charges against Hu Feng. Angered by Hu Feng's sarcastic remarks about the campaign to promote his "Yan'an Talks" in wartime Chongqing, Mao published heavy-handedly edited and annotated excerpts of the letters in *People's Daily* with a scathing editorial he personally wrote in which he labeled the Hu Feng group as an "anti-Party clique." As another ominous phrase "antirevolutionary" was quickly added to the label, the struggle against the Hu Feng group was catapulted from the cultural arena to the political stage and what remained to be done to the fallen prey was bare-knuckled punishment. Within days Hu Feng and ninety-two of his associates were thrown into prison, followed by the persecution of hundreds more. What would eventually happen to these people—exile, solitary confinement, physical and mental abuse, political discrimination, and so on—constituted one of the most deplorable tragedies in modern Chinese history.

Mao Zedong's ruthless persecution of the *Qiyue* school, the first large-scale purge after 1949, effectively closed the space for open dissent in the cultural field. The world of leftist literature, never completely independent of the influence of politics, was now subjugated by a dictatorship that resorted to both indoctrination and brutal violence to maintain its ideological dominance. Without the balance of any institutional restraints, the dictator judged any disagreement with his authority in antagonistic terms of class struggle and stripped those branded as enemies of their right to defend themselves. In order to discredit the opponents completely, a demagogic approach was adopted and the opponents' views and historical records were invidiously distorted for the sake of inciting the masses emotionally. To make things worse for any opposition, Chairman Mao, matching his firm belief in uninterrupted revolution with his changing perceptions of political priorities, often struck out at unpredictable moments and on unpredictable issues. Given the Communist regime's emphasis on authority and obedience, the illegitimacy of opposition and the compounded hazards that came with the erratic use of absolute power and the capricious definitions of opposition, ideological conflicts became highly risky and they had to be carried out in a roundabout, often cryptic, manner.[3]

The *Qiyue* school, if we recall, had existed in an environment marked by relative freedom in the cultural world. With its dissident predisposition tolerated in this environment, it was able to dispute the leftist mainstream on important issues and, in so doing, maintain its ideological independence as an institution. Since the cultural world in which it had existed was not entirely under the sway of practical politics, it could engage itself in long-term historical projects without having to worry about the immediate political consequences of its actions. When the cultural world was subsumed into the political world and literature came under the discipline of a fickle dictatorship after 1949, neither the dissident stance of the *Qiyue* group nor its cherished long-term projects would stand a chance of survival. The purge of the *Qiyue* group might not be a premeditated maneuver in itself, since its course was influenced by many unforeseeable incidents, but it was certainly part of a large campaign Chairman Mao launched to bring intellectuals to toe the Party line. As Mao successfully stamped out the *Qiyue* group, the last obstacle to his supremacy in the cultural world was removed. From then on his literary directives, as indisputable mandates, would encounter no public challenge.

Though in the end brutally wiped out by the highest CCP leader, the *Qiyue* school did produce a significant impact on the Chinese literary scene during its existence. At a time when most of the leftist writers were overwhelmed first by patriotism and then by the theorems of Marxism, *Qiyue* members managed to pluralize and enrich the cultural world with their adherence to the agenda of cultural criticism. In the larger historical and intellectual context the school signaled a combative attitude toward the ethic of subservience. If we agree with Vera Schwarcz that what defines modern intelligentsia is the public use of critical reason,[4] we may argue that, as they used critical reason to debunk nationalist myth and Communist ideology, *Qiyue* writers created a model of conscious resistance. What is most significant about this model is that, intent on revealing the nonidentity between idea and lived experience, it forcefully demonstrated, in various areas, that the ultimate source of political and artistic perception lay inside the writer, not with any external authorities.

Echoes of this stance could still be heard in China decades after the purge of the *Qiyue* writers, when the political situation began to undergo significant changes in the wake of economic reforms. A case in point is the sustained discussions on subjectivity (zhutixing) conducted by the contemporary literary critic Liu Zaifu since 1985. Essentially holding a position similar to Hu Feng's advocacy of the "subjective fighting spirit," Liu stresses the active participation of subjectivity in the social sphere. Here is Liu Zaifu's explication of subjectivity:

> Subjectivity describes the essential force within the Subject that is exclusively human and is manifest in the Object world. Subjectivity is not only a function of subjective consciousness, but the entire essence of the Subject's existence. Therefore, Subjectivity is the essential human force that is intrinsic to the Subject's existence and embodied in the Object world. . . .
>
> The world is thus an Objectification of essential human forces, a world of meaning. Without understanding Objectification there is no way of understanding Subjectivity.[5]

Regarding the issue of subjectivity as first and foremost an ontological issue and emphasizing the transformative power of subjectivity, Liu Zaifu further argues that in the sphere of literature subjectivity embodies itself as a valuative existence rather than a function of mimesis. This call for a "paradigm change" to remedy dogmatic and formulaic literary production, as we can see, bears a strong resemblance to the practice of the *Qiyue* school.

Keeping in view some of the cultural phenomena in contemporary China, for instance such events in the 1980s as the discussions on

Epilogue

socialist alienation and voluntarism, the reflections on feudal tradition and Chinese enlightenment sparked off by *Yellow River Elegy* (*Heshang*), and the attack on the Mao discourse, we may argue that, as long as the struggle between heresy and orthodoxy does not come to an end, dissent and its attendant interplay between content and form will remain an important part of the Chinese cultural scene. As one of the earliest examples of dissent that had kept confronting a burgeoning Communist orthodoxy, the *Qiyue* school certainly still retains its relevance, perhaps even inspiration now that its works are once again available to the public, in the ongoing contention between dissenters and the Communist ideological establishment. With its retrieval of *Qiyue* writers' noncomformist voices, I hope the present study will contribute in its own way to our understanding of intellectual dissent in modern China.

NOTES

Introduction

1. For a detailed account of Chinese resisters' use of the spoken drama, the cartoon, the news report as well as popular literature to wage a concerted battle against the invading Japanese, see Chang-tai Hung's *War and Popular Culture*.
2. Pierre Bourdieu, "The Field of Cultural Production, or: The Economic World Reversed," *The Field of Cultural Production: Essays on Art and Literature*, p. 30.
3. Pierre Bourdieu, *The Rules of Art*, p. 267.
4. Pierre Bourdieu defines the *habitus* as a set of durable, transposable dispositions that, acquired and internalized through practice, generates, regulates, and reproduces further practices without any reference to conscious intention. For Bourdieu's definition see, for example, his *Outline of a Theory of Practice*, pp. 72–95.
5. Michel Hockx, "The Literary Association (Wenxue yanjiu hui, 1920–1947) and the Literary Field of Early Republican China," *China Quarterly* 153 (March 1998): 54–55.
6. I was informed of this by Shu Wu in an interview I conducted in June 1995.
7. Karl Mannheim, "The Problem of Generations," *Essays on the Sociology of Knowledge*, p. 298.
8. For a detailed account of the influence of Fukumotoism on the debate over revolutionary literature and on the attacks on Lu Xun from the Creation and Sun Societies, see Wang-chi Wong's *Politics and Literature in Shanghai: The Chinese League of Left-Wing Writers, 1930–1936*, pp. 19–28.
9. Max Weber, "The Nature of Charismatic Authority and Its Routinization," *On Charisma and Institution Building*, p. 48.

10. Karl Mannheim, "Competition as a Cultural Phenomenon," *Essays on the Sociology of Knowledge*, pp. 203–7.
11. For Liu Kang's view in this regard, see his essay "Hegemony and Cultural Revolution," *New Literary History* 28 (1997): 80–85.
12. For a summary of Denton's views, see his *The Problematic of Self in Modern Chinese Literature: Hu Feng and Lu Ling*, pp. 1–24.

Chapter 1. From a May Fourth Youth to Lu Xun's Ally

1. Hu Feng, "Lixiang zhuyi zhe shidai de huiyi" (May 1934), *Hu Feng pinglunji*, 1:251.
2. Here and elsewhere in this book the biographical information on Hu Feng is mainly drawn from following sources: Hu Feng's *Hu Feng huiyilu*, Ma Tiji's *Hu Feng zhuan*, Dai Guangzhong's *Hu Feng zhuan*, and Xiao Feng's *Jiusi weihui: Hu Feng zhuan*.
3. Karl Mannheim, "The Problem of Generations," *Essays on the Sociology of Knowledge*, p. 309.
4. For Denton's views, see, for example, his *The Problematic of Self in Modern Chinese Literature: Hu Feng and Lu Ling*, pp. 108–16.
5. Vera Schwarcz offers an excellent account of the institutionalizations of May Fourth in a chapter, "May Fourth as Allegory," in her book *The Chinese Enlightenment: Intellectuals and the Legacy of the May Fourth Movement of 1919*, pp. 240–82.
6. Hu Feng, "Ruguo xianzai ta hai huozhe," *Hu Feng pinglunji*, 2:172.
7. Hu Feng, "Lixiang zhuyi zhe shidai de huiyi" (May 1934), *Hu Feng pinglunji*, 1:248.
8. Ibid., 1:253.
9. In his autobiographical sketch "Lixiang zhuyi zhe shidai de huiyi" Hu Feng tells us that in his student days *Symbols of Agony* was one of the books that had "totally overwhelmed" him. Ibid., 1:252.
10. Hakuson, *Kumen de xiangzheng*, *Lu Xun yiwenji*, 3:14.
11. Ibid., p. 32.
12. Leo Ou-fan Lee, *The Romantic Generation of Modern Chinese Writers*, p. 295.
13. Hu Feng, *Hu Feng huiyilu*, pp. 1–2.
14. For a detailed account of the influence of Fukumotoism in this period, see Wang-chi Wong's *Politics and Literature in Shanghai: The Chinese League of Left-Wing Writers, 1930–1936*, pp. 19–32.

15. Li Huoren, "Hu Feng de 'zhuguan zhandou jingshen'" *Zhanzheng yu Zhongguo shehui zhi biandong,* pp. 193–221.

16. Gareth Stedman Jones, "The Marxism of the Early Lukács," *Western Marxism: A Critical Reader,* p. 33.

17. Georg Lukács, "What Is Orthodox Marxism?" *History and Class Consciousness,* pp. 10–11.

18. Georg Lukács, "Class Consciousness," ibid., p. 52.

19. Georg Lukács, "Reification and the Consciousness of the Proletariat," ibid., p. 186.

20. Georg Lukács, "The Changing Function of Historical Materialism," ibid., pp. 231–39.

21. Hu Feng, "Wo de xiaozhuan," *Xinwenxue shiliao* 1(1981):101.

22. Zhou Yang, "Guanyu shehui zhuyi de xianshi zhuyi yu geming de langman zhuyi," *Zhou Yang wenji,* 1:110–11.

23. Ibid., p. 104.

24. Qu Qiubai, "Makesi, Engesi he wenxue shang de xianshi zhuyi," *Qu Qiubai wenji,* wenxue bian, 4:4–5.

25. Hu Feng, "Zhang Tianyi lun," *Hu Feng pinglunji,* 1:36–37.

26. Hu Feng, "Shenme shi 'dianxing' he 'leixing'," *Hu Feng pinglunji,* 1:96–98.

27. Zhou Yang, "Xianshi zhuyi shilun," *Zhou Yang wenji,* 1:155–59.

28. Hu Feng, "Dianxinglun de hunluan," *Hu Feng pinglunji,* 1:353.

29. Hu Feng, "Renmin dazhong xiang wenxue yaoqiu shenme," *Hu Feng pinglunji,* 1:375.

30. Lu Xun, "Lun xianzai women de wenxue yundong," *"Liang-ge kouhao" lunzheng ziliao xuanbian,* 1:389.

31. Ibid., p. 390.

32. Zhou Yang, "Guangyu guofang wenxue," ibid., p. 235.

33. C. T. Hsia, *A History of Modern Chinese Fiction,* p. 299.

34. Theodore Huters, "Hu Feng and the Critical Legacy of Lu Xun," in *Lu Xun and His Legacy* (ed. Leo Ou-fan Lee), p. 150.

35. Hu Feng, "Yuan he duzhe yitong chengzhang—*Qiyue* dai zhici," *Hu Feng pinglunji,* 2:7.

36. For Lu Xun's literary sponsorship, see Howard Goldblatt's "Lu Xun and Patterns of Literary Sponsorship," in *Lu Xun and His Legacy* (ed. Leo Ou-fan Lee), pp. 199–215.

Notes

Chapter 2. Antidote to Wartime Heroics

1. For a discussion of some of the international influences on Chinese leftist reportage in the 1920s and 1930s, see "Literary Reportage in the Left-Wing Movement of the 1920s and 1930s" in Rudolf Wagner's *Inside a Service Trade: Studies in Contemporary Chinese Prose,* pp. 325–57. A fuller treatment of Chinese literary reportage in the same period is offered by Charles Laughlin in his unpublished dissertation *"Narrating the Nation: Aesthetics of Historical Experience in Chinese Reportage Literature, 1919–1966."*

2. An abridged version of *One Day in China: May 21, 1936* is available in English, translated, edited, and introduced by Sherman Cochran and Andrew C. K. Hsieh with Janis Cochran.

3. Mao Dun, "Guangyu baogao wenxue," *Zhongliu,* 11 (Feb. 20, 1937). Cited from *Baogao wenxue lunji* (ed. Zhou Guohua), p. 6.

4. Yi Qun, "Kanzhan yilai de Zhongguo baogao wenxue," rpt. *Zhongguo kangri zhanzheng shiqi dahoufang wenxue shuxi* (ed. Lin Mohan et al.), 3:1377–78.

5. Hu Feng, "Lun suxie," *Hu Feng pinglunji,* 1:67–69.

6. Lu Xun, "Lun xianzai women de wenxue yundong," *"Liangge kouhao" lunzheng ziliao xuanbian,* 1:390.

7. Lu Xun, "Zhe ye shi shenghuo," *Lu Xun quanji,* 6:601.

8. Hu Feng, "Lun zhandouqi de yige zhandou de wenyi xingshi," *Hu Feng pinglunji,* 2:16–24.

9. *Qiyue* 2 (November 1937): 39.

10. Cao Bai, "Xie zai *Qiyue* yi zhounian," *Huxi,* pp. 87–88.

11. Cao Bai, "Houji," ibid., p. 239.

12. For a summary of Ban Wang's views on the politics and aesthetics of the sublime in modern Chinese literature, see his *The Sublime Figure of History: Aesthetics and Politics in Twentieth-Century China,* pp. 1–16.

13. Cao Bai, "Lihu x riji," *Huxi,* pp. 76–77.

14. Ban Wang provides a good analysis of Lu Xun's celebration of the body of power in his *The Sublime Figure of History: Aesthetics and Politics in Twentieth-Century China,* pp. 59–70.

15. "Xianshi wenyi huodong yu *Qiyue,*" *Qiyue* 15 (June 1938): 76–80.

16. Quoted from Zhao Xiaqiu, *Zhongguo xiandai baogao wenxue shi,* p. 266.

17. *Qiyue* 6 (January 1938): 166.
18. Andrew Rutherford, *The Literature of War: Studies in Heroic Virtue*, p. 163.
19. *Qiyue* 7 (January 1938): 201.
20. For example, Zhao Xiaqiu considers it a reportage piece in his *Zhongguo xiandai baogao wenxueshi*, p. 266.
21. Qiu Dongping, "Yige lianzhang de zhandou zaoyu," *Qiyue* 13 (May 1938): 21.
22. Qiu Dongping, "Yige lianzhang de zhandou zaoyu," *Qiyue* 14 (May 1938): 47.
23. Ibid., p. 48.

Chapter 3. From Reflection to Lyricism

1. Critics, as well as catalogers, generally treat the Wuhan period as the starting point of *Qiyue*. The works I have discussed so far were all published after the journal moved to Wuhan.
2. S. M. (A Long), "Wo xie 'zhabei dale qilai'," *Qiyue* 16 (June 1938): 113.
3. S. M. (A Long), "Zhabei dale qilai," *Qiyue* 15 (June 1938): 67–68.
4. See Roland Barthes, "The Reality Effect," *French Literary Theory Today: A Reader* (ed. Tzvetan Todorov), pp. 11–17.
5. S. M. (A Long), "Wo xie 'zhabei dale qilai'," *Qiyue* 16 (June 1938): 114.
6. S. M. (A Long), "Zhabei dale qilai," *Qiyue* 16 (June 1938): 111.
7. S. M. (A Long), "Cong gongji dao fangyu," *Qiyue* 21 (October 1939): 119.
8. S. M. (A Long), "Zhen—guanyu zhanzheng wenxue," *Qiyue* 28 (April 1941): 142.
9. Lü Yuan, "Xu," *Nanjing xueji*, p. 4.
10. A Long, ibid., p. 35.
11. A Long's meticulous concern with the truthful depiction of battle scenes can be seen, for example, in his description of the complicated procedure of firing a mortar in his postface to *Nanjing*. See A Long, "Houji," ibid., p. 225.
12. A Long, ibid., p. 209.
13. Roman Jakobson, "Linguistics and Poetics," *Language in Literature*, p. 66.

Notes

14. Kate Hamburger, *The Logic of Literature,* p. 83.
15. A Long, *Nanjing xueji,* p. 227.
16. Theodore Huters, "Blossoms in the Snow: Lu Xun and the Dilemma of Modern Chinese Literature," *Modern China,* 10. 1 (January 1984): 66.
17. Jia Zhifang, "Ren de bei'ai," *Jia Zhifang xiaoshuoxuan,* pp. 1–2.
18. Ibid., pp. 22–3.
19. Leo Ou-fan Lee, *Voices from the Iron House,* p. 64.
20. Jia Zhifang, "Shenyu jiazhilun," *Jia Zhifang xiaoshuoxuan,* p. 65.
21. Jia Zhifang, "Woxiang," ibid., p. 78.

Chapter 4. Image Making, Legacy Clarification, and Agenda Formulation

1. Hu Feng, "Beitong de gaobie," *Hu Feng pinglunji,* 1: 335–40.
2. Hu Feng, "Guanyu Lu Xun jingshen de ersan jidian," *Hu Feng pinglunji,* 2:9–10.
3. Ibid., p. 11.
4. David Holm, "Lu Xun in the Period 1936–1949: The Making of a Chinese Gorki," in *Lu Xun and His Legacy* (ed. Leo Ou-fan Lee), p. 153.
5. Mao Zedong, "Mao Zedong lun Lu Xun," *Qiyue* 10 (March 1938): 289.
6. Hu Feng, "Guoke xiaoshi," *Hu Feng pinglunji,* 2:92–94.
7. Hu Feng, "Ruguo ta hai huozhe," ibid., pp. 169–70.
8. Hu Feng, "Cong 'you yifen re, fa yifen guang' shengzhang qilai de," ibid., p. 338.
9. Ibid., pp. 339–40.
10. David Holm, "Lu Xun in the Period 1936–1949," pp. 153–79.
11. Lin Yü-sheng, *The Crisis of Chinese Consciousness,* pp. 26–27.
12. Hu Feng, "Wusi shidai de yimianying," *Hu Feng pinglunji,* 1:114–27.
13. For a summary of the views expressed in the debate, see Marián Gálik's "Main Issues in the Discussion on 'National Forms' in Modern Chinese Literature," *Asian and African Studies* 10 (1974): 97–112. Theodore Huters offers an analysis of some of Hu Feng's views in the debate in "Hu Feng and the Critical Legacy of Lu Xun," in *Lu Xun and His Legacy* (ed. Leo Ou-fan Lee), pp. 142–50.

Notes

14. Mao Zedong, "The Role of the Chinese Communist Party in the National War" (October 1938), *Selected Works of Mao Tse-tung*, 2:209–10.
15. Hu Feng, "Wenxue shang de wusi," *Hu Feng pinglunji*, 2:122–24.
16. Hu Feng, "Duiyu wusi geming wenyi chuantong de yi lijie," *Lun minzu xingshi wenti*, ibid., 2:232–34.
17. Ibid., p. 241.
18. For example, Vera Schwarcz cites such an acknowledgment by Ai Siqi, one of Hu Feng's opponents in the debate over "national forms." See Vera Schwarcz's *The Chinese Enlightenment*, p. 234.
19. Mao Zedong, "The May Fourth Movement," *Selected Works of Mao Tse-tung*, 2:237–40.
20. Hu Feng, "Minzu zhanzheng yu xin wenyi chuantong," *Hu Feng pinglunji*, 2:136–37.
21. Hu Feng, "Yige yaodian beiwanglu" (January 13, 1941), ibid., p. 133.
22. See, for example, Lin Yü-sheng's comment on Ah Q's lack of an interior self in his "The Morality of Mind and Immorality of Politics: Reflections on Lu Xun, the Intellectual" in *Lu Xun and His Legacy* (ed. Leo Ou-fan Lee), p. 111, and Leo Ou-fan Lee's similar comment in *Voices from the Iron House*, p. 77.
23. Hu Feng, "Minzu zhanzheng yu xin wenyi chuantong," *Hu Feng pinglunji*, 2:146–47.
24. Hu Feng, "Yi 'Kuangren riji' wei qidian," *Hu Feng pinglunji*, 3:223.
25. G. T. Shea, *Leftwing Literature in Japan*, p. 234.
26. Hu Feng, "Zhang Tianyi lun" (May 1935), *Hu Feng pinglunji*, 1:36–37.
27. Hu Feng, "Wei chuzhibizhe de chuangzuotan," ibid., p. 225.
28. *Qiyue* 27 (December 1940): 97.
29. See "Zuojia de zhuguan yu yishu de keguanxing" (Zuotan bilu), *Zhongguo kangri zhanzheng shiqi dahoufang wenxue shuxi* (ed. Lin Mohan et al.), 3:853.
30. Georg Lukács, "Narrate or Describe?" *Writer and Critic and Other Essays*, p. 143.
31. Hu Feng, "Wenyi gongzuo de fazhan jiqi luli fangxiang," *Hu Feng pinglunji*, 3:10–13.
32. See *Hu Feng huiyilu*, p. 309.

33. Hu Feng, "Zhishen zai wei minzhu de douzheng limian" (October 1944), *Hu Feng pinglunji*, 3:19.

Chapter 5. Different Modes of Intellectual Intervention

1. Cited from Lu Ling's letter to Hu Feng dated February 27, 1941, *Hu Feng Lu Ling wenxue shujian* (ed. Xiao Feng), p. 9.
2. See Zhu Hengqing's "Lu Ling shenshi de chongxin xushu," *Xinwenxue shiliao* (1997) 1: 171–75.
3. For a discussion of the lyrical visions of these two traditional novels, see Yu-kung Kao's "Lyric Vision in Chinese Narrative Tradition: A Reading of *Hung-lou Meng* and *Ju-lin Wai-shih*," *Chinese Narrative: Critical and Theoretical Essays* (ed. Andrew H. Plaks), pp. 227–43.
4. See Lu Ling, "Wo yu waiguo wenxue," *Waiguo wenxue yanjiu* (1985) 2: 3.
5. Hu Sheng, "Ping Lu Ling de duanpian xiaoshuo," *Dazhong wenyi congkan* 1 (March 1948), rpt. *Lu Ling yanjiu ziliao* (ed. Yang Yi et al.), pp. 97–117.
6. Lu Ling, "Jia" (April 1941), *Qingchun de zhufu*, p. 43.
7. Dorrit Cohn, *Transparent Minds*, pp. 100–101.
8. Lu Ling, "Xiemeitai xia," *Qingchun de zhufu*, p. 247.
9. Émile Benveniste, "The Correlations of Tense in the French Verb," *Problems in General Linguistics*, pp. 208–9.
10. Julie Kristeva, *Powers of Horror*, p. 4.
11. Herbert Marcuse, *Eros and Civilization*, pp. 99–102.
12. Ban Wang, *The Sublime Figure of History*, pp. 107–14, 123–54, 185–93, and 229–61.
13. Hu Feng, "Xianshi zhuyi zai jintian," *Hu Feng pinglunji*, 2:319–23.
14. Régine Robin, *Socialist Realism: An Impossible Aesthetic*, p. 264.
15. For a discussion of the socialist realist novel as a parabolic genre, see Katerina Clark's "Socialist Realism *with* Shores: The Conventions for the Positive Hero," in *Socialist Realism Without Shores* (ed. Thomas Lahusen and Evgeny Dobrenko), pp. 27–50.
16. Hu Feng, "Yige nuren he yige shijie" (June 1942), *Hu Feng pinglunji*, 2:382.
17. For Kirk Denton's views in this regard, see *The Problematic of Self in Modern Chinese Literature*, pp. 243–55.
18. Zhu Hengqing, "Lu Ling zaoqi de wenxue huodong," *Xinwenxue shiliao* 1(1995):156.

Notes

19. Lu Ling's letter to Hu Feng dated May 12, 1942, *Hu Feng Lu Ling wenxue shujian* (ed. Xiao Feng), p. 37.
20. Lu Ling, *Ji'e de Guo Su'e*, pp. 11–12.
21. Hu Feng, "Xu," *Ji'e de Guo Su'e*, p. 6.
22. Julia Kristeva, *Powers of Horror*, p. 11.
23. Liu Kang, "The Language of Desire, Class, and Subjectivity in Lu Ling's Fiction," *Gender and Sexuality in Twentieth-Century Chinese Literature and Society* (ed. Tonglin Lu), p. 75.
24. For a succinct account of the vicissitude of the crowd in Chinese leftist fiction, see Marston Anderson's *The Limits of Realism*, pp. 180–202.
25. Ji Pang, "Ai Lu Ling," *Xinwenxue shiliao* 1(1995):138.
26. Lu Ling, "Qifeng dishou," *Qiu'ai*, p. 47.
27. Wayne Booth, *The Rhetoric of Fiction*, p. 164.

Chapter 6. Manifestations of Self-Transcendence

1. Hu Feng, "Xu," *Caizhu de ernumen*, p. 1.
2. Lu Ling, "Tiji," ibid., p. 2.
3. Ibid., pp. 2–3.
4. Lu Ling's formal education came to a stop when he was sixteen, before he could finish high school. In a recent letter dated June 29, 1998, Shu Wu, his roommate at the time of writing *Children of Wealth,* informs the present author that Lu Ling had only read an extremely limited number of Chinese classics and had obtained his knowledge about literature entirely from reading foreign masterpieces in Chinese translation.
5. Lu Ling was working full-time as a librarian at the time and could only write in his spare time, yet he finished, for example, the second volume of his novel—more than seven hundred printed pages—in just six months. Even if we completely discount his habit of writing several works at the same time, to write so much in such a short time means he had to write, on average, approximately 2,370 characters every evening without any time for revision. A further, and obviously extreme, proof of his extraordinary pace can be found in his letter to Hu Feng dated May 13, 1945, in which he tells Hu Feng that he had dashed off 130,000 characters in eighteen days as he was finishing his novel. (See *Hu Feng Lu Ling wenxue shujian* [ed. Xiao Feng], p. 88.) In his recent letter Shu Wu also tells the present author Lu Ling

usually wrote two to three thousand characters every evening at the time.

6. For Kirk Denton's interpretations, see *The Problematic of Self in Modern Chinese Literature,* pp. 221–43.

7. For Kirk Denton's interpretation of Jiang Chunzu, see his *The Problematic of Self in Modern Chinese Literature,* pp. 101–220. For Kang Liu's view on the novel, see his "Mixed Style in Lu Ling's Novel *Children of the Rich*," *Modern Chinese Literature* 7 (1993): 61–87.

8. Lu Ling, "Tiji," *Caizhu de ernumen,* p. 1.

9. Lu Ling, *Caizhu de ernumen,* p. 101.

10. Kang Liu, "Mixed Style in Lu Ling's Novel *Children of the Rich*," *Modern Chinese Literature,* 7 (1993): 70.

11. In his letter to Hu Feng dated October 15, 1942, Lu Ling mentioned that he had not read *Jean Christophe* and that he was ready to send to Hu Feng the first volume of his own novel. See *Hu Feng Lu Ling wenxue shujian* (ed. Xiao Feng), p. 62.

12. See Hu Feng, "Xu," *Caizhu de ernumen,* p. 7, and Yang Yi, "Lu Ling zhuanlue," *Xinwenxue shiliao* 1(1987):196.

13. Lu Ling, *Caizhu de ernumen,* 1:312.

14. Susan Rubin Suleiman, *Authoritarian Fictions,* p. 7.

15. Ibid., p. 10.

16. Hu Feng, "Xu," *Caizhu de ernumen,* p. 5.

17. Lu Ling, *Caizhu de ernumen,* p. 599.

18. Ibid., p. 520.

19. Roland Barthes, "From Work to Text," *Textual Strategies* (ed. Josue V. Harari), pp. 74–76.

20. Lu Ling, *Caizhu de ernumen,* p. 385.

21. Jaroslav Průšek, "Reality and Art in Chinese Literature," *The Lyrical and the Epic,* p. 93.

22. Lu Ling, *Caizhu de ernumen,* p. 440.

23. Ibid., pp. 652–53.

24. Kirk A. Denton, *The Problematic of Self in Chinese Literature,* pp. 224–28.

25. Lu Ling, *Caizhu de ernumen,* p. 736.

26. Roland Barthes, *S/Z,* pp. 18–20.

27. Lu Ling, *Caizhu de ernumen,* p. 2.

28. David Wang, "Lianyi biaomei," *Xiaoshuo zhongguo,* p. 78.

29. Leo Ou-fan Lee, *The Romantic Generation of Modern Chinese Writers,* p. 287.

Notes

30. Kirk Denton, *The Problematic of Self in Modern Chinese Literature*, pp. 194–97 and 217–18. Denton also quotes the same remarks by Lu Ling, but he translates the Chinese phrase "duixiang" in the first sentence as "opponents" and, perhaps because of that, comes to the conclusion that Lu Ling expresses decided approbation for his protagonist. In consideration of the context, the phrase "duixiang," I believe, should be understood as "targeted readers."

31. Lu Ling, *Caizhu de ernumen*, pp. 478–79.

32. For a recent discussion on the tropes and modality of socialist realism, see Régine Robin's *Socialist Realism: An Impossible Aesthetic*, pp. 245–96.

33. Lu Ling, *Caizhu de ernumen*, p. 928.

34. Ibid., pp. 1113–4.

35. Lydia H. Liu, "The Discourse of Individualism," *Translingual Practice*, pp. 77–99.

36. Franco Moretti, *The Way of the World*, p. 208.

37. Lu Ling, *Caizhu de ernumen*, p. 1002.

Chapter 7. (Re)presentation of Historical Particularities

1. Theodore Huters, "Lives in Profile," *From May Fourth to June Fourth*, p. 271.

2. Ibid., p. 272.

3. Ji Pang, *Zou yelu de renmen*, p. 472.

4. Ji Pang, "Shi," *Xiwang* 1.1 (December 1945): 56.

5. Hu Feng, "Zhishen zai wei minzhu de douzheng limian" (October 1944), *Hu Feng pinglunji*, 3:20.

6. See Tzvetan Todorov's "An Introduction to Verisimilitude," in his *The Poetics of Prose*, pp. 80–88, and Jonathan Culler's *Structuralist Poetics*, pp. 138–60.

7. Ji Pang, "Chujian he yongjue," *Xinwenxue shiliao* 4 (1987):94.

8. Ji Pang, *Zou yelu de renmen*, p. 471.

9. Peter Brooks, *Reading for the Plot*, p. xi.

10. Slavoj Žižek, *The Sublime Object of Ideology*, p. 140.

11. See Ban Wang's *The Sublime Figure of History*, particularly the chapter "Desire and Pleasure in Revolutionary Cinema," pp. 123–54.

12. For Lacan's interpretations of the Symbolic order, see, for example, his "On a question preliminary to any possible treatment of psychosis," in *Écrits*, pp. 179–225.

13. Malcolm Bowie, *Lacan*, p. 93.
14. Ji Pang, *Zou yelu de renmen*, p. 24.
15. David Der-wei Wang, *Fictional Realism in Twentieth-Century China*, pp. 242–45.
16. Ji Pang, *Zou yelu de renmen*, p. 448.
17. Ibid., p. 453.
18. Ibid., p. 221.
19. Ibid., p. 325.
20. Ibid., pp. 424–25.
21. Ibid., pp. 468–69.
22. Ji Pang, "Zaiban fuji," ibid., p. 472.
23. Pierre Bourdieu, "Price Formation and the Anticipation of Profits," *Language and Symbolic Power*, p. 66.

Epilogue

1. Hu Feng, "Xiezai houmian" (April 1951), *Hu Feng pinglunji*, 3:367.
2. Dai Guangzhong, *Hu Feng zhuan*, pp. 274–75.
3. For an analysis of the Communist politics in China, see James R. Townsend and Brantly Womack's *Politics in China*, pp. 1–195.
4. Vera Schwarcz, *The Chinese Enlightenment*, p. 292.
5. Liu Zaifu, "The Subjectivity of Literature Revisited," *Politics, Ideology, and Literary Discourse in Modern China* (ed. Liu Kang and Xiaobing Tang), pp. 57–58.

BIBLIOGRAPHY

A Long 阿垅. *Nanjing Xueji* 南京血祭 (Nanjing Blood Sacrifice). Beijing: Renmin wenxue chubanshe, 1987.
Anderson, Marston. *The Limit of Realism: Chinese Fiction in the Revolutionary Period.* Berkeley: University of California Press, 1990.
Bakhtin, M. M. *The Dialogic Imagination: Four Essays.* Ed. Michael Holquist. Trans. Caryl Emerson and Holquist. Austin: University of Texas Press, 1981.
———. *Problems of Dostoevsky's Poetics.* Ed. and trans. Caryl Emerson. Minneapolis: University of Minnesota Press, 1984.
Barthes, Roland. *S/Z.* Trans. Richard Miller. New York: Hill and Wang, 1974.
———. "From Work to Text." In *Textual Strategies*, ed. Josue V. Harari. Ithaca, N.Y.: Cornell University Press, 1979, 73–81.
———. "The Reality Effect." In *French Literary Theory Today: A Reader*, ed. Tzvetan Todorov. Cambridge: Cambridge University Press, 1982, 11–17.
Baxandall, Lee, and Stefan Morawski, eds. *Marx and Engels on Literature and Art: A Selection of Writings.* St. Louis: Telos Press, 1973.
Becker, George J., ed. *Documents of Modern Literary Realism.* Princeton: Princeton University Press, 1963.
Benveniste, Émile. *Problems in General Linguistics.* Trans. Mary Elizabeth Meek. Coral Gables, Fla.: University of Miami Press, 1971.
Booth, Wayne C. *The Rhetoric of Fiction.* 2nd ed. Chicago: University of Chicago Press, 1983.
Borland, Harriet. *Soviet Literary Theory and Practice during the First Five-Year Plan 1928–1932.* Rpt. New York: Greenwood Press, 1969.
Bourdieu, Pierre. *Outline of a Theory of Practice.* Trans. Richard Nice. Cambridge and New York: Cambridge University Press, 1977.
———. *Language and Symbolic Power.* Cambridge: Harvard University Press, 1991.

———. *The Field of Cultural Production: Essays on Art and Literature.* New York: Columbia University Press, 1993.
———. *The Rules of Art: Genesis and Structure of the Literary Field.* Trans. Susan Emanuel. Stanford, Calif.: Stanford University Press, 1996.
Bowie, Malcolm. *Lacan.* Cambridge: Harvard University Press, 1991.
Brooks, Peter. *Reading for the Plot: Design and Intention in Narrative.* Cambridge: Harvard University Press, 1984.
Cao Bai 曹白. *Huxi* 呼吸 (Breathing). Rpt. Shanghai: Shanghai wenyi chubanshe, 1983.
Chatman, Seymour. *Story and Discourse: Narrative Structure in Fiction and Film.* Ithaca, N.Y.: Cornell University Press, 1978.
Chow, Rey. *Woman and Chinese Modernity: The Politics of Reading between West and East.* Minnesota: University of Minnesota Press, 1991.
Chow Tse-tsung. *The May Fourth Movement: Intellectual Revolution in Modern China.* Cambridge: Harvard University Press, 1960.
Clark, Katerina. "Socialist Realism with Shores: The Conventions for the Positive Hero." In *Socialist Realism without Shores*, ed. Thomas Lahusen and Evgeny Dobrenko. Durham, N.C.: Duke University Press, 1997, 27–50.
Cochran, Sherman et al., trans. and eds. *One Day in China: May 21, 1936.* New Haven: Yale University Press, 1983.
Cohn, Dorrit C. "Narrated Monologue: Definition of a Fictional Style." *Comparative Literature* 18:2 (Spring 1966): 97–112.
———. *Transparent Minds: Narrative Modes for Presenting Consciousness in Fiction.* Princeton, N.J.: Princeton University Press, 1978.
Culler, Jonathan. *Structural Poetics.* Ithaca, N.Y.: Cornell University Press, 1975.
Dai Guangzhong 戴光中. *Hu Feng zhuan* 胡风传 (A Biography of Hu Feng). Yinchuan: Ningxia renmin chubanshe, 1994.
Denton, Kirk A. *The Problematic of Self in Modern Chinese Literature: Hu Feng and Lu Ling.* Stanford, Calif.: Stanford University Press, 1998.
Department of Chinese Literature, Beijing University, et al., eds. *Wenxue yundong shiliaoxuan* 文学运动史料选 (An Anthology of historical documents on literary movements), 4 vols. Shanghai: Shanghai jiaoyu chubanshe, 1980.
Ermolaev, Herman. *Soviet Literary Theories 1917–1934: The Genesis of Socialist Realism.* Rpt. New York: Farrar, Straus & Giroux, 1977.
Fokkema, Douwe Wessel. *Literary Doctrine in China and Soviet Influence, 1956–1960.* London: Mouton & Co. 1965.

Gálik, Marián. "Main Issues in the Discussion on 'National Forms' in Modern Chinese Literature." *Asian and African Studies* 10 (1974): 97–112.

Goldblatt, Howard. "Lu Xun and Patterns of Literary Sponsorship." In Leo Ou-fan Lee, *Lu Xun and His Legacy*, 199–215.

Goldman, Merle. "Hu Feng's Conflict with the Communist Literary Authorities." *China Quarterly*, 12 (October 1962): 102–137.

———. *Literary Dissent in Communist China*. Cambridge: Harvard University Press, 1967.

———. ed. *Modern Chinese Literature in the May Fourth Era*. Cambridge: Harvard University Press, 1977.

Gotz, Michael. "The Pen as Sword: Wartime Stories of Qiu Dong-ping." In *La Littérature Chinoise au Temps de la Guerre de Résistance Contre le Japon (de 1937 à 1945): Colloque International*. Paris: Éditions de la Fondation Singer-Polignac, 1982, 101–16.

Gramsci, Antonio. *Selections from the Prison Notebooks of Antonio Gramsci*. Ed. and trans. Quintin Hoare and Geoffrey Nowell Smith. New York: International Publishers, 1971.

———. *Selections from Cultural Writings*. Ed. David Forgacs and Geoffrey Nowell Smith, trans. William Boelhower. London: Lawrence and Wishart, 1985.

Hakuson, Kuriyagawa 厨川白村. *Kumen de xiangzheng* 苦闷的象征 (Symbols of Agony). Trans. Lu Xun. In *Lu Xun yiwenji* (Translations by Lu Xun). Beijing: Renmin wenxue chubanshe, 1958, 3: 3–94.

Hamburger, Kate. *The Logic of Literature*. Rev. ed. Trans. Marilynn Rose. Bloomington: Indiana University Press, 1993.

Hockx, Michel. "The Literary Association (Wenxue yanjiu hui, 1920–1947) and the Literary Field of Early Republican China." *China Quarterly* 153 (March 1998): 49–81.

Holm, David. "Lu Xun in the Period 1936–1949: The Making of a Chinese Gorki." In Leo Ou-fan Lee, *Lu Xun and His Legacy*, 153–79.

Hsia, Chih-tsing. *A History of Modern Chinese Fiction*. 2nd ed. New Haven: Yale University Press, 1971.

Hsia Tsi-an. *The Gate of Darkness: Studies on the Leftist Literary Movement in China*. Seattle: University of Washington Press, 1968.

Hu Feng 胡风, ed. *Qiyue* 七月 (July). October 1937 – September 1941.

———, ed. *Xiwang* 希望 (Hope). December 1945 – October 1946.

――. "Wo de xiaozhuan" 我的小传 (An autobiographical sketch). *Xinwenxue shiliao* 1 (1981): 101–4.

――. *Hu Feng pinglunji* 胡风评论集 (Collected Essays of Hu Feng). 3 vols. Beijing: Renmin wenxue chubanshe, 1984.

――. *Hu Feng huiyilu* 胡风回忆录 (Memoirs of Hu Feng). Beijing: Renmin wenxue chubanshe, 1993.

Hu Sheng 胡绳. "Ping Lu Ling de duanpian xiaoshuo" 评路翎的短篇小说 (A Critique of Lu Ling's Short Stories), *Dazhong wenyi congkan* 1 (March 1948). Rpt. *Lu Ling yanjiu ziliao*, ed. Yang Yi et al., 97–117.

Hung, Chang-tai. *War and Popular Culture: Resistance in Modern China, 1937–1945*. Berkeley: University of California Press, 1994.

Huters, Theodore. "Blossoms in the Snow: Lu Xun and the Dilemma of Modern Chinese Literature." *Modern China* 10.1 (January 1984): 49–77.

――. "Hu Feng and the Critical Legacy of Lu Xun." In Leo Ou-fan Lee, *Lu Xun and His Legacy*, 129–52.

――. "Lives in Profile: On the Authorial Voice in Modern and Contemporary Chinese Literature." In *From May Fourth to June Fourth: Fiction and Film in Twentieth-Century China*, ed. Ellen Widmer and David Der-wei Wang. Cambridge: Harvard University Press, 1993, 269–94.

Jakobson, Roman. *Language in Literature*. Cambridge: Harvard University Press, 1987.

Jenner, W. J. F. "Lu Xun's Last Days and After." *China Quarterly* 91 (September 1982): 424–45.

Ji Pang 冀汸. *Zou yelu de renmen* 走夜路的人们 (Night Travellers). Shanghai: Zuojia shuwu, 1951.

――. "Chujian he yongjue" 初见和永诀 (First Meeting and Final goodbye). *Xinwenxue shiliao* 4 (1987): 93–96.

――. "Ai Lu Ling" 哀路翎 (Mourning Lu Ling). *Xinwenxue shiliao* 1 (1995): 137–54.

Jia Zhifang 贾植芳. *Jia Zhifang xiaoshuoxuan* 贾植芳小说选 (A Selection of Fiction by Jia Zhifang). Nanjing: Jiangsu renmin chubanshe, 1983.

Jones, Gareth Stedman, "The Marxism of the Early Lukács." In *Western Marxism: A Critical Reader*, ed. New Left Review. Norfolk, England: Lowe & Brydone Printers, 1977, 11–60.

Kao, Yu-kung. "Lyric Vision in Chinese Narrative Tradition: A Reading of *Hung-lou Meng and Ju-lin Wai-shih."* In *Chinese Narrative: Critical and Theoretical Essays*, ed. Andrew Plaks. Princeton, N.J.: Princeton University Press, 1977, 227–43.

Korsch, Karl. *Marxism and Philosophy*. Trans. Fred Halliday. London: New Left Books, 1970.

Kristeva, Julie. *Powers of Horror: An Essay on Abjection*. Trans. Leon S. Roudiez. New York: Columbia University Press, 1982.

Lacan, Jacques. *Écrits*. New York: W.W. Norton, 1977.

Lan Hai 蓝海. *Zhongguo kangzhan wenyi shi* 中国抗战文艺史 (A History of the Literature in China's War of Resistance). Shanghai: Xiandai chubanshe, 1947.

Laughlin, Charles. "Narrating the Nation: Aesthetics of Historical Experience in Chinese Reportage Literature 1919–1966." Ph.D. dissertation. Columbia University, 1996.

Lee, Leo Ou-fan. *The Romantic Generation of Modern Chinese Writers*. Cambridge: Harvard University Press, 1973.

———. "Literature on the Eve of Revolution: Reflections on Lu Xun's Leftist Years, 1927–1936." *Modern China* 2.3 (July 1976): 277–326.

———, ed. *Lu Xun and His Legacy*. Berkeley: University of California Press, 1985.

———. *Voices from the Iron House: A Study of Lu Xun*. Bloomington: Indiana University Press, 1987.

Li Huoren 黎活仁. "Hu Feng de zhuguan zhandou jingshen" 胡风的主观战斗精神 (Hu Feng's "Subjective Fighting Spirit"). In *Zhanzheng yu Zhongguo shehui zhi biandong* 战争与中国社会之变动 (War and the Changes in Chinese Society), ed. Danjiang daxue zhongwenxi. Taipei: Taiwan xuesheng shuju, 1991, 193–221.

Li Ruiteng 李瑞腾, ed. *Kangzhan wenxue gaishuo* 抗战文学概说 (A Survey of the War of Resistance Literature). Taipei: Wenxun yuekan zazhishe, 1987.

Lin Mohan 林默涵 et al., eds. *Zhongguo kangri zhanzheng shiqi dahoufang wenxue shuxi* 中国抗日战争时期大后方文学书系 (A Compendium of Literary Works Published in the Interior during China's War of Resistance against Japan). Chongqing: Chongqing chubanshe, 1989.

Lin, Yü-sheng. *The Crisis of Chinese Consciousness: Radical Antitraditionalism in the May Fourth Era*. Madison: University of Wisconsin Press, 1979.

———. "The Morality of Mind and Immorality of Politics: Reflections on Lu Xun, the Intellectual." In Leo Ou-fan Lee, *Lu Xun and His Legacy*, 107–28.

Liu, Kang. "Subjectivity, Marxism, and Culture Theory in China." *Social Text* 31/32 (1992): 114–40.

———. "Mixed Style In Lu Ling's Novel *Children of the Rich*: Family Chronicle and *Bildungsroman*." *Modern Chinese Literature* 7 (1993): 61–87.

———. "The Language of Desire, Class, and Subjectivity in Lu Ling's Fiction." In *Gender and Sexuality in Twentieth-Century Chinese Literature and Society*, ed. Tonglin Lu. Albany: State University of New York Press, 1993, 67–83.

Liu, Kang, and Xiaobing Tang, eds. *Politics, Ideology, and Literary Discourse in Modern China*. Durham, N.C.: Duke University Press, 1993.

———. "Hegemony and Cultural Revolution." *New Literary History* 28 (1997): 69–86.

Liu, Lydia H. *Translingual Practice: Literature, National Culture, and the Translated Modernity—China 1900–1937*. Stanford, Calif.: Stanford University Press, 1995.

Liu Zaifu. "The Subjectivity of Literature Revisited." In Kang Liu and Xiaobing Tang, *Politics, Ideology, and Literary Discourse in Modern China*, 56–69.

Lu Kuiran 鲁喟然. *Hu Feng shijian de qianyin houguo* 胡风事件的前因后果 (The Causes and Consequences of the Hu Feng Incident). Hong Kong: Nanfeng chubanshe, 1956.

Lu Ling 路翎. *Ji'e de Guo Su'e* 饥饿的郭素娥 (Hungry Guo Su'e). Rpt. Beijing: Renmin wenxue chubanshe, 1988.

———. *Qingchun de zhufu* 青春的祝福 (The Blessings of Youth). Chongqing: Xiwangshe, 1945.

———. *Qiu'ai* 求爱 (In Search of Love). Shanghai: Haiyan shudian, 1946.

———. *Zai tielian zhong* 在铁链中 (In Iron Chains). Shanghai: Haiyan shudian, 1949.

———. *Caizhu de ernumen* 财主的儿女们 (Children of Wealth). Rpt. Beijing: Renmin wenxue chubanshe, 1985.

———. "Wo yu waiguo wenxue" 我与外国文学 (Foreign Literature and I). *Waiguo wenxue yanjiu* 2 (1985):3–8.

———. "Aidao Hu Feng tongzhi" 哀悼胡风同志 (Lamenting Comrade Hu Feng's Death). *Wenhui yuekan* 9 (1985):53–55.

Bibliography

———. *Chuxue* 初雪 (First snow). Yinchuan: Ningxia renmin chubanshe, 1981.
Lu Xun 鲁迅. *Lu Xun quanji* 鲁迅全集 (Collected Works of Lu Xun). Beijing: Renmin wenxue chubanshe, 1981.
Lukács, Georg. "Narrate or Describe?" In *Writer and Critic and Other Essays*, ed. Arthur Kahn. London: Merlin Press, 1970, 110–48.
———. *History and Class Consciousness*. Trans. Rodney Livingstone. Cambridge: The MIT Press, 1971.
Lyell, William A. "Lu Ling's Wartime Novel: *Hungry Guo Su-e*." *La Littérature Chinoise au Temps de la Guerre de Résistance Contre le Japon (de 1937 a 1945): Colloque International*. Paris: Éditions de la Fondation Singer-Polignac, 1982, 267–82.
Ma Tiji 马蹄疾. *Hu Feng zhuan* 胡风传 (A Biography of Hu Feng). Chengdu: Sichuan renmin chubanshe, 1989.
Mannheim, Karl. *Essays on the Sociology of Knowledge*. Ed. Paul Kecskemeti. London: Routledge & Kegan Paul, 1964.
Mao Zedong 毛泽东. "The Role of the Chinese Communist Party in the National War." In *Selected Works of Mao Tse-tung* [Mao Zedong]. Peking: Foreign Languages Press, 1965, 2: 195–211.
———. "The May Fourth Movement." In *Selected Works of Mao Tse-tung* [Mao Zedong]. Peking: Foreign Languages Press, 1965, 2: 237–40.
———. "Talks at the Yan'an Forum on Literature and Art." In *Selected Works of Mao Tse-tung* [Mao Zedong]. Peking: Foreign Languages Press, 1965, 3: 69–98.
Marcuse, Herbert. *Eros and Civilization: A Philosophical Inquiry into Freud.* New York: Random House, 1962.
Moretti, Franco. *The Way of the World: The Bildungsroman in European Culture*. London: Verso, 1987.
Průšek, Jaroslav. *The Lyrical and the Epic: Studies of Modern Chinese Literature*. Ed. Leo Ou-fan Lee. Bloomington: Indiana University Press, 1980.
Qin Xianci 秦贤次, ed. *Kangzhan shiqi wenxue shiliao* 抗战时期文学史料 (Historical Data on the Literature during the War of Resistance). Taipei: Wenxun yuekan zazhishe, 1987.
Qiu Dongping 丘东平. *Diqilian* 第七连 (The Seventh Company). Rpt. Shanghai: Xiwangshe, 1947.
Qu Qiubai 瞿秋白. *Qu Qiubai wenji* 瞿秋白文集 (A Collection of Works by Qu Qiubai). Beijing: Renmin wenxue chubanshe, 1986.

Robin, Régine. *Socialist Realism: An Impossible Aesthetic.* Trans. Catherine Porter. Stanford, Calif.: Stanford University Press, 1992.

Rutherford, Andrew. *The Literature of War: Studies in Heroic Virtue.* 2nd ed. London: Macmillan Press, 1989.

Schwarcz, Vera. *The Chinese Enlightenment: Intellectuals and the Legacy of the May Fourth Movement of 1919.* Berkeley: University of California Press, 1986.

Shea, G. T. *Leftwing Literature in Japan: A Brief History of the Proletarian Literary Movement.* Tokyo: The Hosei University Press, 1964.

Su Guangwen 苏光文. *Dahoufang wenxue lungao* 大后方文学论稿 (Studies of the Literature in the Interior). Chongqing: Xinan shifan daxue chubanshe, 1994.

Suleiman, Susan Rubin. *Authoritarian Fictions: The Ideological Novel as a Literary Genre.* Princeton, N.J.: Princeton University Press, 1993.

Todorov, Tzvetan. *The Poetics of Prose.* Trans. Richard Howard. Ithaca, N.Y.: Cornell University Press, 1977.

Townsend, James R. and Brantly Womack. *Politics in China.* 3rd ed. Glenview, Ill.: Scott, Foresman and Company, 1986.

Wagner, Rudolf G. *Inside a Service Trade: Studies in Contemporary Chinese Prose.* Cambridge: Harvard University Press, 1992.

Wang, Ban. *The Sublime Figure of History: Aesthetics and Politics in Twentieth-Century China.* Stanford, Calif.: Stanford University Press, 1997.

Wang, David Der-wei. *Fictional Realism in Twentieth-Century China: Mao Dun, Lao She, Shen Congwen.* New York: Columbia University Press, 1992.

———. *Xiaoshuo Zhongguo: Wanqing dao dangdai de Zhongwen xiaoshuo* 小说中国: 晚清到当代的中文小说 (Fictional China: Fiction in Chinese from the Late Qing to the Present). Taipei: Maitian chuban gongsi, 1993.

Weber, Max. *On Charisma and Institution Building.* Chicago: The University of Chicago Press, 1968.

Wen Tianxing 文天行. *Guotongqu kangzhan wenxue yundong shigao* 国统区抗战文学运动史稿 (A Draft History of the Wartime Literary Movements in Guomindang-Controlled Areas). Chengdu: Sichuan jiaoyu chubanshe, 1988.

Wen Zhenting 文振庭 and Fan Jiyan 范际燕, eds. *Hu Feng lunji* 胡风论集 (A collection of essays on Hu Feng). Beijing: Zhongguo shehui kexue chubanshe, 1991.

Wong, Wang-chi. *Politics and Literature in Shanghai: The Chinese League of Left-Wing Writers, 1930–1936*. Manchester, England: Manchester University Press, 1991.

Wu Zimin 吴子敏. "Lun qiyue liupai" 论七月流派 (On the *Qiyue* School). *Wenxue pinglun* 2 (1983): 72-85.

Xiao Feng 晓风, ed. *Hu Feng shuxinji* 胡风书信集 (A Collection of Hu Feng's letters). Tianjin: Baihua wenyi chubanshe, 1989.

———, ed. *Hu Feng Lu Ling wenxue shujian* 胡风路翎文学书简 (Letters on Literature between Hu Feng and Lu Ling). Hefei: Anhui wenyi chubanshe, 1994.

———. *Jiusi weihui: Hu Feng zhuan* 九死未悔: 胡风传 (Nine Deaths without Regret: A Biography of Hu Feng). Taipei: Yeqiang chubanshe, 1996.

Yang Shuxian 杨淑贤. "Qiu Dongping zhuanlue" 丘东平传略 (A Biographical Sketch of Qiu Dongping). *Xinwenxue shiliao* 3 (1987): 200–11.

Yang, Yi 杨义. "Lu Ling–linghun aomi de tansuo zhe" 路翎–灵魂奥秘的探索者 (Lu Ling—An Explorer of the Soul). *Wenxue pinglun* 5 (1983): 114–127.

———. "Lu Ling zhuanlue" 路翎传略 (A biographical sketch of Lu Ling). *Xinwenxue shiliao* 1 (1987): 193–204.

Yang, Yi, et al., eds. *Lu Ling yanjiu ziliao* 路翎研究资料 (Research Data on Lu Ling). Beijing: Shiyue wenyi chubanshe, 1993.

Yi Men 亦门 (A Long). *Diyiji* 第一击 (The First Stroke). Shanghai: Haiyan shudian, 1947.

Zhao Xiaqiu 赵遐秋. *Zhongguo xiandai baogao wenxue shi* 中国现代报告文学史 (A History of Modern Chinese Reportage). Beijing: Zhongguo renmin daxue chubanshe, 1987.

Zhongguo shehui kexueyuan wenxue yanjiusuo xiandai wenxue yanjiushi 中国社会科学院文学研究所现代文学研究室, ed. *"Liangge kouhao" lunzhan ziliao xuanbian* "两个口号"论战资料选编 (A Selection of Documents on the Debate over the "Two Slogans"). Beijing: Renmin wenxue chubanshe, 1982.

Zhou Guohua 周国华 et al., eds. *Baogao wenxue lunji* 报告文学论集 (A Collection of Essays on Reportage). Beijing: Xinhua chubanshe, 1985.

Zhou Yang 周扬. *Zhou Yang wenji* 周扬文集 (A Collection of Works by Zhou Yang). Beijing: Renmin wenxue chubanshe, 1984.

Zhu Hengqing 朱珩青. "Lu Ling zaoqi de wenxue huodong" 路翎早期的文学活动 (Lu Ling's Early Literary Activities). *Xinwenxue shiliao* 1 (1995): 154–60.

———. "Lu Ling shenshi de chongxin xushu" 路翎身世的重新叙述 (A New Account of Lu Ling's Family Background). *Xinwenxue shiliao* 1 (1997): 171–75.

Žižek, Slavoj. *The Sublime Object of Ideology*. London: Verso, 1989.

Index

A
A Long (Chen Shoumei), 48, 56, 63, 65–66, 80, 109, 176. Works: "Fighting Started at Zhabei," 66–69, 70; "From the Offensive to the Defensive," 69–71; "How I Wrote 'Fighting Started at Zhabei'," 67, 68; *Nanjing Blood Sacrifice*, 73–79; "Tangential Encounter," 71–73
A Ying, 45
abjection, 116
activism, 28
Ai Siqi, 189n18
alazon, 127
Anderson, Marston, 191n24
Arishima Takeo, 27
"atomistic competition," 11

B
Ba Jin, work: *Family*, 145
Bakhtin, M. M., 123, 133, 153, 170
Barbusse, Henri, 59
Barthes, Roland, 67, 137, 144
Benveniste, Émile, 114
Bergson, Henri, 27
Bildungsroman, 58, 150–151, 159–160, 164
Booth, Wayne, 126
Bourdier, Pierre, 5, 6, 9, 172
Bowie, Malcolm, 162
Brooks, Peter, 160
Bukharin, Nikolai Ivanovich, 31

C
Can Xue, 118
Cao Bai (Liu Pingruo), 48, 56, 63, 80; and Hu Feng, 50; and Lu Xun, 49–50; self-image, 53–54; and *zawen*, 50, 52. Works: "Here, Life Is Also Breathing," 50–51; "In the Shadow of Death," 51–52; "Seizing the 'Living Soul'," 51–52; "Yang Kezhong," 52–53
Chang, Eileen, 117
Chekhov, Anton, 124
Chinese Communist Party (the CCP): relationship to the *Qiyue* group, 4. *See also* Mao Zedong
Chinese Writers' National Anti-Aggression Association, 73, 103
Clark, Katerina, 190n15
Cohn, Dorrit, 111
Comintern, 37
Creation Society, 8, 27, 29
critical realism, 10, 39, 46, 63, 93, 108, 119, 156
Culler, Jonathan, 156

D
Dai Guangzhong, 194n2
Denton, Kirk, 18, 25, 120, 130, 131, 143, 146, 150
Ding Ling, work: "Flood," 123, 169
Dream of the Red Chamber, 110, 134
Duanmu Hongliang, 41, 55

E
Eguchi Kiyoshi, 29
emotive function, 78
Engels, Friedrich, 13, 33, 34, 36, 176

Index

F
Feng Naichao, 56
Feng Xuefeng, 24, 38, 40
formulism, 2, 10, 31, 34, 40, 50, 115, 154
Freud, Sigmund, 27, 117–118

G
Gálik, Marián, 188n13
Gannu (Nie Gannu), 54–55
generation entelechy, 25
Goldblatt, Howard, 185n36
Gorky, Maxim, 110
Gramsci, Antonio, 14–17

H
habitus, 6
Hamburger, Kate, 79
He Qifang, 103
Hegel, Georg Wilhelm Friedrich, 34, 122
hegemony, 15
hermeneutic code, 144
Hockx, Michel, 6
Holm, David, 90, 92
Hsia, C. T., 40
Hu Feng, 4, 7, 13, 23, 38, 52, 65, 74, 87, 109–110, 115, 120, 129, 133, 136, 154, 176, 177; and antitraditionalism, 7, 25; as a charismatic leader, 9; criticism of traditional literature, 95; and the debate over "national forms," 94–96; and the debate over the "Two Slogans," 37–38, 40–41; and the debate with Zhou Yang over "typical characters," 35; early experience, 24; comparison with the Frankfurt School, 32; and Fukumotoism, 7–8, 29–30; and Guo Moruo, 7; interpretations of Lu Xun, 88–93, 97–98; interpretations of May Fourth, 93–99; and Japanese proletarian literature, 29, 100; and Lu Xun, 26, 36–37; and Lukács, 30–32, 101–103; and Mao Dun, 7, 29; and Mao Zedong's "Yan'an Talks," 103; and Marxist aesthetics, 32–33; and May Fourth literature, 24, 27; and the New Culture, 25–26; petition to the CCP, 44, 177–178; and popular culture, 17; position among leftists, 8–9; on reportage, 47–49; and socialist realism, 34; and the "subjective fighting spirit," 99–105; voluntarist view on literature, 27–29, 34–35, 36; and Zhou Yang, 6–7, 177. Works: "Arising from 'Emanating a Ray of Light As Long As There Is an Ounce of Heat'," 92; "A Brief Explanation of 'The Passerby'," 91; "A Critique of Zhang Tianyi," 34–35, 100–101; "A Discussion on Writing for Beginning Writers," 101; "A Grievous Good-bye," 89; "If He Were Still Alive," 91–92; "May Fourth in Literature," 95; "The National War and the Tradition of the New Literature," 97–98; "On a Combative Literary Genre in Wartime," 48, 52; *On the Direction of Realism,* 176; "On a Few Fundamentals of the Spirit of Lu Xun," 89–90; *On the Issue of National Forms,* 95; "On the Sketch," 47; "Putting Ourselves into the Struggle for Democracy," 104, 155–156; "Realism Today," 119; "Taking 'A Madman's Diary' As a Starting Point," 98; "Time Has Begun," 176; "What Are 'Typical Characters' and 'Stereotypes'," 35; "What Do the Masses Demand of Literature?" 38, 40; "Willing to Grow with Our Readers," 40–41
Hu Sheng, 111
Hung, Chang-tai, 183n1
Huters, Theodore, 40, 79–80, 153, 188n13

I
individualism, 149–150

206

Index

J
Jakobson, Roman, 78
Ji Pang, 5, 11, 99, 105, 124, 156, 158; and Hu Feng's "subjective fighting spirit," 154–155. Works: *Night Travellers*, 153–173; "Oath," 154
Jia Zhifang, 80–81. Works: "Human Sadness," 81–82; "My Hometown," 84–85; "Surplus Value," 82–84
Jones, Gareth Stedman, 30

K
Kao, Yu-kung, 190n3
Kawaguchi Hiroshi, 44
Kobayashi Takiji, 29
Korsch, Karl, 14–15, 30. Work: *Marxism and Philosophy*, 14, 30
Kristeva, Julia, 116, 122
Kurahara Korehito, 100
Kuriyagawa Hakuson, 27–28, 91–92, 100. Works: *Outside the Ivory Tower*, 92; *Symbols of Agony*, 27–28

L
Lacan, Jacques, 162
Lake Side Poems, 24–25
Lao She, work: *Four Generations under One Roof*, 145
Laughlin, Charles, 186n1
League of Left-Wing Writers, 37, 44
Lee, Leo Ou-fan, 28, 82, 146, 189n22
Lenin, Vladimir Ilyich, 13, 36
Li Huoren, 30, 101
Liang Qichao, 44
Lin Yü-sheng, 93, 189n22
Literary Association, 6, 27
Literary Battlefield, 43, 44
Liu Baiyu, 103
Liu Bannong, 93
Liu Kang, 16, 123, 131, 133, 150
Liu, Lydia, 149–150
Liu Na'ou, 75, 117
Liu Zaifu, 180
Lou Shiyi, 56

Lu Ling (Xu Sixing), 5, 11, 76, 79, 99, 105, 115, 176; early experience, 108–109; enunciative style, 114; focus on neuroses, 116–117; portrayal of intellect and the intellectual, 113–114; presentation of the subconscious, 118; revolt against the revolutionary sublime, 118; revolt against socialist realism, 119–120; treatment of violence, 123; use of the narrated monologue, 111; use of the reliable narrator, 111–112, 132; use of satire, 123–128. Works: "After Withdrawing from the 'Fortress'," 109; "Autumn Night," 127; "A Blind Man," 127; *Children of Wealth*, 109, 113, 129–151, 153, 173; "The Coffins," 110, 117; "Family," 110, 111; "Grandfather's Job," 110; "He Shaode Came under Arrest," 110; *Hungry Guo Su'e*, 120–123; "An Important Letter," 127–128; "In Iron Chains," 117; "The Night China Won the Victory," 126; "Novel Amusement," 126; "Old Woman Wang and Her Piglet," 117; "Under the Loading Dock," 112, 116–117; "Valley," 113; "A Well-Matched Chess Game," 125
Lu Xun, 8, 40, 47, 80, 171; and the debate over the "Two Slogans," 37–39; and Zhou Yang, 37–38. Works: *Call to Arms*, 26; "In the Tavern," 82–83; "A Madman's Diary," 61; "Medicine," 81; "My Old Home," 84, 171; "New Year's Sacrifice," 171; "On the Power of *Mara* Poetry," 54, 99; "Public Display," 125; "Random Thoughts," 98; "This Too Is Life . . . ," 47, 50; "The True Story of Ah Q," 61; *Wandering*, 82, 125
Lü Ying, 101
Lü Yuan, 74
Lukács, Georg, 13, 14, 30–32, 33, 101. Works: *History and Class Consciousness*, 30–32; "Narrate or Describe," 101, 102–103

Index

M
Mannheim, Karl, 7, 11, 25
Mao Dun, 38, 44, 139, 140; on reportage, 45
Mao Zedong, 94, 176, 179; on Lu Xun, 90–91; on May Fourth, 96–97; persecution of the Hu Feng group, 178. Works: "On New Democracy," 96; "Talks at the Yan'an Forum on Literature and Art," 88, 175, 178
Marco Polo Bridge Incident, 1, 43
Marcuse, Herbert, 118
Marx, Karl, 13, 30, 31, 33, 34, 36, 176
"method of dialectic materialism," 33, 100
Moretti, Franco, 150
Mu Shiying, 75, 117

N
nationalism, 1
Nationalist Party (the Guomindang), 3
naturalism, 10
New Fourth Army Incident, 65
New Perceptionists, 75, 117

O
"objectivism," 7, 154

P
Pan Mohua, 24
"primitive vitality," 120, 158, 163
proairetic code, 144
Průšek, Jaroslav, 140

Q
Qiu Dongping, 48, 56, 109. Works: "A Company Commander's War Experience," 60–63; "An Impression of Ye Ting," 57; "The Seventh Company," 57–59; "We Were Defeated There," 59–60; "Wu Luxun and His Wife Kiko," 57
Qiyue, 1, 8, 40, 41, 43–44, 50, 55, 65, 107; as a "journal for the likeminded," 55–56

Qu Qiubai, 44. Work: "Marx, Engels, and Realism in Literature," 33–34

R
RAPP (Russian Association of Proletarian Writers), 30, 32, 33, 100
reality effect, 67
Rectification Campaign, 88
reification, 31
reportage, 44–46
Resistance Literature, 43, 44
Robin, Régine, 119, 193n32
Rolland, Romain, work: *Jean Christophe*, 133, 145
roman à thèse, 135
romanticism, 36
Ropshin, V., 26
Rutherford, Andrew, 59

S
Scholars, 110
Schwarcz, Vera, 180, 184n5
Second International, 29
semic code, 144
Sha Ting, 123
Shea, G. T., 100
Shen Congwen, work: "Xiaoxiao," 163
Shi Zhicun, 117
Shu Wu, 151, 176, 177, 178, 191n4, 191n5
socialist realism, 10, 13, 33, 34, 39, 100, 103, 108, 118, 119, 147, 159
"subjective fighting spirit," 7, 10, 14, 79, 80, 82, 88, 98, 108, 128, 131, 132, 146, 149, 173, 180. *See also under* Hu Feng
"subjectivism," 7
Sudermann, Hermann, 26
Suleiman, Susan Rubin, 135
Sun Ling, 46
Sun Society, 8, 29
Symbolic order, 162

Index

T
Tai'erzhuang Campaign, 46
"third-category" writers, 30, 100
Todorov, Tzvetan, 156
Tolstoy, Leo, works: *Resurrection* 26; *War and Peace*, 133–134, 138, 140
Townsend, James R., 194n3

V
verisimilitude, 63, 139, 156

W
Wagner, Rudolf, 186n1
Wang, Ban, 52, 118, 161, 186n14
Wang, David Der-wei, 145, 163
Wang Jingzhi, 24
Wang Tongzhao, 24–25
Weber, Max, 9
Womack, Brantly, 194n3
Wong, Wang-chi, 183n8, 184n14
Work and Study, 81, 88
Wu Zuxiang, 123, 139

X
Xiang Linbing (Zhao Jibin), 94–95
Xiao Hong, 41
Xiao Jun, 41
Xie Bingying, 44, 46
Xiwang, 4, 104

Y
Yamakawa Hitoshi, 29
Yang Yi, 133
Ye Zi, 123
Yi Qun, 46
Ying Xiuren, 24
Yu Hua, 118

Z
zawen, 47, 80
Zhang Tianyi, 123
Zhao Xiaqiu, 187n20
Zhdanov, Andrei, 13
Zhou Enlai, 4
Zhou Yang, 8, 37; and "National Defense Literature," 37; and the persecution of Hu Feng, 178. Works: "On National Defense Literature," 39; "On Socialist Realism and Revolutionary Romanticism," 33; "A Preliminary Discussion on Realism," 35
Zhu Hengqing, 120, 190n2
Žižek, Slavoj, 161